Citizenship in America and Europe

Citizenship in America and Europe

Beyond the Nation-State?

Editors

Michael S. Greve and Michael Zöller

The AEI Press

Publisher for the American Enterprise Institute

WASHINGTON, D.C.

Distributed to the Trade by National Book Network, 15200 NBN Way, Blue Ridge Summit, PA 17214. To order call toll free 1-800-462-6420 or 1-717-794-3800. For all other inquiries please contact the AEI Press, 1150 Seventeenth Street, N.W., Washington, D.C. 20036 or call 1-800-862-5801.

Library of Congress Cataloging-in-Publication Data

Citizenship in America and Europe : beyond the nation-state? / Michael S. Greve and Michael Zöller, editors.
    p. cm.
  Includes bibliographical references and index.
    ISBN-13: 978-0-8447-4310-3
    ISBN-10: 0-8447-4310-0
  1. Citizenship—Europe. 2. Citizenship—United States. I. Greve, Michael S. II. Zöller, Michael.
  JN40.C571 2009
  323.6094—dc22

                                                                2009028119

13 12 11 10 09   1 2 3 4 5

Printed in the United States of America

Contents

Preface

Citizenship in America and Europe: Beyond the Nation-State? was produced under the auspices of the Transatlantic Law Forum (TLF), a joint venture of the American Enterprise Institute's Legal Center and the American-European Council on Public Policy, based in Bayreuth, Germany. The forum's principal purpose is to build an international community of scholars, lawyers, judges, policymakers, and journalists with a serious interest in deepening the understanding of constitutionalism, constitutional democracy, and the legal culture on both side of the Atlantic. Prominent among the forum's programs is a series of annual conferences, alternating between the United States and Europe, on salient issues of public policy and their legal and constitutional dimensions.

The essays in this book were originally presented at the TLF's inaugural event in the United States, an international conference entitled "Citizenship in Europe and the United States" held at the American Enterprise Institute in October 2008. The authors subsequently revised their contributions in light of the conference discussions. The "conversation" among European and American observers (see chapter 5) is an edited transcript of two panel discussions on the public and political debate over citizenship in Europe and in the United States, respectively.

The conference featured exceptionally informative and lively debates among the presenters and discussants. We hope that our compressed, formal, and "academic" book format still provides a flavor of the candor and inquisitiveness that made for an uncommonly fruitful event. Still, we fear—in fact, we know—that much nuance and value have been lost in the translation from conference to book. A full transcript of the event, including the full program and a list of the distinguished participants, is available at http://www.aei.org/event1787 and http://www.council.uni-bayreuth.de/index.pl?lang=en&id=16641.

This project was supported through the Transatlantic Program of the Federal Republic of Germany, with funds from the European Reconstruction Program of the Ministry for Economics and Technology.

MICHAEL S. GREVE
John G. Searle Scholar
American Enterprise Institute

MICHAEL ZÖLLER
Chairman
Council on Public Policy

Washington, D.C./Bayreuth
June 2009

Introduction:
Citizenship on Two Continents

Michael S. Greve and Michael Zöller

In a sense, the essays collected in this volume need no introduction. Citizenship is in fashion nowadays, for good and not-so-good reasons. Due to its common usage and perhaps its legalistic connotations, "citizenship" has been made to carry a heavy load of political and ideological commitments—to participatory democracy, communitarianism, internationalism, and egalitarian rights, among others. Though not all the cargo on the good citizenship is contraband, removing some baggage would bring clarity to the discussion of what citizenship is, ought to be, and can achieve. This volume is a step toward that clarity: it explores citizenship from historical, legal, and other perspectives; considers the connection of citizenship to patriotism and nationality; and weighs what citizenship has meant in the past and what it might mean in the future, in the United States and in Europe.

"Citizenship" connotes both universalism and particularism—both general principles of liberal democracy, and belonging to a particular political community. This interplay creates tensions and contradictions—a sort of Hegelian dialectic. Hegel himself had a decided view on it:

> It is part of education . . . that I am apprehended as a *universal* person, in which [respect] *all* are identical. A *human being counts as such because he is a human being*, not because he is a Jew, Catholic, Protestant, German, Italian, etc. This consciousness . . . is of infinite importance—[it is] inadequate only if it adopts a fixed position—for example, as *cosmopolitanism*—in opposition to the concrete life of the state.[1]

1

Hegel suggests where the "infinitely important" consciousness of universal personhood comes from. His phraseology echoes Paul's letters (although as usual, Hegel misquotes from memory).[2] And the passage is situated in a chapter about the rise of a capitalist society and its spiritual twins—the Enlightenment and political liberalism. There is, Hegel insists, no going back behind that heritage and the "hard, infinite struggle" of Reason it embodies— the recognition of equal personhood as the irreducible essence of law and lawfulness. Still, Hegel insists that abstract personhood has a chance in real life only when actual, individual persons become citizens of an actual political organization. As he puts it elsewhere, the individual comes into his just and rightful place only by being a citizen of a good state.[3] The German term for citizenship—*Staatsbuergerschaft*—suggests the point.

If one point of agreement emerges with perfect clarity from the transatlantic conversation in this book, it is the authors' uniform sense that Americans have a much less complicated, more pragmatic approach to citizenship and its difficult dialectic than do Europeans. Perhaps that is because America is sufficiently lucky to have been spared Europe's decaying castles and, for the most part, its Hegelian speculations. Or perhaps it is because those two quintessentially Western traditions—our Judeo-Christian heritage, and our classical liberalism—are more robust in the United States than in Europe, where learned opinion now widely dismisses them as atavistic and "neoliberal," respectively. (To which Americans are in turn prone to respond: "Too God damn bad.") But the best way of crystallizing the differences may be to begin with what Hegel calls "cosmopolitanism"—that is, the temptation of marching universalist abstractions into battle against "the concrete life of the state."

Cosmopolitanism still has a very hard time in the United States, where foreign observers unfailingly note the omnipresence of patriotic symbols and rituals. One need not look far to realize that Americans' expressions of affection for the concrete life of *their* state signal a deeper, politically salient sentiment. "For the first time in my adult life, I am proud of my country," Mrs. Obama commented (in an unguarded moment) on her husband's rising fortunes in the 2008 presidential campaign. When her much-quoted remark was taken, rightly or wrongly, to suggest an attitude at some variance with an uncomplicated, everyday patriotism,[4] the Obama campaign launched an energetic counteroffensive, knowing how damaging the impression might become if it were allowed to sink in. Europe, in contrast, is much drawn to cosmopolitan abstractions. By all appearances, the peoples of Europe—most of them, at any rate—retain firm loyalties to their own countries and governments. Their politicians and opinion leaders, however, no longer believe in a sovereign, democratic state with citizens, institutions, and a concrete life of its own. For them, the public's lack of enthusiasm for the European project is a constant source of consternation and lament.

We hasten to acknowledge that the divide is not altogether so sharp. On the American side, for example, a vast network of human rights organizations with an explicit, professional fixation on universal, abstract personal rights enjoys broad support among the public, as well as the media and law schools. Conversely, on the European side, even committed advocates of international law and human rights eventually recognize the need to confront the question of who and what will make those abstractions real *if not* a citizen-protective state. Those internal debates are of great help in sustaining a transatlantic exchange that is a dialogue, not a clash of political civilizations. Even so, the differences remain real, and they run through the citizenship issues covered in this book.

The book begins with chapters by Josef Joffe and William Galston that explore the idea of "constitutional patriotism." The next section, on European citizenship, begins with chapters by Francesca Strumia and Markus Kotzur, includes a "transatlantic conversation" among experts, and concludes with remarks on citizenship in the United States by Judge Diane P. Wood, and in Europe, by Judge Jean-Claude Bonichot and Francois-Henri Briard. The final section of the book, which treats different conceptions of rights, includes chapters by Peter H. Schuck, Adam Tomkins, and Robert R. Gasaway and Ashley C. Parrish. A short conclusion by Kenneth W. Starr reflects on some of the large points raised in earlier chapters. Below, we offer our own thoughts on the authors' splendid contributions.

Between Cosmopolitanism and National Identity: Constitutional Patriotism?

Equal citizenship based on universal principles need not be in fixed opposition to citizenship in a particular state. A well-ordered modern state will respect persons as persons *and* as individual citizens—with particular interests and talents, with families, with varying religious beliefs, with vibrant civic institutions ("corporations," in Hegel's terminology). That state will in turn command a kind of easy-going, confident, affectionate loyalty on the part of its citizens. That disposition Hegel describes as *Verfassungspatriotismus*, or constitutional patriotism.[5]

Verfassungspatriotismus has since had a long history in Germany. In the postwar era, the notion was propounded first by the political scientist Dolf Sternberger and then by Germany's omnipresent public intellectual, Jürgen Habermas. (Habermas has since attempted to mobilize the concept as a basis for Europe and European citizenship.[6]) Josef Joffe ably chronicles the concept's origins, trajectory, and uses in chapter 1 of this volume; in chapter 2, William Galston looks at constitutional patriotism in the United States, where the "American creed" constitutes a potent form of and opportunity for national self-identification.

Both Joffe and Galston readily acknowledge constitutional patriotism's humane attractions. Both, however, worry that it might not be enough to sustain engaged citizenship and political allegiance—that it might be too "thin," as democracy theorists put it. Then again, both worry that more particularistic attachments to nationhood might be dangerous, or at least problematic.

It is worth pondering further some of the points Joffe and Galston raise.

Postwar Germany, Joffe observes, had no usable political past, and so constitutional patriotism emerged as the only plausible patriotism. But Joffe doubts its patriotic content. "Constitutional patriotism," he writes, "is not a theory of allegiance, but almost a contradiction in terms." Liberal democracy exists in many countries: what, other than the sheer accident of birth, should prompt allegiance to one liberal democracy rather than another? The thinness of constitutional patriotism is suggested by the fact that following the war, the most powerful symbols of German self-identification were the *Wirtschaftswunder* (economic miracle) and the D-Mark, not the accompanying *Demokratiewunder* (tellingly, not a term in common usage).[7] And mind you: Germany's constitutional order has had its enemies. Leftist critics sneeringly acronymed the *freiheitlich-demokratische Grundordnung*—the constitutional, liberal-democratic order Sternberger defended—the "FDGO." As the Marquis de Sade eventually discovered, though, it is difficult to defile sacred objects without implicitly affirming their sacredness: without it, desecration becomes pointless vandalism. By that same token, snarled-at institutions may have more force and dignity than either their critics or their diffident defenders perceive. This appears to be the case in Germany, where, with the exception of the *Bundesverfassungsgericht* (constitutional court) in its better moments, Germany's political institutions and elites have made little effort to remind citizens of postwar Germany's democratic and constitutional achievements.[8] Perhaps constitutional patriotism in Germany suffers less from the thinness of the concept itself than from the mindset of the country's governing elites.

America's problem is more attenuated. As Galston puts it, "The idea of a unity that is creedal rather than ethnic is in our bones." Moreover, America's constitutive understanding and constitutional culture reflect a particular, concrete, and (yes) exceptional constitutional history. Americans have managed to synthesize abstract ideals and concrete nationhood into constitutional patriotism and citizenship because the synthesis was there at the beginning, in a constitutional moment. It was there, Kenneth W. Starr's concluding remarks remind us, in the confident, candid assertion of "self-evident truths" in the Declaration of Independence. The "We the People" of the United States Constitution knew who they were—former colonists who had declared their independence from the motherland, fought a violent war to defend it, and, in a conclusive, constitutive act of a single sovereign, established a constitution to secure the blessings of liberty for themselves and their posterity.

That marriage of particularity and universal principle, of course, was marred by the shameful compromise with slavery. America needed, and achieved at great cost, a second founding. Tellingly, though, that second founding did not seek to trump the original synthesis but to make good on it. The Civil War was fought not to make America more similar to other nations but to vindicate her exceptional character and promise. (Lincoln's famous phrase—"the last best hope of earth"—precisely captures the symbiosis of particularity and universalism.) And the principal constitutional product was designed not to shower new rights upon citizens but to extend well-recognized rights of national citizenship to previously excluded individuals. That pattern has prevailed throughout: citizenship in the United States has always been about inclusion, not identity. Americans, to repeat, know who they are.

Galston ends up worrying whether they will *remember*. As he cheerfully volunteers, that concern is itself something of an American tradition.

Americans have perennially worried about their ability to imbue millions of immigrants, and new generations of youthful slackers, with sufficient patriotic affection. And as Galston perceptively adds, the attractive logic of American citizenship has a privatistic downside: once people have been given their rights of inclusion, no one seems to care a whole lot about what they do with those rights.[9] But the worriers have always been proven wrong. Why? We offer two guesses, unsupported by empirical evidence but suggested by some of our contributors, and in any event morsels for thought.

First, America's cultural worriers operate in a vibrant private sector of nonprofit and for-profit institutions (such as the publishers of bestsellers on the founding fathers and of some sixteen thousand books on Abraham Lincoln). In her remarks on citizenship in chapter 5, Ayaan Hirsi Ali emphasizes the contrast between the Netherlands' officially sponsored cultural dialogue and America's free-wheeling nonprofit sector, and some of her interlocutors' comments seem to bear her out. Similarly, as near as we can tell, no one in the intense German debate over a *Leitkultur* (a "lead culture," a logical home for constitutional patriotism) supposed that such an effort could or would be anything but a governmental enterprise, steered and funded by the *Kulturminister*. Americans, especially those professionally committed to the propagation of constitutional patriotism, are likely to suspect that a secretary of culture would pursue a policy analogous to that of the secretary of agriculture—raise prices, reduce output, and turn his sector of American society into a producer cartel. The prospect is unlikely.[10]

Second, we suspect that constitutional patriotism's virility in the United States and its limpness in Germany may have the same explanation—elite attitudes and politics. In the United States, the synthesis of universalism and nationhood in a constitutional moment is no mere partisan trope and, in particular, no conservative "America First" trope. The rehabilitation of America's constitutional moments has, over the past generation, largely been the work of progressive scholars.[11] And the country is now led by a Democratic president who is an ardent admirer and serious student of that greatest of Republicans and presidents, Abraham Lincoln. There are real differences of opinion among American elites about the precise meaning and import of the American creed, but precisely that argument keeps the constitutional synthesis and moment alive. The United States may face all sorts of problems. Forgetfulness is not among them.

European Citizenship?

For reasons too obvious to enumerate, no other nation has had, or will ever again have, America's constitutional moment, or moments. (It is not even to be wished for. America paid for her supposedly easy-going constitutional patriotism *ex ante*, with two bloodbaths.) That need not mean, though, that no other genuine constitutional experience is possible. Catastrophic military defeat as well as liberation from colonial or Soviet rule may prompt an authentic constitutional politics and, in turn, constitutional loyalties.[12] Those constitutional experiences and experiments, however, remain tied to particular places, experiences, and moments. The question is whether citizenship and constitutionalism can have meaning and purchase without any such connection. The cosmopolitan proposition that they *can* be so disconnected from concrete life has a name: the European Union (EU). Markus Kotzur makes the case for that proposition in chapter 4.

With admirable clarity, Kotzur begins with the central juxtaposition—America's constitutional moment of "reflection and choice," versus the European deliberations over the union. The crucial differences, Kotzur elaborates, are two. First, America's constitutional choice was that of the citizens addressed by *The Federalist*. In Europe, the reflecting and choosing are done by the member states' political leaders. Second, the American model is a decisive choice: up or down with the Constitution.[13] The European model, in contrast, is a gradual process within a matrix of citizens, regions, national governments, intergovernmental institutions, and other stakeholders (such as a governmentally organized European "public" of non-government organizations). Europe's citizens, the theory goes, may and indeed ought to retain loyalties to their home countries, regions, towns, or religions, while developing affection for and a sense of belonging to Europe. In that process, out of that matrix, the "House of Europe" will evolve.

This model—constitutionalism and citizenship as a process—has enormous currency among Europeanists on both side of the Atlantic, and Kotzur presents and defends it ably and more soberly than most of its proponents. Some problems with the model, however, emerge in chapter 3, by Francesca Strumia. Strumia offers an instructive microanalysis of the citizenship rules administered by EU member states and the EU vis-à-vis third-country nationals. Those individuals, she notes, have no means of becoming European citizens without first becoming citizens of a member state, a process that entails residency requirements of varying duration. For that duration, immigrants are rendered largely immobile within the EU—despite the fact that potent considerations (such as labor market rigidities) would seem to counsel a more liberal policy. She notes in addition that naturalizing third-country nationals swear a loyalty oath to the country of immigration, not to the EU—and that the typical oath in effect rules out any competing loyalty to that body. As Judge Diane P. Wood notes in chapter 7, the legal framework for American citizenship is hardly free from inconsistencies; but they do not seem of quite the same order. The uneasy suggestion behind Strumia's analysis is that constitution-and-citizen-building-by-process is not a progressive approximation but rather an inherently paradoxical affair.

One potent illustration of that suggestion is the prominent role of the European Court of Justice (ECJ)—the union's least democratic institution—in the development and definition of European citizenship, noted by Judge Jean-Claude Bonichot (chapter 6). More broadly, though, "paradoxical" may characterize not only the question of legal citizenship but the EU project as a whole. The EU's major current initiative, the yet-to-be-ratified Lisbon Treaty, was originally conceptualized and advertised as an explicitly *constitutional* project. The unwieldiness of the existing intergovernmental arrangements and the prospect of the EU's enlargement certainly played a role in the undertaking. Equally clearly, though, its architects and promoters—Joschka Fischer, Juergen Habermas, Jacques Chirac, Lionel Jospin—insisted that the "Monnet method" of improvising toward an "ever closer union" had reached the end of its useful and defensible life. Sooner rather than later, the politicians would have to let their citizens know where the experiment would lead. And so, the grand constitutional experiment began—with a declaration (in Laeken), with fanfare and comparisons to Philadelphia, with a convention.

Which of the many failures of this enterprise constitutes the biggest debacle—the convention, which was promptly hijacked by warring Brussels bureaucracies? The constitutional document itself, whose embarassments begin with the first words of the preamble ("His Majesty, the King of the Belgians") and continue for several hundred pages? Its rejection in popular referenda in France and, of all places, the Netherlands? The German chancellor's ultimatum to the president of the Czech Republic, issued from Berlin with the support of EU officials from Austria and Spain, to sign a document in support of a constitutional rescue operation within forty-eight hours (*or else*), lest European peace and progress falter yet again on Czech hang-ups about sovereignty?[14] The EU member states' defiant attempt to implement the rejected "constitution," in substantially identical form, by means of a treaty amendment? The rejection of even that maneuver by the Irish voters? The French president's imperious insistence that *les malentendus* will be made to vote again, until they get it right? The fact that everyone understands that the instrument will be put into effect eventually, regardless of what any citizen of any country may think?[15]

This jarring conflict between process and promise—Strumia's problem on a large scale—is central. In seeking to remedy its much-maligned "democracy deficit," the EU confronts a process deficit: it cannot get from here to there without political means that contradict the purported ends. James Madison and Alexander Hamilton staked their fortunes and their honor on the defense of the Constitution. Should it fail (they knew), they would have an awful lot to answer for. The champions of the failed European Constitution, in contrast, staged their project with an implied the-show-must-go-on immunity. Europe's political class will grant citizens no reflection, let alone a choice, with respect to their political future. If the price of European citizenship is contempt for actual citizens; if more transparent institutions can be produced only surreptitiously; if Europe's constitutional process can no longer be distinguished from a cabal, or its supposed citizens-in-the-making from dupes, no one will say so. In Europe's stifling atmosphere, "even dogs cease to bark."[16]

The tensions and contradictions of the process might be tolerable if one could be confident that they will eventually yield to a comforting web of loyalties and the sense of belonging described by Kotzur. Can one? Will they? Nested, complementary loyalties are an ordinary fact of life. They are in the normal course of events easily manageable for individuals and for liberal democracies. (In light of that experience, Hobbesian hostility to intermediary institutions has long given way to Tocquevillean enthusiasms about families, townships, churches, and bowling leagues as the social glue that holds an atomistic society and a liberal state together.) Europe's cosmopolitan project, however, is to mobilize multiplicity for the purpose of severing the connection between citizenship and the (nation-)state. That orientation tends to ignore that at the end of the day, citizens with multiple loyalties "have only one life to live, or to give."[17] The state, as traditionally conceived, had the ability, and at all events the political obligation, to ensure its citizens' physical safety. It could in turn demand citizens' allegiance and, in the extreme case, sacrifice. It had a right to ask: Whose side are you on?

The sacrifice question seems remote. The European Union has no army and no military duty, and while EU member states have contributed troops and supplies to multinational military operations (some more so than others), no one will die for the European Union as a political entity any time soon. The allegiance question, in contrast, is acute, as the conversation with Jürgen Kaube, Robert von Rimscha, Martin Klingst, Ayaan Hirsi Ali, and Peter Skerry (chapter 5) demonstrates. What has brought the problem to the forefront on both sides of the Atlantic is the Muslim question.

As Peter Skerry notes, "Whose side are you on?" is an impolite, divisive question. (This may be one reason why most countries still administer loyalty oaths, quaint and ritualistic though they may seem: one does not want to have to ask the question too often at a time when the answer is needed.) Skerry hopes, as do we, that America will not have to ask that question of Muslims, or anyone else. But if it has to ask at some point, we are tolerably confident— perhaps more confident than Skerry—that it will be a "terror question," not a "citizenship question," a law enforcement issue, not a matter of identity politics.

Here again, Europe's predicament is far more difficult. In part, that is a function of geography and numbers. Unlike the United States, the European Union has Muslim countries on its borders, and many millions of Muslim immigrants, residents, and citizens. In part, it reflects the lower absorptive capacity and cultural resilience of European countries. In yet another part, we fear, it reflects the European political and opinion elites' long-standing refusal to think about questions of citizenship and allegiance with sufficient hard-headedness and realism. It should surprise no one that many of the most dramatic conflicts over Islamism and citizenship should have arisen in the Netherlands: that most internationalist of EU countries suffers the cultural contradictions of cosmopolitanism in their most acute form. Tolerance, forbearance, and openness hold real attraction—so long as all recognize that the bargain must run both ways. But what of people who do not accept the implied civic obligation? And what of countries that belatedly come to the grim realization that such people are in their midst?

It is clear, though hardly comforting, that European governments and Muslim communities now feel insecure about one another. When European governments invite a foreign Muslim leader to initiate a "dialogue" with *their own citizens*, that supposed gesture of goodwill is bound to signal that the host governments trust neither themselves nor their Muslim citizens—who are then bound to return the favor. Due to different histories and political and demographic conditions, European countries confront the dilemma in somewhat varying forms; but in trying to manage it, none seems to have much to draw on. With respect to Germany, Jürgen Kaube's contribution to the conversation in chapter 5 shows that the dominant political and economic strategies—expansive welfare state guarantees, coupled with a failure to instill a culture of achievement—have only exacerbated problems that were initially caused by short-sighted immigration policies. Kaube's declared intention is to dial down a heated debate to empirical, policy-driven questions. We wholeheartedly support his ambition, but worry about its traction. Germany's welfare state has confronted a series of wrenching shocks, from a loss of competitiveness in the 1980s to reunification in the 1990s. Time and again, the welfare state has triumphed. Perhaps the country flees into ethereal debates over *Leitkultur* and multiculturalism because the truly intractable problems are on the policy side.

Rights

Citizenship is commonly understood in terms of rights. (Obligations of citizenship, several authors in this volume note, have receded into the background.) In chapter 8, Peter H. Schuck elaborates three models that underlie discourses about citizenship: a nationalist model, which ties rights to citizenship in a nation-state; an internationalist, human rights model, which severs that connection; and a "Marshallian" welfare-rights model (after the British sociologist T. H. Marshall, who famously posited a progression from property to participatory to positive rights as the substance of citizenship). The distinctions, Schuck cautions, do not mark a strict trichotomy: the nationalist-internationalist distinction goes to the "who" of rights, whereas the Marshallian notion goes to the "what." But while the Marshallian notion is technically compatible with either of the "who" accounts, Schuck notes a natural affinity between welfare rights and internationalism. He predicts that internationalism and Marshallianism will remain dominant in Europe (though he also believes that the prospect of "ever-greater de-territorialized inclusiveness and expanding welfare-state citizenship . . . seems to be receding" there); America, on the other hand, will maintain a liberal, individualistic, privatistic form of nationalist citizenship, even as it modestly increases Marshallian welfare rights.

Adam Tomkins introduces an additional distinction in chapter 9 by demonstrating how different ways of conceiving constitutions inform notions of citizenship. The British constitution, he argues, is "political rather than legal." British citizenship is about having a representative, and Parliament becomes "the institutional embodiment of citizenship in Britain." Robert R. Gasaway and Ashley C. Parrish introduce a third level of contrast and comparison in chapter 10, starting with the difference between American and European constitutional thought. According to the authors, the United States Constitution achieves a "reconciliation" both among individual rights and between rights and representative democracy. It does this through certain structural principles—among them, a limited inventory of rights that leaves the regulation of private primary conduct, by and large, to the "give and take of the democratic process." Europeans, Gasaway and Parrish elaborate, follow a different, "rights-proliferating approach," assuming that more is better. This strategy empowers legal elites because it leaves the weighing and balancing of rights to judges and other interpreters.

Tomkins and Gasaway/Parrish explicate coherent and theoretically compelling political alternatives to the dominant, rights-driven view of citizenship. The great value of their contributions is to broaden a debate that in its rights-centeredness takes too much for granted. Yet the authors themselves seem to wonder how much real-world traction their preferred models still have. Reviewing a recent government study on questions of citizenship in Britain, Tomkins notes with an understandable air of perplexity that the document makes absolutely no reference to the traditional British model. In a somewhat different vein, what Gasaway and Parrish call "rights proliferation" may now warrant a "European model" moniker. At its inception in the 1960s, however, it was an *American* model, and constitutional courts around the globe have taken their inspiration from the U.S. Supreme Court. Intriguingly, Gasaway and Parrish suggest that even constitutional "originalism," an influential American school of thought that opposes judicial activism at the rights front, has done a poor job in expounding the Constitution's true structure. Europeans may not understand American constitutionalism very well. As Gasaway and Parrish forthrightly acknowledge, though, Americans may no longer understand themselves very well.

What accounts for the real-world weakness of those models of citizenship and constitutionalism? In a word, they are *political*, and they presuppose a great deal of confidence in democratic politics. In modern mass democracies (even in advanced democracies, to say nothing of deeply divided societies), most people find that confidence hard to sustain. The rise of rights consciousness and of powerful constitutional courts is probably linked to that loss of confidence.[18]

The impulse to compensate for a distrust of democracy with a cornucopia of rights appears uncontrollable both at the level of day-to-day judicial politics and even, perhaps especially, at the level of constitutional politics. The United States Constitution consists of seven articles and twenty-seven amendments. Modern constitutions, in contrast, routinely clock in at several hundred articles, many of them containing rights and rights-like guarantees. Gasaway and Parrish have some reason to hope that the U.S. Constitution's parsimony and internal coherence still exert some gravitational pull: in pushing back against rights proliferation, they push back to a foundational text that has a coherent structure, provided one understands it correctly. Modern democracies, in contrast, commit to rights proliferation *ex ante* and *ab ovo*.

That, of course, is particularly true of the Lisbon Treaty. In that unique case, though, rights consciousness coincides with a genuine perplexity: on what basis other than rights could European citizenship possibly be constructed? Not nationality, obviously. Representation and democracy? That conception, Adam Tomkins shows, is becoming attenuated and complemented with very different notions even in Britain; and in any event, the European project will forbid anything like it for many decades to come. History? Much mutual warfare there, and not much commonality—except Christianity, which is a distinct, common heritage and, moreover, resonates with universal aspirations (recall the Hegel passage with which we began). Initially, in fact, the European Community was a discernibly Catholic project. But that memory has passed, and even an easy-going, ecumenical version now looks unavailable. Over centuries past, Christianity emptied Valhalla;[19] with much greater dispatch, modern Europe has emptied the churches.

What remains are the orientations identified by Schuck: cosmopolitan commitments to international law and human rights; and the welfare state or, more grandiosely, the "European way of life."[20] As Jürgen Habermas, a principal proponent of this agenda, has candidly acknowledged, the platform of internationalism and welfare statism has a distinctly social-democratic flavor.[21] It has the advantage of resting on a broad political consensus and, perhaps, the added advantage of having a foil: quite purposefully, it encapsulates what America is not. And perhaps this is the best that Europe can do. One wonders, however, about the coherence of a vision that attempts to disconnect citizens from the state but then encourages them to expect everything of it. On a more practical but also more alarming note, one wonders about the long-term stability of an enterprise that imposes extravagant demands on legal elites and on an overburdened economy. Should either fail to deliver the promised goods, what happens?

Conclusion

It is altogether proper and fitting that we should have ended our ruminations with a question mark. Our opinionated remarks should be taken for what they are—the urgent, inquisitive questions of entrepreneurial but nonexpert academics. We care enough to organize a transatlantic dialogue on citizenship; we know better than to shade, let alone monopolize, a debate that is best left to far more knowledgeable and insightful authors. We confidently commit readers to their care.

Notes

1. G. W. F. Hegel, Elements of the Philosophy of Right 240 (Allen W. Wood ed., 1991).

2. Galatians 3:28: "There is neither Jew nor Greek, there is neither slave nor free man, there is neither male nor female; for you are all one in Christ Jesus." Colossians 3:11: "Here there is no Greek or Jew, circumcised or uncircumcised, barbarian, Scythian, slave or free, but Christ is all, and is in all."

3. Hegel, *supra* note 1, at 196. For the "hard, infinite struggle" *see* G. W. F. Hegel, Reason in History (Robert S. Hartman ed., 1997).

4. *See, e.g.*, Peggy Noonan, *Try A Little Tenderness*, Wall St. J., Feb. 22, 2008.

5. Hegel, *supra* note 1, at 288.

6. Juergen Habermas, *The European Nation-State: On the Past and Future of Sovereignty and Citizenship*, in The Inclusion of the Other: Studies in Political Theory 105 (Claran Cronin & Pablo De Greiff eds., 1998).

7. Recent history casts serious doubt on neo-Schmittian contentions, often heard in the 1960s and 1970s, that Germany's political stability has been altogether dependent on the economy. *See, e.g.*, Ernst Forsthoff, Der Staat der Industriegesellschaft (1971). The D-Mark long ago disappeared in the Euro, and the economic miracle has been buried under the burgeoning costs of an expansive welfare state and of reunification. Yet Germany has remained remarkably free and stable.

8. Among the European national courts, the *Bundesverfassungsgericht* has been the most adamant in defending national constitutional prerogatives and principles against the European Union.

9. *See also* Judith Shklar, American Citizenship: The Quest for Inclusion (1998).

10. Cass R. Sunstein, then still in a vaguely Habermasian mood, did some time ago propose such a "New Deal" for free speech. *See* Sunstein, Democracy and the Problem of Free Speech ch. 2 (1993). That, though, was sixteen years and many books ago, and nothing has come of Sunstein's or similarly inspired proposals.

11. *See especially* Bruce A. Ackerman, We the People: Foundations (1993).

12. For a brief overview of the burgeoning literature on constitutional politics, *see* Nathan Brown, *Reason, Interest, Rationality, and Passion in Constituion Drafting*, 6 Perspectives on Politics 675 (2008).

13. The in-between choice—an incremental improvement over the Articles of Confederation—seemed a plausible option to many at the time. *The Federalist* argued strenuously against it. *See* The Federalist No. 16 (Alexander Hamilton).

14. *See* Hugh Williamson, *Merkel aims to win over Klaus on EU treaty*, Financial Times, Apr. 16, 2007.

15. For a harsh critique of the ratification process from a distinctly European point of view, *see* Declan Ganley, *A Vision for a New Europe*, Speech to the Henry Jackson Society (Feb. 10, 2009).

16. *Cf.* The Federalist No. 11 (Alexander Hamilton) ("[European philosophers] have gravely asserted, that all animals, and with them the human species, degenerate

in America; that even dogs cease to bark, after having breathed a while in our atmosphere").

17. Susan Shell, Kant and the Limits of Autonomy (2009).

18. Martin Shapiro and Alec Stone Sweet, On Law, Politics, and Judicialization (2002).

19. G. W. F Hegel, *On the Positivity of the Christian Religion*, in Early Theological Writings, 80 (T. M. Knox ed., 1971).

20. Lionel Jospin, Speech to the Foreign Press Association, Paris (May 28, 2001).

21. Jürgen Habermas, *Why Europe Needs a Constitution* 11 New Left Rev. 12 (2001).

PART I
Constitutional Patriotism

1

Verfassungspatriotismus: Wrong Concept, Right Country

Josef Joffe

Only a postwar West German—in this case the political scientist Dolf Sternberger—could have invented the idea of *Verfassungspatriotismus*, "constitutional patriotism." Why? A quick answer is given by another German thinker, Max Horkheimer, on the why and wherefore of this unwieldy (at least in English) concept. "No civilized country," he opined in 1959, "has as little reason to celebrate patriotism as does Germany, and nowhere have its citizens questioned patriotism less than in Germany, where it has caused the very worst. . . . German patriotism is so dreadful because it is so unjustified."[1]

This was West Germany's founding myth, at least from a left-liberal perspective. The past was sheer evil, and the evil had fed on patriotism/nationalism gone mad—to the extremes of chauvinism, racism, and annihilationism. This founding myth bears some structural resemblance to the American one: the past also had been evil, an endless string of oppression, injustice, and tyranny. It would be transcended in America, where free citizens praying unhindered to their God would turn their back on a corrupt past and build an ideal community—a "cittie uppon a hill" or a "New Jerusalem." Note, too, how the theme of the Pilgrims replicates an *ur*-myth of humanity (at least of its Judeo-Christian part): revolt against Pharaonic slavery, Exodus, freedom regained, redemption in the Promised Land.

In fact all three founding myths describe the transcendence of evil, the passage from an insufferable yesterday to a bright and shining tomorrow. In the German case, though, the evil to be overcome had a very special quality: It was not done *to* the Germans, as it was done to the Israelites and Puritans by wicked pharaohs both ancient and modern. It was done *by* the Germans.

This is the implicit message of the quotation from Horkheimer, and it emerges, much more faintly, in Sternberger's original essay on *Verfassungspatriotismus*. "Our sense of nationhood [*Nationalgefühl*]," Sternberger wrote, "remains wounded, we don't live in a Germany that is whole. But we live in a constitution that is whole, and this is in itself a kind of a Fatherland."[2] Another inkling of the evil wrought by Nazism can be found in an aphorism from La Bruyère, whom Sternberger quotes approvingly: "There is no fatherland in despotism." Sternberger adds: "Once the air of liberty has been sucked out, the voice of the fatherland can no longer be heard."[3]

So *Verfassungspatriotismus* is above all a reactive concept, lodged in a specific time and place, namely postwar Germany. The reactive component, which Sternberger only hints at, perhaps with a sense of shame, is not hard to explain. Those normal elements that go into the making of a national identity and consciousness were tainted with the blood of millions and thoroughly discredited in the case of postwar Germany. Race? Ethnicity? The *Volk*? No way, not after the orgy of racist nationalism unleashed by the Nazis. Place—the German lands, on which so much of the idea of Deutschland was grounded? West Germany was but a sliver of the original Reich. Gone was practically half the former country—absorbed by the Soviets, by the Poles, and by Bonn's Communist counterstate, the German Democratic Republic. History? That, too, was hardly a source of pride from the vantage point of a postwar West German.

Which history was there to celebrate? Hitler's Twelve-Year *Reich* could not be an object of emotional attachment. The Weimar Republic? Weimar was a nice try at democracy, but it had failed miserably both politically and economically and thus provided a springboard for Nazi totalitarianism. The *Kaiserreich*? Not so great either, this haven of authoritarianism, racism, and expansionism—especially not after the empire had lost World War I and collapsed into chaos and revolutionary mayhem. It is hard to love a loser, especially since in the left-liberal imagination the Wilhelmine Empire was practically a precursor of the Third Reich, as vitriolically satirized in Heinrich Mann's highly influential novel *Der Untertan* (*The Loyal Subject*.)

Bismarck? He was a national hero, having unified twenty-five states and mini-states into the Second Reich. But Bismarck was also tainted as an authoritarian *Junker* who had suppressed the liberties of the rising middle classes while propping up imperial and aristocratic power. Prussia? Though past generations had learned to venerate the Hohenzollerns, especially Frederick the Great, Prussia was suddenly a broken mirror. It had been abolished by the four victorious powers of World War II as the original source of all evil. Besides, as German kids would soon learn from their post-Nazi teachers, Prussia was the scourge of liberty, having suppressed the revolutions of 1830 and 1848. History, in short, was no more a solace than *Volk* or territory.

What was left? *Kultur*, of course. Beethoven and Brahms, Hölderlin and Handel, Goethe and Lessing, Heine and Börne, Einstein and Planck, Theodor Fontane and Thomas Mann—and all those greats who had written the first chapter of the cinematographic canon: Papst, Lang, Billy Wilder. . . . But wait: Einstein was a Jew, and he had been driven out. Heine and Börne were Jews, too, though Heine had converted. These avatars of coming modernity weren't quite, how shall we put it, *German*. Freud (himself a Jew) and Wittgenstein, Germans in the wider sense of a culture that encompassed Vienna and Prague, had made their mark not in Germany, but in Anglo lands. Thomas Mann? A German for sure, but an ambivalent one, what with his antidemocratic leanings after World War I and his conversion to liberal democracy during his American exile. The filmmakers? Gone to Hollywood. There were too many broken strands of too many hues in the tangled web of German culture to serve as a firm foundation for a new national identity.

It was arguably preordained, then, that somebody like Sternberger, and later Jürgen Habermas, who borrowed from Sternberger, would bestride the stage. They came with a precious gift in hand: a patriotism, or collective identity, unsullied by all the ingredients of nationhood and nationalism that defined national identity and pride in other countries but had become tainted, if not radioactive, in the German case.

Constitutional patriotism had a nice ring to it because it lacked all traces of toxicity. It was as immaculate as a freshly wiped blackboard, and it was practically ahistorical. It invoked the transcendence of a new beginning like the Promised Land bequeathed to the Israelites and Puritans. An additional advantage, according to Jürgen Habermas (who stood way to the left of Sternberger), was that *Verfassungspatriotismus* made for a cozy relationship with three of the four World War II victors, who had suddenly turned protectors and parole officers: "Constitutional Patriotism is the only patriotism that will not alienate us from the West."[4] Look, America, Britain, and France—we are like you.

In short, constitutional patriotism offered a postnational and posttraditional identity. But what exactly did it mean? Sternberger, the inventor of *Verfassungspatriotismus*, remained sibylline. His essay quotes the eighteenth-century writer Thomas Abbt:

> If I join a state by dint of birth or voluntary decision, whose salutary laws I accept, I shall call it Fatherland—on condition that these laws do not take more from my liberty than necessary for the good of the State.[5]

Here we have a key element of *Verfassungspatriotismus*: obligation to the state as long as it maximizes freedom. Very nice, absolutely no debate—and very much in the liberal English tradition first defined by John Milton. What else? Sternberger avers that by "constitution" he does not mean a "juridical document as such," like the West German Basic Law with its (then) 146 articles. Rather, he means the "liberal-democratic order" as "object of attachment or loyalty." This order would "exclude all arbitrary or coercive rule" while including the "*Rechtsstaat*" (more or less: rule of law), self-determination, and majority rule bounded by the principles of freedom and equality. Then he runs down the list: individual freedoms, representative institutions, checks and balances, an independent judiciary, rules-bound alternation in power, civic participation, civil society.[6]

Having enumerated these mainstays of the liberal-democratic state, Sternberger asks the obvious: "Can such an entity elicit attachment, affections and patriotism?" His answer: "Actually, this is a rhetorical question. History has answered it long ago, though in other regions than in our own." He lists the two obvious examples. One is Switzerland, which "is not a nation, but held together by her constitution." The other, of course, is the United States: "She is unified by nothing but her constitution and the patriotic feelings that are bestowed on that constitution."[7]

So the constitution is the object of identification, affection, and, one supposes, obligation. There is some truth to this, but only some. The truth is that Swiss and American patriotism today do not rest on a common ethnicity, let alone race or religion or even language (in the case of the quadrilingual Swiss). It is also true that American nationhood is defined in terms of documents like the Declaration of Independence, the Constitution, and the Gettysburg Address. By signing on to them, so to speak, anybody, whatever his color, creed, or bloodline, can become an American citizen. "Signing on" is done by pronouncing an oath of naturalization:

> I hereby declare, on oath, that I absolutely and entirely renounce and abjure all allegiance and fidelity to any foreign . . . state . . . of which I have heretofore been a . . . citizen; that I will support and defend the Constitution and laws of the United States of America against all enemies, foreign and domestic; that I will bear true faith and allegiance to the same; that I will bear arms on behalf of the United States . . . and that I take this obligation freely without any mental reservation or purpose of evasion; so help me God.[8]

Yet this affirmation ignores some basics which, as we shall see, collide with the all-too-abstract idea of a document-based patriotism. One is an obvious logical conundrum. In a world with more than one liberal-democratic order, constitutional patriotism cannot deliver a reason for attachment to a particular country, let alone for obligation to that state. Unless one believes in national polygamy—that a person can love many countries and encounters no conflict between these attachments—Verfassungspatriotismus becomes meaningless. Since Germany, Britain, and America are all liberal democracies, why should I prefer one to the other? Why should I feel obligated to one or the other? "Patriotism" comes from "patria," the Latin for "fatherland." So why this rather than that "patria"?

Constitutional patriotism, to put it unfairly, is a permit for promiscuous patriotism. Now, there is nothing wrong with "rootless cosmopolitanism" (a term which Russians still use when they accuse Jews of lacking allegiance to the Rodina), if you are a committed cosmopolitan or "one-worlder." In that case, you simply don't believe in the nation-state. But, by definition, you cannot be a patriot, which implies selective loyalties and allegiances. So a patriot must choose to whom to accord his feelings, and logically, that cannot be done in terms of a political order shared by many countries.

There is also a historical problem with the "documentary" conception of patriotism and national identity when applied to the United States. It does not hold water. While Americans define their national identity in terms of a "creed," that creed does not come out of nowhere; it is not just a pallid broth cooked up by Locke, Montesquieu, Hutchinson, and Hume that any country could ingest. Samuel Huntington explains why:

> America is a founded society created by seventeenth- and eighteenth-century settlers almost all of whom came from the British Isles. Their values, institutions, and culture provided the foundation for and shaped the development of America in the following centuries. They initially defined American in terms of race, ethnicity, culture, and most importantly religion. Then, in the eighteenth century, they also had to define America ideologically to justify their independence from [Britain]. . . . By the latter years of [the nineteenth] century, the ethnic component had been broadened to include Germans, Irish, and Scandinavians. By World War II and the assimilation . . . of southern and eastern immigrants . . . , ethnicity virtually disappeared as defining component of national identity. So did race [after the civil rights legislation of the 1960s]. As a result, by the 1970s, American identity was defined in terms of culture and the Creed.[9]

True, America was founded on the basis of the "Creed": liberty, equality, democracy, individualism, rights, rule of law, and private property. These were the bricks, so to speak. But the mortar that held the American nation-state together was an Anglo-American Protestant nationalism that was racial, ethnic, religious, and ideological. That mortar was unique and separate, and not a kind of universal constitutionalism. Over time, America has become a "universal" nation in the sense that it embraces many religions, cultures, and ethnicities. But it remains exceptional in the sense that there is a peculiarly *American* political culture, ethos, and sense of history that have been passed on from the earlier Americans to successive immigrant groups.[10] These have shaped an identity that proclaims "We are Americans," and not "We are constitutional patriots."

From all this flows a sense of obligation that makes Americans fight in wars and share their wealth with fellow Americans more than with others. This is why fire stations fly oversized American flags and policemen sew a replica on their sleeves. The flag does stand for the Constitution, but surely in a remote and abstract way. The far more immediate and dominant message refers to powerful and inchoate feelings of affection and pride, of "we" and community. What about the Swiss (Sternberger's other example of a people held together by something other than national identity), who are bound by neither language nor ethnicity nor religion? One should never generalize from small countries on the periphery of the drama of nations, but it is nevertheless clear that, like the Americans, the Swiss possess a sense of nationalism and exceptionalism that is *not* based on constitutional principles alone.

Constitutional patriotism is not a theory of allegiance, but almost a contradiction in terms. Hence, Jürgen Habermas's attempt to salvage it from logical ruin does not really work. "Contrary to widespread misunderstanding," Habermas writes, "*Verfassungspatriotismus* means that citizens do not accept the principles of the constitution simply on the basis of abstract content, but in the context of their peculiar national history."[11] Behind this convolution lurks a simple insight: people do not draw their identity from universal values and procedures, but from specialness deriving from the usual suspects of national consciousness: history, culture, and difference.

And yet. Writing about nationhood, national identity, and nationalism at the beginning of the twenty-first century, at least in the democratic West, has a very different flavor than it had during the age of nationalism, circa 1789–1945. There is a strong whiff of postnationalism in the air. What has changed?

First, the fires of nationalism that used to drive millions into the trenches have burned out; mass-based bloodthirstiness is no longer part of the Western ethos. Second, the intelligentsia, once the ideological engine of nationalism, has sputtered and then reversed directions: intellectuals today are antinationalists. Third, the very idea of "Americanness" or "Germanitude" has weakened, to the point where significant segments of the political class will feel reluctant, if not ashamed, to wave a flag (hence, in Germany, the coinage *Leitkultur*—"dominant culture"—as a way of describing a country's culture without reference to national identity). An endless debate in the West, including the United States, revolves around the extent to which immigrants should be forced to accept the cultural mores, even the language, of their new homelands. (In Germany, the word "immigrant"—*Einwanderer*—is now shunned in favor of *Migrant*, meaning a wanderer who may or may not stay and should thus not be asked to relinquish his cultural identity.)

Fourth, the postmodern reluctance to keep the admissions price of membership high goes hand in glove with a larger distaste for "Westernism" or "Europeanism." Hence, the epithet "Eurocentrism," a term that evokes a long and murderous history of colonization, racism, and oppression. Finally, the postmodern or postnational state tends to emphasize rights and entitlements over obligations and sacrifice. Political rhetoric is now dominated by the language of disbursement—to groups and individuals (subsidies, tax credits, and entitlements enforceable in court). In Western Europe, the language of sacrifice was probably heard last in Winston Churchill's wartime Britain ("blood, sweat, and tears").

In the Western world, from Berlin to Berkeley, the integralism that today dominates the Muslim world is gone and passé. Does this mean that we are all constitutional patriots now? No, that has not come to pass, and for these reasons:

First, some Western nations are more nationalist than others. Two come to mind immediately: America and Israel, strangely two countries whose nationality is totally multiethnic and firmly based on documents such as the Constitution and the Hebrew Bible. (The latter should not be confused with religion per se, as the majority of Israelis are secular.) To sharpen the paradox: the less a nation defines itself in terms of ethnicity, race, or bloodline, and the more it does so in terms of a "creed," the stronger its sense of identity and nationalism.

Second, the longer a nation has had its nationality repressed, the stronger its nationalism. This pertains to Europe's former East Bloc members, as well as the states and statelets that have emerged from imperial domination by the Soviet Union and Yugoslavia. This is what Isaiah Berlin calls "bent-twig" nationalism.

Third, where nationalism reemerges, it is not the aggressive, expansionist, "*Deutschland über alles*" type, but *defensive*. Defensive nationalism is a feature of rich countries that act as a magnet for poor or persecuted foreigners who seek to secure their livelihood or their lives, and who are often resented as aliens threatening the host countries' identity and resources. Defensive nationalism is also directed against abstract enemies: outsourcing, offshoring, and importing—in short, against globalization.

All that said, it is still clear that the age of nationalism is over in much of the West, and hence the peculiarly German idea of *Verfassungspatriotismus* may have been ahead of the times. The first significant straw in the wind was *Afroyim v. Rusk*, where the Supreme Court held that the government cannot take citizenship from a naturalized American just because he has voted in a foreign election, served in a foreign army, or even held high office in another country.[12] This despite the exclusivist naturalization oath cited earlier. Since then, nationality laws in Western countries have been successively loosened and diluted, to the point where even bloodline countries like Germany now bestow naturalization as a result of mere residence (plus a simple citizenship test). Dual nationality, once a no-no, is not quite routine, but expanding. The trend has been well described by Stanford scholars Gerhard Casper and Stephen Krasner: "Individuals may hold multiple passports. Their affection may be torn among a number of different polities. In a globalized society, however, the most skilled will gravitate toward public spaces in which they can exercise their talents."[13]

This is the essence of postmodernity: anybody can go anywhere because talent beats territory, and because Western states can no longer demand exclusive allegiance from their inhabitants. What shall we call this? Certainly not constitutional patriotism; it is rather conditional patriotism. Having argued postnationalistically, Casper and Krasner close on an ambivalent note, which is actually quite fitting: "Over time those who stay will internalize at least core American values, individualism, democracy, and a free market—values that will have served their own individual self-interest as well."[14]

So, is it "core American values"—distinct and separate? Or is it the oldest definition of patriotism on the books, variously ascribed to Aristophanes and Cicero: *Ubi bene, ibi patria*—My fatherland is where I am doing well? If so, say hello to the postnational (Western) state and to opportunistic, rather than constitutional, patriotism.

Notes

1. Max Horkheimer, *Hinter der Fassade*, in Nation, Nationalismus, Nationale Identität (1988), available at http://www.tguv.de/~baustein/PDF/C7-Horkheimer.pdf. In the original German: "Nirgendwo in zivilisierten Ländern ist sowenig Grund zum Patriotismus wie in Deutschland, und nirgendwo wird von den Bürgern weniger Kritik am Patriotismus geübt als hier, wo er das Schlimmste vollbracht hat. . . . Der Patriotismus in Deutschland ist so furchtbar weil er grundlos ist."

2. Dolf Sternberger, *Verfassungspatriotismus*, Frankfurter Allgemeine Zeitung, May 23, 1979, at 1. The piece was written on the occasion of the thirtieth anniversary of the West German Basic Law. The term was first used in an article in the same paper dated January 27, 1970. It reemerged in a much longer piece in the *Frankfurter Allgemeine Zeitung*, also called "*Verfassungspatriotismus*" and dated August 31, 1982. A reproduction of Sternberger's address appeared in the *Bayerischer Landtag* on June 29, 1982. All subsequent quotations are from this version and are cited as *Verfassungspatriotismus II*.

3. Sternberger, *Verfassungspatriotismus II*.

4. Jürgen Habermas, *Apologetische Tendenzen*, in Eine Art Schadensabwicklung 123 (Jürgen Habermas ed., 1987).

5. Quoted in Sternberger, *Verfassungspatriotismus II*.

6. *Id.*

7. *Id.*

8. Oath of Renunciation and Allegiance, 8 U.S.C.§ 1448.

9. Samuel P. Huntington, Who Are We? The Challenges to American Identity 38 (2004).

10. There is a parallel here with the Jewish "creed." Each year at Passover, which celebrates the Exodus, historical memory is passed on to the children during the seder, the festive meal. This is how we suffered, how we escaped, how we became a people. . . .

11. Jürgen Habermas, *Vorpolitische Grundlagen des demokratischen Rechtsstaates*, in Zwischen Naturalismus und Religion 111 (2005).

12. *Afroyim v. Rusk*, 387 U.S. 253 (1967).

13. Unpublished paper on file with author, 2008.

14. *Id.*

2

The Meaning of American Citizenship: What We Can Learn from Disputes over Naturalization

William Galston

During the past two decades, the idea of "constitutional patriotism" has been much discussed in European intellectual and political circles. The core of this idea is the proposition that political attachment should focus on "the norms, the values, and . . . the procedures of a liberal democratic constitution." So understood, patriotism steers a middle course between cultural and ethnic particularism on the one hand, and cosmopolitanism on the other. By helping to decouple the idea of national solidarity from that of adherence to a dominant majority culture, it can enhance the possibility of inclusiveness in increasingly multicultural societies.[1]

Given the unhappy history of ethnic and cultural particularism in Europe (not least in Germany), it is not hard to understand why this approach has gained some traction. But many Americans wonder what the fuss is all about. As a nation of immigrants, we instinctively believe that while ethnic loyalties have a legitimate place in civil society, they cannot work as the basis of national solidarity. The idea of a unity that is creedal rather than ethnic is in our bones, even if we find it difficult to say exactly what our creed might be.

A moment's reflection, however, suggests that matters are not so simple.

Reason and Emotion in Citizenship

Throughout American history, creedal and cultural definitions of national identity have vied for dominance. Immigrants who spoke languages other than English, who came from non-European stock, or who professed religions other than dissenting Protestantism were viewed with suspicion and often oppressed, especially in times of war. Recently, Samuel Huntington has challenged the belief that creed alone would suffice to maintain American unity. "History and psychology," he argues, "suggest that it is unlikely to be enough to sustain a nation for long. America with only the Creed as a basis for unity could soon evolve into a loose confederation of ethnic, racial, cultural, and political groups."[2] The reason is this, says Huntington: "People are not likely to find in political principles the deep emotional content and meaning provided by kith and kin, blood and belonging, culture and nationality. These attachments may have little or no basis in fact but they do satisfy a deep human longing for meaningful community." Moreover, America's shared Anglo-Protestant culture created the "people" that claimed its right to separate from Great Britain, assume its equal station among other nations, and ordain a new constitution for the new nation. It is from this culture that the American creed first flowed, and upon which it continues to rest today. And thus, Huntington concludes, a multicultural America will inevitably become a multicreedal America.[3]

The situation in Europe is no less tangled. Ethnic divisions stoked the tragic conflicts in the Balkans and have sustained the Basque insurgency against Spain. Czechs and Slovaks found it impossible to live together in a single political community, and Belgium is in danger of splitting up over ethnic and linguistic issues. In the Baltic states, divisions between majority populations and Russian-speaking minorities have created instability (occasionally violence) and may yet serve as a pretext for Russian intervention. And even in Germany, the advocates of constitutional patriotism run up against very different understandings of national unity and identity. A personal story will illustrate my point.

A few years ago I was invited to a conference in Munich on the topic "Religious America, Secular Europe?" For most of the meeting, I did not understand why the title contained a question mark, because all the quantitative sociological evidence speakers presented suggested that Max Weber's secularization thesis applied to Europe but not the United States. On the afternoon of the final day, though, a distinguished German law professor spoke about his country's conception of citizenship. For half an hour his discourse traveled a predictable path. But then, out of the blue, he began talking about Turkey's effort to join the European Union. "This is out of the question," he declared. I expected him to cite the impact of Turkish accession on the political composition of the EU, or its financial stability. Instead, he said, the case against this step was cultural. Despite its secular constitution, Turkey is an Islamic nation, while the heart of European civilization was Christianity. The EU's legal and economic unification rested on a broad cultural consensus, which Turkey would fatally disrupt. During a break in the proceedings, I walked around the hall and chatted with members of the audience. I could find no one who disagreed with the speaker.

None of this proves that Huntington is right about America, or that German (or European) identity is indissolubly linked to Christianity. It seems undeniable, however, that citizenship requires a measure of emotional identification with a particular community. While constitutional democracies may share some basic principles that command reasoned assent, citizens are members of, and are attached to, particular communities, not to constitutional democracies in general.

In his first inaugural, Lincoln closed with references to civic friendship, to the "bonds of affection" that united Americans despite their differences, to the "mystic chords of memory" that would, he hoped, "swell the chorus of the Union."[4] This was an unabashed appeal to patriotic emotions and to the shared experiences that linked Americans, one to another. These commonalities did not suffice to avert separation and war, of course. But Lincoln's appeal to them did illuminate the key role they play in real-world citizenship.

Lincoln's rhetoric points to a larger truth, obvious but sometimes overlooked and even resisted. Every political community is bounded not only by geography but also by population and constitutive understandings, which are elements of particularity that citizens are called upon to accept and endorse. There is nothing anomalous about such a requirement. While we owe a general respect to age, for example, we are asked to honor our own fathers and mothers in a special way. Similarly, while we are not permitted to be indifferent to the needs of children, we are allowed, indeed expected, to give preference and special care to our own. While many local norms lack general validity, they may still be binding on us; we follow long-established family traditions while recognizing that other families do things differently, and legitimately so.

It is easy to see what motivates mistrust of particular attachments. They can insulate us from, even render us indifferent to, wider obligations. They can foster mutual incomprehension and mistrust. At their worst, they can lead to violence and war. But cosmopolitanism is not a realistic remedy for these ills. Not only is there no cosmopolis of which we could be members, but if there were, we would quickly discover how a world-state could threaten liberty. The challenge is to combine what is valid in cosmopolitanism— the moral reality of shared humanity—with what is valuable in particularity—the satisfactions of communities of sentiment—into a sustainable practice of constitutional citizenship.

A leading American constitutional scholar, Sanford Levinson, has explored the analogy between constitutional communities and faith communities.[5] One of the many parallels between them is the commitment of their members to the interpretation of fundamental texts as a guide to practice. This commitment does not mean that members will agree among themselves. Indeed, each community typically contains leading thinkers who subscribe to varying methods of textual interpretation leading to divergent conclusions about the meaning of the text. In the case of Judaism, for example, views of the Torah run the gamut from literalism to existentialism—from understanding the words as literally dictated to Moses by God, on the one hand, to seeing them as a human response to the overwhelming experience of divine presence, on the other. And even among literalists there is a range of interpretative strategies.

Nonetheless, the members of the community must have something in common beyond the text itself. They must be jointly and severally committed, first, to the interpretative process, and second, to some authoritative mechanism for the resolution of disputes touching on belief and practice. In Judaism, as in many constitutional courts, controversies among those qualified by learning and experience to participate in them were settled in favor of the majority (with minority opinions faithfully recorded for future reference and possible use). Just as we can speak of the Talmudic tradition, we can speak of a constitutional tradition within a specific political community, which Jan-Werner Muller has called a "constitutional culture."[6]

This source of civic unity and particularity is much cooler and more cerebral than the mystic chords of memory, for which it is no substitute. For peoples as for families, participation in a shared history, filled with tales of triumph and tragedy and depictions of virtue and vice, is the emotional core of the common venture. Another personal story will illustrate the point.

Although (or perhaps because) I was on the staff of Walter Mondale's presidential campaign, I will never forget Ronald Reagan's address on the fortieth anniversary of D-Day. He spoke on Pointe du Hoc, a cliff overlooking one of the Normandy beaches and the site of one of the most heroic feats of that remarkable day. Under intense fire, with no cover, U.S. Army Rangers had scaled the cliff and seized the high ground, silencing the German machine guns and clearing the way for the American forces. As President Reagan spoke, the camera showed grainy black and white footage of the young, superbly conditioned soldiers as they made their way up the face of the cliff. As the film ended, the television camera panned around to the hobbled, white-haired survivors of that day, seated in rows of chairs in front of the president. He gestured toward them and said, "These are the boys of Pointe du Hoc." As he uttered that sentence, tears welled up in my eyes. I was standing in a crowd in the Mondale campaign's press office. I looked around me and saw that everyone was crying. I realized then that we could not win the election because we were up against a man with an unerring ability to find and tap the emotional core of his country. But I realized something else as well—that these emotions are as much a part of citizenship as are the shared principles we embrace.

This is a not altogether comfortable truth, in part because unscrupulous leaders can manipulate the emotional side of citizenship against its rational side. And it raises another set of troubling questions: Can adults who choose to join a community ever share fully in the constitutive experiences of those who were born and bred within it? And if not, can they be treated as full and equal citizens?

Here again, Levinson's analogy between religious and political communities is illuminating. Ovadyah, a convert to Judaism, wrote to Moses Maimonides asking whether he was allowed to participate in prayers and rituals that appeared ethnocentric. Could he utter the phrase "God of our fathers"? Did he have the right to claim to have been "chosen"? Could he say that God took "us" out of Egypt or that he was a member of the group for whom God had performed miracles? Maimonides replied that he could. Abraham had rejected idolatry and discovered monotheism through his own efforts and had persuaded others to join him. The founder of Judaism, then, was a convert and had converted others. As James Diamond puts it, Maimonides eliminated the gap between converts and the Jewish community "by replacing the biological father-son model with a pedagogical teacher-disciple one."[7] In fact, Maimonides suggested, converts may be more fully Jewish than are many born into the community—if their decision to become Jewish rests on knowledge and reasonable belief rather than on (say) emotional ties to a Jewish spouse. This is not to say that a community one rationally chooses to join cannot also become a locus of sentiment. (Recall the book of Ruth.) Immigrants may come to America in search of freedom and opportunity, but their gratitude and loyalty often exceeds that of native-born citizens.

Maimonides' rationalist account of community membership did not go unchallenged. Both Judah Halevy and writers in the Jewish mystical tradition propounded theories of an inherited spiritual property that distinguished Jews at birth from other peoples. It followed that converts, however knowledgeable and loyal, could never be fully equal to "native-born" Jews, an essentialist thesis that has influenced strands of Orthodoxy down to the present day.[8] And many Jews who reject essentialism nonetheless believe that Judaism is more than correct belief, or even orthopraxy, but consists as well of an ensemble of cultural assumptions, absorbed osmotically from birth, that structure a distinctive way of looking at the world and of treating other human beings. These culturalists suspect (even if they do not admit it) that converts are never quite at one with the people they have decided, however wholeheartedly, to join.

Similar considerations figured in the long-running American debate about Catholic participation in American life. There was a question of principle: was the Pope a "foreign potentate," allegiance to whom would require conscientious American Catholics to divide their loyalties and dilute their allegiance to the Constitution? But there were cultural issues as well. Didn't "Americanism" embody individualism and suspicion of authority? Wasn't Catholicism essentially communitarian, hierarchical, and dominated by authorities whose writ was not to be questioned? It took more than a century, and important changes in both Catholicism and American society, before these divisions could be set aside.

Naturalization and U.S. Citizenship

I want to use the process of naturalization as a prism through which to view the American conception of citizenship. But as Aristotle argued in the *Politics*, we cannot understand competing views without first clarifying what we mean by citizenship in general. One of Aristotle's key theses is that enjoying what we now call the "equal protection of the laws" is not a sufficient condition. Citizenship also requires the right and ability to engage in important public functions. In his view two were key—judging and deliberating, or in our terms, participating as a juror in the administration of justice and as a voter in the selection of officials who make the laws and decide questions of war and peace. Although it would be a stretch to describe Aristotle as a partisan of democracy, he acknowledged that his definition of citizenship corresponded most closely to the definition operative in democracies, where participation in judging and deliberating is most widely shared.[9] The controversies throughout American history over voting rights and jury service attest to the continuing relevance of the Aristotelian framework.

Modern constitutional democracy is in many respects representative rather than direct. This raises the possibility that qualifications for "office" may not be the same as for citizenship in general. And indeed, there are special qualifications for most national offices established under the Constitution. To serve in the House of Representatives, nonnative citizens must be naturalized for at least seven years; to serve in the Senate, at least nine years. And no matter how long they have been citizens, individuals who obtain U.S. citizenship through naturalization are ineligible for the presidency.[10]

It is instructive to return to the constitutional convention of 1787 to find out why. The issue was most fully debated on August 8. The draft before the body required members of the House to have been citizens for at least three years. George Mason objected on two grounds. First, he argued, citizenship for only three years "was not enough for ensuring that local knowledge" that each representative should possess. And second, a three-year standard might not be enough to guarantee loyalty to the United States. Indeed, foreign countries could send emissaries to become naturalized as sleeper agents who would pursue "insidious purposes" against the interests of their adopted country.[11] Speaking the next day in support of Gouverneur Morris's proposal to require fourteen years of naturalized citizenship for senators, Charles Pinckney emphasized the special importance of loyalty for senators, who would after all have the power of ratifying treaties and helping the executive manage foreign policy (235). Pierce Butler added a third consideration: people who come to the United States from other countries bring with them "not only attachments to other countries, but ideas of government so distinct from ours that in every point of view they are dangerous" (236).

Although there was general agreement that three years was too short a requirement for House members and that seven years would be appropriate, the proposal to require fourteen years for senators met significant resistance. Both James Madison and Benjamin Franklin objected to giving the new Constitution what Madison labeled a "tincture of illberality" (236). Besides, they argued, many foreign countries were sympathetic to the new nation, and many foreigners had rendered great service during the Revolutionary War. They had proved their devotion and should not be discouraged from immigrating to the United States by public marks of mistrust. Even worse, argued John Randolph, overly lengthy exclusion from the possibility of office might strike erstwhile sympathizers as a breach of faith and drive them into hostility to the new regime.

Speaking as a non-native-born citizen, James Wilson offered personal and heartfelt reflections. The fourteen-year requirement, he argued, would be interpreted as "degrading discrimination" and generate a sense of "discouragement and mortification" on the part of those excluded from high office for so long. Indeed, he himself had experienced the consequences of such legal incapacities. "To be appointed to a place," he remarked, "may be a matter of indifference. To be incapable of being appointed, is a circumstance grating, and mortifying" (237).

Wilson's remarks prompted a remarkable intervention from the sponsor of the fourteen-year amendment. "The lesson we are taught," retorted Morris, is that "we should be governed as much by our reason, and as little be our feelings, as possible." Generosity was one thing, imprudence another. Experience shows that attachments to one's country of origin are shed only with difficulty, and slowly. This is not to be regretted: "The men who can shake off their attachments to their own country can never love any other. These attachments are the wholesome prejudices which uphold all governments." It follows that the absence of such prejudices is inconsistent with the maintenance of order and good government. Cosmopolitanism is a political vice, Morris concluded, not proof of superior virtue. He did not wish to see any of those "philosophical gentlemen," those self-styled "citizens of the world," in the public councils of the United States; their lack of attachment to a particular place meant that they could not be trusted (237–38). The requirements for office that the constitutional convention ultimately adopted represent an effort to acknowledge the partial validity of, and achieve a workable balance among, these competing understandings of membership in a political community.

Prior to the Civil War, the dominant understanding of citizenship ran along two separate tracks. On the one hand, for native-born Americans, citizenship in a particular state was the necessary and sufficient condition for being a citizen of the United States.[12] On the other hand, Article I, Section 8 of the Constitution gives Congress the power to establish a "uniform rule of naturalization," a power it exercised during the First Congress in 1790 and that it has exercised ever since. No individual state can devise and employ its own standards for naturalization. Transforming an "alien" into a "citizen" is a national act. This represents one of the clearest instances of the differences between "we the people" and "we the states." From this perspective, citizenship through naturalization has functioned throughout American history as a counterweight to local attachments; immigrants are "coming to America," not to New York or Virginia. And it is through the requirements for naturalization that Americans clarify—not just to the world, but for themselves—how they understand the essentials of citizenship.

Conditions laid down in the Immigration and Nationality Act of 1952 and incorporated into the United States Code reduce to four essentials. After admission to permanent residence, applicants for citizenship must have resided in the United States for at least five years, and continuously after applying for citizenship. Applicants must be of "good moral character," that is, they must be law abiding. They must be "well disposed to the good order and happiness of the United States," that is, they must genuinely care about the well-being of the political community they wish to join. And finally, they must be "attached to the principles of the Constitution of the United States."[13]

Let us dwell on this final, quietly paradoxical condition. On the one hand, it establishes beyond doubt that America officially understands itself as a creedal community unified by belief rather than blood. On the other hand, it does not specify the content of the creed. The Constitution itself does not set forth its principles, or even incorporate them by reference. We may infer some from the text. "We the people" are the ultimate source of legitimate authority, and only they may ordain and establish a constitutional order. The Constitution exists to further certain purposes but not others—for example, security and liberty, not virtue or piety. To guard against tyranny and safeguard liberty, powers are separated and distributed among competing individuals and institutions; there is therefore a powerful presumption against concentrated power. And the defense of liberty does not stop with the separation of powers. In addition, constitutional democracy both hedges its commitment to pure majority rule and spells out certain rights that majorities cannot legitimately invade.

To embrace these principles is not to endorse the letter of the Constitution, however, which leaves open the possibility that candidates for naturalization may conceivably favor radical changes in the existing constitutional order. Consider a scholarly applicant for U.S. citizenship who had written articles in favor of establishing a unicameral national legislature or electing the president by direct popular vote. It is hard to imagine that such a candidate would be rejected for inadequate attachment to constitutional principles.

But how far can we push the distinction between the document's spirit and its letter? The case of *Schneiderman v. United States* raises precisely this issue. The petitioner was a member of the Communist Party at the time of his naturalization and thereafter. The government sought to revoke his citizenship on the grounds that it had been fraudulently procured: petitioner's Communist affiliation and activities proved that he was not attached to the principles of the Constitution. A five-member majority of the Supreme Court disagreed. Article V, the justices pointed out, excluded almost no provisions of the constitution from possible amendment: "This provision and the many important and far-reaching changes made in the Constitution since 1787 refute the idea that attachment to any particular provision or provisions is essential, or that one who advocates radical changes is necessarily not attached to the Constitution."[14] And they quoted from Justice Holmes's dissent in *United States v. Schwimmer*: "Surely it cannot show lack of attachment to the principles of the Constitution that [one] thinks it can be improved."[15] Our "primary attachment" must be to the right of "free discussion and free thinking," which the majority in effect specifies as the core principle of the Constitution itself.[16]

It would seem to follow then, that as long as an applicant is willing to obey the law and to change the Constitution through peaceful processes, he has met the statutory conditions for citizenship. The counsel for the petitioner (one Wendell Willkie, the recently defeated Republican candidate for president) urged just that position. The Court declined to follow its logic to the end, arguing instead that if Congress had considered Communism ground for exclusion from citizenship, it would have said so. After all, it had specifically excluded anarchists and polygamists, among others. The statute's silence about Communism, whose tenets were well known to Congress, therefore had to be construed as leaving the question open, and there was insufficient reason to conclude that petitioner's personal mode of adhering to Marxist doctrine was incompatible with peaceful change in our constitutional order.[17]

Writing in dissent, Chief Justice Stone, whose credentials as a civil libertarian were beyond reproach, professed incredulity. He was joined by an indignant Felix Frankfurter as well as Justice Roberts. Congress had first used the operative phrase—"the principles of the Constitution"—in the Naturalization Act of 1795, and among its drafters were men who had participated in the constitutional convention and could be presumed to know what they were talking about. The chief justice proceeded to offer his own gloss, which diverged in some respects from the definition of constitutional principles the government had propounded in its brief. He discussed at considerable length the history, beliefs, and practices of the Communist Party, which in his view were not only incompatible with any acceptable account of constitutional principles but also revealed an intention to change the constitution by force and violence rather than peaceful amendment if circumstances permitted.[18]

Reading the opinions, it is hard to avoid the impression that Stone had the better of it. Nonetheless, he did not prevail, and his position has had rough going ever since. One reason for this is that the majority appealed to a classic American principle—freedom of conscience—that was enjoying something of a revival in the 1940s. Indeed, *Schneiderman* was handed down exactly one week after the more famous *West Virginia v. Barnette* decision overturning the mandatory flag salute and recitation of the Pledge of Allegiance as applied to Jehovah's Witnesses.[19] In his majority opinion, Justice Jackson had declared, "If there is any fixed star in our constitutional constellation, it is that no official, high or petty, can prescribe what shall be orthodox in politics, nationalism, religion, or other matters of opinion." For the government to do so, Jackson continued, would be to invade "the sphere of intellect and spirit which it is the purpose of the First Amendment to our Constitution to reserve from all official control."[20] To be sure, Jackson was speaking of what government could not rightly do to *citizens*. It is not unreasonable, one might object, to impose standards at the threshold of membership in the community that one might not deploy against current members. Still, how a community understands the beliefs and practices required of citizens is bound to affect its standards for admission. The more capaciously (civil) libertarian the former, the more open and permissive are the latter likely to be.

We thus encounter a fact poised uneasily between anomaly and outright paradox. G. K. Chesterton once remarked that America is "the only nation founded on a creed" and is "a nation with the soul of a church."[21] If the United States is a creedal community, if membership in the community is seen primarily as assent to the creed and not the facts of descent or geography, then we would expect the creed to be clearly stated and fiercely guarded. But to judge from the authoritative pronouncements of our Supreme Court, we would seem to have shared procedures but no common creed, or perhaps a creed that gives pride of place to arguing about its meaning. From time to time, to be sure, we mount crusades against "un-American" activities and beliefs. For the most part, we espouse principles of civil liberty and freedom of conscience without worrying much about their limits.

Indeed, we seem not to worry much about the meaning of citizenship. We are notably ineffective in teaching our history and civic traditions to our children; we hardly try. Nor do we expect much of adult citizens—not voting, not military service, not paying taxes adequate to defray the costs of government. Most of us manage to avoid jury duty, and most of those who disregard notices to appear are not punished with any severity. We are coming closer and closer to the view of citizenship that Aristotle dismissed as manifestly inadequate—the right to sue and be sued.

The jeremiad is a classic American literary tradition, and the reader may be forgiven for concluding that I have repaired to it without warrant. Americans' ignorance about their country is matched only by their patriotic attachment to it. Despite the soft temptations of a wealthy commercial society, the United States has never been short of men (and now women as well) who are willing to fight and die for their country. And in the face of great challenges, Americans can always be counted on to do the right thing, though only after they have tried everything else, as Winston Churchill once remarked.

All true, and yet it is probably true that the ratio of light to heat in our national debates would rise considerably if we worked a bit harder to refine our conception of citizenship. Consider immigration policy. We lurch from a generous open door to fear-based restrictions and back again. We see languages other than English as threats in one generation, and in the next deplore our inability to speak languages other than our own. Despite oft-repeated platitudes about a nation of immigrants, we cannot seem to decide whether today's new entrants are strengthening or weakening us. Like citizenship itself, our policy disputes inevitably blend reason and passion. But understanding better what we expect from naturalized citizens, and why we have worried throughout our history that we might not get it, would be a large step toward a steadier and more sustainable balance.

Notes

1. Jan-Werner Muller & Kim Lane Scheppele, *Constitutional Patriotism: An Introduction*, 6 Int'l J. Const. L. 67, 67–68 (2008).

2. Samuel P. Huntington, Who Are We? The Challenges to America's National Identity 19 (2004).

3. *Id.*, 339–40.

4. Abraham Lincoln, *First Inaugural Address, March 4, 1861*, in Abraham Lincoln: Speeches and Writings, 1859–1865 (1980), 215, 224.

5. Sanford Levinson, Constitutional Faith (1988).

6. Jan-Werner Muller, *A General Theory of Constitutional Patriotism*, 6 Int'l J. Const. L. 80 (2008).

7. James A. Diamond, *Maimonides and the Convert: A Juridical and Philosophical Embrace of the Outsider*, 11 Medieval Phil. & Theology 127 (2003).

8. On this disagreement, *see* David Hartman, Israelis and the Jewish Tradition: An Ancient People Debating Its Future (2000); *see also* Menachem Kellner, Maimonides' Confrontation with Mysticism (2006).

9. Politics 3.1 (1275a22–23).

10. There appear to be no constitutional restrictions for service on the Supreme Court, the only part of the judiciary established by the Constitution. In principle, then, statutes could open up the federal bench, including the Supreme Court, to noncitizens.

11. The Records of the Federal Convention of 1787, volume 2 (Max Farrand, ed, 1966) 216. Subsequent quotations from this work are cited with a parenthetical page number in the text.

12. The *Dred Scott* case represented a constitutional revolution in part because it challenged this understanding. According to Chief Justice Taney's majority opinion, "It does not by any means follow, because [an individual] has all the rights and privileges of a citizen of a State, that he must be a citizen of the United States." *Dred Scott v. Sanford*, 60 U.S. 393 (1857).

13. 8 U.S.C. §§ 1427, 316 (2002).

14. *Schneiderman v. United States*, 320 U.S. 118, 137 (1943).

15. *United States v. Schwimmer*, 279 U.S. 644, 654 (1929) (Holmes, J., dissenting).

16. *Schneiderman*, 320 U.S. at 139.

17. *Id.* at 132, 140.

18. *Id.* at 170–97. (Stone, C. J., dissenting.) *See especially* Chief Justice Stone's sketch of the principles of the Constitution at 181.

19. 319 U.S. 624 (1943).

20. *Id.* at 642.

21. The Collected Works of G. K. Chesterton, vol. 21, 41 (1990).

PART II
Citizenship

3

European Citizenship: Mobile Nationals, Immobile Aliens, and Random Europeans

Francesca Strumia

European citizenship, a dormant alter ego of nationality, becomes active and consequential when a resident of an EU member country moves to or visits a country other than her own. An Ethiopian national who has lived and worked in Italy for eight years faces very different prospects for legal inclusion, labor market access, nondiscrimination guarantees, and family reunification than, say, a French national with an identical residency and employment record in Italy. In this context, European citizenship maneuvers invisible but significant boundaries, which still mark the nominally borderless space of the European Union. It turns a blind eye to immigrants' claims that in some way they belong to the European Union. As the main source of mobility rights, European citizenship creates two Europes, one for the more European, and one for the less, without achieving any clear definition of what it means to belong to Europe. It intensifies insider/outsider divisions that have been drawn by member states and, in so doing, waives much of its integrative potential. To reward deserving immigrants while discouraging the undeserving, we should rethink the criteria of Europeanness, and extend to resident foreigners some of the Europe-wide benefits of European citizenship.

European Citizenship and Mobility

European citizenship is a skinny legal construct, but it relates to important concerns—legitimacy, democracy, identity, immigration, and diversity—that are at the center of incendiary debates in the European Union.

The idea of a citizenship for Europe is closely tied to a notion of a European people, the ghostly *demos* that many students of European integration have been unable to find, and whose absence leaves the future of Europe on shaky grounds.[1] While the "democratic deficit" of the European Union has institutional, procedural, political, and constitutional aspects, its hard core is the disinclination of European citizens to endorse the institutions of Europe as their legitimate, autonomous agents and democratic representatives. (In June 2008, for instance, the Irish rejected the Lisbon Treaty, which was supposed to remedy some of the shortfalls of democracy in Europe.) The distance between the citizens of Europe and the EU has to do in part with issues of identity. The question is whether citizens of Europe can develop some sort of European identity based on civic commonality or on a common cultural heritage. There are many views on the extent to which a European identity exists, and on how such an identity could be developed.[2] So far, however, little in the way of a European identity seems to have been created by a treaty-based European citizenship.

Ideally, European citizenship would address the problem of diversity in Europe. European citizens speak twenty-three official languages; and they celebrate national holidays on different days, recalling on those days different collective memories. (Some may recall a victory, others a defeat.) As children they learn different national histories, or different sides of the same one; and they may worship differently or belong to different churches. Immigration waves add color to the diversity of Europe. Through the prospect of naturalization in a member state, immigrants represent an important pool of candidates for European citizenship. About 19 million non-European citizens are legally resident in the EU. Every year, between 1.5 and 2 million new ones enter the EU legally, and estimates suggest that an additional 500,000 persons enter illegally. Different member states attract different immigrant groups. For instance, the largest group of resident foreigners in Germany is made up of Turks (about 1.8 million). In Spain, it is Moroccans (about 600,000); in Italy, Albanians (about 400,000); in Portugal, Brazilians (about 70,000).[3]

One has to scratch the surface quite hard, then, to reveal the Europeanness of European citizens. Hence a citizenship of Europe that gave meaning to European belonging could help tackle many of the issues connected to diversity—by accommodating claims for membership of the old and new European minorities; by giving a political voice to all groups; and by rationalizing and rethinking the generous welfare systems of European countries. It is in the interest of the member states to facilitate the long-term inclusion and upward social mobility of immigrants.[4] Low birthrates throughout Europe have led to declining populations in several member states, which in turn threaten their welfare system, their long-term decisional weight within the EU, and more generally the international influence of the European Union. Immigration represents the main way for Europe to cope with this demographic crisis—but only if immigrants have a channel to legal integration, and one that offers the prospect of upward mobility, so that they can become substantial contributors to national welfare systems.[5]

Citizenship can be an important tool in addressing the issues raised by diverse European populations. It sets the criteria that distinguish between insiders and outsiders, and it ties claims and rights to that distinction. It also creates a method for bringing outsiders inside, and in fact encourages those being excluded to seek inclusion. But European citizenship at present does not perform these functions. Being simply additional and complementary to national citizenship, it distinguishes between the rights of citizens and noncitizens, without distinguishing the degree to which either group belongs to Europe. As a result, it produces a distribution of rights and mobility options that often looks undeserved, inconsistent, or arbitrary.

According to the European Community treaty, a European citizen is any person who holds the nationality of a member state.[6] There are three ways of becoming a European citizen: first, being born a national of a member state, either by birth on the territory of one of the member states with some qualifying link to its community or by being born in another corner of the globe but having family links to some EU country national;[7] second, naturalizing as a citizen of one of the EU member states after having complied with all the relevant requirements; and third, being a national of a country that joins the European Union, and whose nationals are thereby collectively vested with European citizenship at the time of their country's entry into the union.[8] In multitier entities, one level of citizenship often derives from another, as is the case in the United States, where state citizenship derives from national citizenship. However, U.S. state citizenship is tied to residence, and thus to a tangible condition of belonging to the territorial and political community of a particular state. European citizenship, in contrast, is not tied to residence or some other obvious indicator of European belonging, to the extent that holding nationality of a member state can be taken as a proxy for belonging to the European Union. Each member state nationality comes equipped with its own affective symbols, membership requirements, and defining characters. European "citizenship," conferred in the penumbra of one of those nationalities, represents legal belonging to a community whose emotional and definitional boundaries are at best fuzzy.

European citizens can move and reside freely in any member state; they can vote in local elections and for the European Parliament in another member state if they reside there; they can claim the protection of the diplomatic authorities of another member state while in a third country; and they can petition some European institutions (which is the only thing they can do as European citizens even if they have not moved anywhere). The right to move to and reside in any other EU member country is the most important right of European citizenship. Free movement within the EU was originally a right for workers and economic actors in the European Common Market. In the words of the European Community treaty, and in the minds of the judges of the European Court of Justice, however, this right has gradually taken the shape of a right of citizenship.

Tying free movement to European citizenship generates a hierarchy of mobility in the European Union. At least three groups may now be distinguished in respect of free-movement rights under European law: fully mobile European citizens; semimobile third-country nationals (TCNs) long resident in Europe; and immobile recently arrived TCNs. European citizenship, therefore, while apparently of little definitional value, entails important rights and distinctions that significantly affect the choices open to European citizens and residents.

European citizens are at the top of the mobility ladder, even if the exercise of their right often depends on the availability of sufficient resources and comprehensive health insurance. Citizens' free movement is a formal right that the European Community treaty confers on them, but it also grows out of the work of the European Court of Justice. In a series of judgments between 1998 and 2005,[9] the ECJ relied extensively on the legal instrument of European citizenship to remedy some "externalities" of a person's right to move to and reside in any EU member state—for instance, to facilitate access to social security systems, as well as permanent residence and family reunification in the host state. Migrant European citizens have increasingly obtained, through the work of the court, rights comparable to those of nationals of the host state. Two judgments exemplify the court's efforts.

In *Baumbast*, the court held that a European citizen who had originally moved to another member state to be employed still preserved a directly effective right to reside in the host state even after he had abandoned his occupational activity there.[10] In this way, the court began to reconceptualize the right to move as a right to resettle rather than a right to sojourn in another member state as a guest worker. *Trojani* confirmed this tendency.[11] The court was faced with the claim of an indigent European citizen who had a domestic-law residence permit in Belgium and was living there to participate in a reintegration program run by the Salvation Army. He had applied to Belgian authorities for a minimum subsistence allowance, but his request had been denied on the basis of his not being a Belgian national. The court held that a European citizen residing on the basis of a domestic-law residence permit in a member state other than that of his nationality could not be denied a social benefit that would have been granted to a host-state national in the same situation. The court referred in its holding to the right to nondiscrimination on the basis of nationality, which European citizens enjoy with respect to subject areas covered by the EU treaties. The judges seemed to be working to ensure that resettling European citizens are treated as insiders in the new state, with the same level of social solidarity enjoyed by nationals of the host member state. Taken together, *Baumbast* and *Trojani* signal a ripening of a right to free movement based on citizenship, which has gradually lost its original connection to employment issues.

As a further confirmation of this metamorphosis, a 2004 European directive delineates the conditions for the exercise of European Community–wide rights to free movement and residence by European citizens.[12] Under the directive, citizens' rights to free movement remain conditioned on the availability of sufficient financial resources and of health insurance. Any European citizen, however, can reside for a maximum period of three months in any other member state, regardless of resources, and with no access to locally provided social protection. Also, a European citizen who has lawfully resided in another member state for five years is entitled to the status of permanent resident there. Permanent residents are not required to comply with resource requirements and are entitled to equal treatment with nationals, even with respect to social protection.[13] European citizens are thus becoming increasingly mobile, and able to resettle in different parts of the EU with few legal constraints. Only a very small percentage of European citizens actually takes advantage of these rights, however. Bureaucratic inefficiencies and administrative ordeals make intra-European mobility quite burdensome even for citizens, as the benefits and undifferentiated treatment promised by the directive are not equally forthcoming in every member state.[14] Still, in terms of movement-related rights, European citizens are unequaled in the EU.

Recently arrived TCNs, meaning foreigners who have lived in any single member state less than five years (even those whose cumulative time of residence in EU countries is longer), are at the opposite extreme of the mobility spectrum. European law grants these individuals some short-term movement rights. It is silent with respect to movement rights for purposes of resettlement in another EU country.

Short-term movement rights are regulated under the Schengen system.[15] Under the Schengen provisions, TCNs may obtain a common visa, which is valid for periods of up to three months and for the entire Schengen area. In addition, even TCNs who are in a Schengen country on the basis of a domestic-law visa can travel freely to any other Schengen country for periods of up to three months. Quick intra-EU visits are thus readily available to everyone who is legally within the borders of the EU, even those who have been there for just a short while. Resettlement, however, is a different matter.[16] European law has been long silent on this point, and while some recently introduced provisions cover long-term resident TCNs, none addresses recent arrivals. For recently arrived TCNs, resettlement within the EU is still largely an experience of immigration from a first host state to a second one, regulated under domestic immigration law.

Long-term resident TCNs enjoy some statutory free-movement rights, which place them in an intermediate category between European citizens and recently arrived TCNs. A 2003 directive provides that TCNs who have gained long-term resident status in a member state by residing there for at least five years can move to a second member state for purposes of study, vocational training, or employment.[17] Financial conditions apply to the exercise of this right, and the second host member state may impose integration requirements on the entering TCNs. While still heavily conditioned, this right of movement for long-term residents approximates the moderately constrained mobility of European citizens.[18] In this sense, the treatment of long-term resident TCNs may reflect the European Council's intent, expressed at a 1999 meeting in Tampere, that the EU should aim at approximating the condition of TCNs to that of European citizens.[19]

Ironically, though, the concrete *exercise* of mobility rights may remove TCNs further from European citizenship. As noted, TCNs can obtain long-term status only through naturalization into the nationality of an EU member state. As most member states require periods of continuous legal residence on their territory as a condition of citizenship, every resettlement within the EU resets the TCN's clock for legal inclusion.

For instance, an Ethiopian who had legally and continuously resided in Italy for eight years would be a long-term resident there under European law and entitled to move to another member state. He would also be two years away from qualifying for citizenship, Italian and European, under Italian nationality law. If at this point he obtained an attractive employment opportunity in, say, Austria, and moved to that country, he would once again be ten years away from qualifying for Austrian and European citizenship at the discretion of Austrian authorities, and a full thirty years away from Austrian and European citizenship under Austrian law. If the Ethiopian's child (born in Italy, perhaps two years earlier) moved to Austria with the father and thus interrupted his period of residence in Italy, the child would lose the right to apply for Italian citizenship when reaching maturity. (Children born to foreign parents in Italy qualify for Italian and European citizenship at maturity if they have uninterruptedly resided in Italy since birth.) The goal for inclusion would be to co-naturalize with the parent in Austria, provided both have resided there for at least ten years.

If father and child returned to Italy after a couple of years, their temporary absence would have set back the clock there: the residence period for citizenship must be *continuous*. The exercise of free-movement rights thus comes at a potentially high cost, despite the promise of the 2003 directive. Contrast the situation just sketched with that of a European (say, French) citizen: after a mere four years of residence in Italy, he would have already qualified for Italian citizenship, thanks to the more lenient naturalization residence requirements for EU citizens. In Austria, he would face a waiting period of six years—not thirty—before having a legal claim to Austrian citizenship. He probably would have much less interest in these naturalizations, though, as he would in any case have some political voice, social benefits claims in both Italy and Austria, and a generally secure status by virtue of his being by origin a European citizen. Even his child, born in Italy, would already be a French and European citizen—with a lower stake in obtaining Austrian or Italian citizenship, but able to obtain either more easily than an Ethiopian child under similar circumstances.[20] In short, the "who" and "what" of inclusion in the EU render seemingly similar rights significantly different in fact. For a person not a citizen of the EU, the choice between exercising free-movement rights and lining up for citizenship in a member state (and thus for European citizenship) can be a delicate trade-off.

It has been suggested that the status of resident foreigners in European nation-states after World War II has gradually come to resemble that of citizens, especially in terms of social rights.[21] The achievement of *legal* citizenship, the argument goes, has lost attraction for immigrants, who are able to gain inclusion in the national community through avenues other than citizenship. However, even if most contributory social benefits are now granted in EU states regardless of citizenship, citizenship does confer special benefits. In some cases it remains the only way to have access to the full range of welfare benefits, including the noncontributory ones. Public service employment is often reserved for citizens. Citizenship confers full political voice, at the national and local level. It grants security of status by annulling or reducing the risk of deportation, and an EU passport means admission on favorable visa conditions in many other countries—all the more important in a society which tends to be increasingly transnational, and where affective and professional ties cut across borders.[22]

The Centrality of the Nation-State

Nationality is a legitimate avenue of distinction between European citizens and noncitizens, and it may represent a valid proxy for a notion of belonging to Europe. Tying conditions of mobility to that distinction may likewise seem fully legitimate. Still, limits on immigrants' mobility interfere with a balanced relation between labor demand and supply throughout the various member states. Immigrants are by definition more prone to movement than local residents, and if allowed they might respond to local employment crises by extending their job search to neighboring states and to EU zones where labor market conditions are more promising. Greater freedom to move might also temper the unsettling effects of large waves of immigration to a particular geographic area.

However, the two-tiered system also entails some important consequences in terms of European-level responses to issues of immigration and diversity. First, the fact that immigrants are bound to a national pocket of the EU reinforces the role of the national community as the main referent for their integration and legal inclusion. This tends to lessen the importance of their becoming *European as well as national* citizens. Second, as the passage from alienage to citizenship (both national and European) happens at different times in different member states, and as it also entails a passage from a condition of immobility to one of mobility, immigrants with similar histories of presence in the EU and residing in the same member state may find themselves at different levels of inclusion. Is there room to rethink the exclusive relationship between European citizenship and nationality? Is it possible to make that relationship less exclusive?

European immigrants are strongly bound to a host nation-state, even if they have all entered the EU area by passing through a stretch of common external borders. Some of them—for instance researchers, students, and possibly in a not-too-distant future highly skilled workers—enter on common EU visas.[23] Immigrants are tied to a specific nation-state first by reduced mobility options. About seven hundred thousand people obtained EU citizenship in 2006, roughly the same number as U.S. naturalized citizens that year.[24] But while naturalized U.S. citizens have achieved their status while potentially moving around in the nine million square kilometers of U.S. territory and potentially resettling across the several U.S. states without encountering significant regulatory or physical barriers,[25] naturalized Europeans have achieved their status by sticking to a member state, to its rules and its territory, with reduced experience of the EU's political, cultural, linguistic, and legal diversity. Mobility within a society fosters exchange and intercommunication among the different parts of that society, especially if the pockets of difference are territorially organized (as is the case in the EU and in part in the United States). This matters particularly because the EU, unlike the United States, cannot count on country-wide communication and awareness, which partially compensate for the de facto immobility of some segments of the population. In the United States, there is a common language and a lively national political debate in the media; in the EU, the media, political debates, and social discourse are too fragmented to create a sense of Europeanness or make up for its lack. Hence the likelihood that immobile immigrants will experience isolation from Europe.

In addition, the immobile immigrants' pathways to naturalization in each member state differ quantitatively and qualitatively, and are not likely to remind prospective citizens that their desired legal status is a supranational one. On the contrary, elevation to citizenship reinforces the link between an immigrant and a specific European nation. The length of the residency requirements varies from member state to member state, from a minimum of three to a maximum of ten years. Some states consider any title to legal residence as valid for purposes of naturalization, while in others "residence" means presence on a permanent residence permit. Some states admit dual nationality, while others insist on a renunciation, release, or loss of any previous citizenship. Some naturalization laws also require prospective citizens to have sufficient and stable resources to support themselves and possibly their families, while others impose no such requirement. As already noted, the country of naturalization also affects the status of children born in the host member state. Some naturalization statutes allow for children of immigrants to acquire nationality at birth if at least one parent has been resident for a while in the state of birth; others allow minor children to co-naturalize only at the time their parents naturalize; still others prohibit naturalization of children before they reach majority. Even when immigrants have obtained a European national citizenship, and hence a European citizenship, their status, though nominally equal, is not equally secure. Some member states provide that naturalized citizens lose their citizenship (including European citizenship) at the occurrence of several events, such as absence from the territory of the naturalizing state for periods of seven years or longer without a positive statement of an intent to remain citizens.[26]

In short, an individual's status as a European is overwhelmed by the national features of the naturalization process. This is evidenced also by the integration requirements that many prospective citizens have to meet. These requirements test the applicant's familiarity with cultural, linguistic, and constitutional features of the receiving polity. They signal that the grant of citizenship represents not only a change in legal status but also admission into a political and affective community, which claims a right to self-definition. While these requirements safeguard local identities and local political autonomy, they also suggest that the idea of the polity exhausts itself at the frontier of the nation-state. Nineteen member states out of twenty-seven require that prospective citizens prove their knowledge or command of (one of) the national languages. Twelve member states also require that citizenship applicants show knowledge of the history, the culture, and/or the Constitution and relevant laws of the adoptive country. The culture, history, and laws that one is called on to learn represent first of all a nation, and only secondarily Europe.[27]

The nation is also central to the oaths or declarations of allegiance that many naturalizing immigrants have to render. Some elements of these oaths are constant: loyalty to the naturalizing state, and commitment to protect its interests. But what if the national interest comes to conflict with the interest of the European Union (into which, to some extent, the immigrant is also naturalizing)? The oaths either ignore these potential tensions or implicitly indicate that the nation prevails over everything.

A prospective Lithuanian, for instance, has to swear "to be loyal to the Republic of Lithuania, to observe the Constitution and Laws of the Republic, to defend the independence of Lithuania, to protect the territorial integrity of the state." She also swears to "respect the state language of Lithuania, its culture and customs, and to strengthen the democratic Lithuanian state." A prospective Hungarian must express his allegiance in the following words: "I do solemnly swear that I shall consider Hungary my country. I shall be a loyal citizen of the Republic of Hungary, shall honor and observe the Constitution and laws thereof. I shall defend my country as far as my strength allows, and shall serve it according to the best of my abilities." A prospective Latvian says: "I pledge that I will be loyal only to the Republic of Latvia. I undertake to fulfil the Constitution and the Laws of the Republic of Latvia in good faith and with all vigour to protect them. I undertake without regard to my life to defend the independence of the State of Latvia and to live and work in good faith, in order to increase the prosperity of the State of Latvia and of the people." And the future Romanian will swear "devotion to the Romanian country and Romanian people" and agree "to defend the rights and national interest [and] respect the Constitution and the laws of Romania."[28] To be sure, these recitations have symbolic and celebratory value, rather than promising concrete action. Still, who would know that when citizenship applicants proffer these words and seal their contract of belonging to Lithuania, Hungary, Latvia, or Romania, they are also sealing their contract of belonging to the European Union?

Even as the EU insists on its political character and longs for the affection, allegiance, and trust of the European people, then, EU immigrants' struggle for integration has the nation as its focus. The centrality of the nation-state as a gateway to membership in the European polity tends to reinforce the primacy of the national people and aspiring nationals over the European people at large. For instance, it is within the boundaries of each nation that battles for entitlements to welfare, housing, education, health care, and political participation come to be fought, and that different recipes to accommodate the potentially competing interests of old members and newcomers are found. It is within these same boundaries that both solidarity and resistance find their stronger expression. The European Union, by setting minimum standards for the treatment of outsiders and by establishing some rules of nondiscrimination, at most sets the broad contours of this confrontation. This may make the escape from Europe's often-lamented democratic deficit even more difficult. The nation-state tends to remain the natural referent for participation, representation, and assimilation. The people of Europe, conscious of their national differences and only casually aware of their Europeanness, have a hard time identifying common interests that can safely be entrusted to the EU.

Nationality remains thus the primary filter of external diversity. There is no way of becoming a European without at the same time acquiring a particular European nationality. Europe remains at a distance. As a result, an emotional vacuum surrounds European citizenship, which individual national attachments cannot fill.

Different European Destinies for Similar Immigration Histories

In addition to reaffirming the central role of the nation, the nationality-dependent distribution of mobility rights in the EU potentially differentiates among otherwise similar immigration histories, distinguishing "more-mobiles" and "less-mobiles" among TCNs who may have spent equal time in the European Union. As a result, TCNs who have been in a certain member state for a short period are potentially more legally included there than TCNs who have been in another member state ever since entering the EU. This depends in part on diverging requirements for nationality and thus for full mobility. To refer to my earlier illustration: suppose our Ethiopian friend had originally left Ethiopia at the same time as his brother, also seeking better fortunes in Europe. While he had found a job and obtained a job permit in Italy, his brother had found a better chance in France. After eight years of legal residence in the EU, the brother's legal situation is potentially quite different. The Italian-resident Ethiopian is still waiting for the ten years necessary for naturalization in Italy to pass. At most, he may have obtained an EU long-term residence permit. The French-resident Ethiopian, in contrast, will long have met France's five-year residence requirement for naturalization. If he has applied for naturalization and obtained French and thus European citizenship, he will be fully mobile, while his brother is still stuck in Italy. The French Ethiopian could immediately move to Italy, provided he found an occupation there or had resources to support himself. Once there, he would enjoy stronger political rights than his brother—who had been resident in Italy eight years longer than he and in the EU for the same length of time.

The French Ethiopian could vote in local elections in the Italian municipality of his new residence and could vote for the European Parliament. His Italian-resident brother would remain fully disenfranchised. What is more, the French Ethiopian brother could sponsor other Ethiopian relatives to come to the EU and to Italy on better conditions than currently apply to his brother, and could obtain a more secure status for them.[29] He could naturalize into Italian citizenship after only four years of residence in Italy. He would also be able to leave Italy and move to a third member state, spending some time there as a job seeker and trying his fortune again. In moving and resettling around the EU, he would not compromise his status as a European citizen in any way, while his Italian-resident brother, if making a similar choice, would sacrifice his options for legal inclusion through citizenship. The issue here is not whether it is desirable or not, fair or not, that a European citizen be treated better than someone who is not a European citizen, or that a European national be treated better than someone who is not a European national. The issue is that European citizenship differentiates among immigrants who, in terms of European belonging, are similar and similarly deserving.

The mobility options and related rights connected to EU citizenship may also differentiate among similarly situated *communities* of immigrants in connection with the political enlargement of the EU. Accession to the European Union means extension of common citizenship to the national population, including members of the entrant population who already reside in an EU member country. In the immigrant community, this cuts across immigration histories, shortening and easing the course to integration for some favored groups in the immigrant pool. The new European citizens suddenly surpass in status other segments of the immigrant community, regardless of how long they have been resident in the host state and regardless of their employment and family histories.

The Albanian and Romanian communities in Italy provide a telling example. The two national groups represent the two most populous immigrant communities in Italy, amounting to 376,000 and 342,000 individuals respectively. The two communities are similar in the collective perceptions of native Italians. They have been present in Italy for roughly the same time. Their members tend to take up similar occupations and, sadly, are among the most regular occupants of Italian jails.[30] Yet in January 2007, with the accession of Romania into the European Union, Italian-resident Romanians suddenly became European citizens, with the result that they can vote in Italian municipal elections, enjoy a range of labor rights and a number of nondiscrimination guarantees, and soon will have full mobility rights.[31] Moreover, they now qualify for a shortened residency requirement of four years (instead of ten) in order to naturalize into Italian citizenship. Albanians, including those who have resided in Italy for much longer than some Romanians, remain aliens.

If in the United States one day all immigrants of Mexican nationality—but they alone—were given preferential treatment on account of their nationality (perhaps including voting rights in local elections, more generous welfare benefits, a preferential channel to sponsor family members, and a shortened path to American citizenship), this would probably raise eyebrows and evoke unpleasant memories of an era when immigration policy was based on national quotas. It would be yet more absurd if Mexicans could move unconstrained among the several states and resettle in any of them, while immigrants of any other nationality had to stay put in their state of first settlement unless they attained American citizenship. In the European Union, the ordinary operation of European citizenship may produce results of this kind.

European Citizenship beyond Nationality?

Addressing in normative terms the inconsistencies in immigration and citizenship experiences requires careful reflection and the weighing of pros and cons. Some of the issues connected to the practical operation of the "who" and "what" of European citizenship, such as the reduced importance of residence-based notions of European belonging and the hierarchy of mobility rights, seem to argue for the extension of full-fledged mobility options to immigrants, a move that would in part decouple European citizenship and nationality. To change the legal requirements underpinning European citizenship, however, is to transform its nature. This might be neither desirable nor politically desired in the European Union, an entity that remains a novel experiment in the sharing of political and economic decision making and that properly has not adopted the defining features of a state entity. The EU's relationship to the people of Europe is still uncertain; the institutions of the EU long for legitimacy and support while the people of the EU are indifferent or hostile. For these reasons, European citizenship as additional and complementary to nation-state citizenship—that is, as it was conceived ever since the Maastricht era—is perhaps its preferable form.[32] The dependency of European citizenship on nationality is a moderate way to introduce an EU-wide legal status without compromising the political and legal distinctiveness of a wide array of national citizenships. To the extent that citizenship can be seen as a marker of local cultural, political, and civic traditions, the current European citizenship regime may be seen as an effective way to realize the European project of "unity in diversity."

Even so, some room might be found to think about attenuating the exclusive link between nationality and European citizenship, for instance, by extending to the immigrant population the mobility rights that are now mainly tied to European citizenship. At present immigrants to the EU are subject to a vertical process of inclusion: they receive national citizenship and only as a result the horizontal, Europe-wide benefits of European citizenship. The horizontal effectiveness of European citizenship could be enhanced to the benefit of outsiders. While member states could retain their naturalization laws and requirements, introducing via European law some measure that recognizes and seeks to minimize disparities across member states might temper many of the tensions highlighted earlier.

In the case of immigrants, a qualifying threshold, alternative to nationality, would be needed to grant rights of movement and mutual recognition. This threshold could be represented by legal residence on EU territory for a minimum period.[33] Once the immigrant had met the qualifying residence requirement, a number of mutual-recognition effects for purposes of specific nationality laws might be triggered. For instance, immigrants could be allowed to count periods of residence in different parts of the European Union for purposes of complying with the residence requirements under individual naturalization laws. Birth on the territory of another member state could be treated as equivalent to birth in the territory of the naturalizing state for purposes of children's naturalization. Knowledge of one of the many languages of the European Union could justify leniency in applying the national requirements for knowledge of another. Demonstrated commitment to the constitutional values of a member state could be considered to corroborate an immigrant's potential for successful integration into the society of another member state. Mutual recognition is a guiding principle in important areas of European law (prominently, the free movement of goods),[34] and it might work well in the area of people's free movement and inclusion.

Alternatively, the European Council's statement at Tampere might be read to encourage the expansion of the rights of aliens through EU law in order to make their status more and more similar to, even if distinct from, citizenship. Aliens in the EU who exercise their mobility rights can significantly delay their access to citizenship. Thus making citizenship less attractive to immigrants by allowing them to claim rights usually exclusive to national citizenship might also contribute to attenuating the dilemmas that currently affect their mobility decisions. This choice is in part impracticable, especially as regards immigrants' political participation at the national level. It would reflect the lingering perception of immigrants as guest workers rather than as new, full-fledged community members. In any case, most new immigrants are in the EU to stay, and keeping them on a separate but equal track vis-à-vis citizens does not serve the purposes of successful integration and harmonious coexistence. Also, expanding citizenship rights without extending citizenship itself poses the danger of devaluing citizenship.[35]

Applying mutual recognition principles and extending mobility to immigrants would not lessen the value of citizenship as a tool for defining both the terms of coexistence in a community and the values embraced by that community. Citizenship is a source not only of rights but also of civic duties. Creating a double threshold for inclusion—one for obtaining mobility, and a second one for obtaining nationality—would not make full inclusion in the community any less selective. The idea of mutual recognition among regimes of membership would be based on a notion of belonging to Europe, and would reflect the view that membership in a European member state, either as national or as resident, has some legal and symbolic value in the rest of the EU.

The extension of mutual recognition to the regime of membership could be tied, though it need not be, to a newly conceived, independent notion of European citizenship. A new European citizenship could be granted based on possession of either nationality of a member state or minimum legal residence in the EU, barring criminal convictions. Its effects might be limited to mobility and mutual recognition matters, while the limited political rights of current European citizenship could be tied to European nationality (meaning nationality of one of the EU member states). Such an approach would help to close the gap between the experience of being an immigrant to a European country and the experience of being a citizen of that country.

Making different elements of nationality interchangeable would reduce the role of the nation in Europe for purposes of assimilation, while maintaining intact the member states' distinctive roads to nationalization. A regime of that description would dilute the sense that there are two Europes, one for insiders and one for outsiders, while at the same time making a Europe without borders more credible and effective. This in turn might be conducive to a better integration of immigrant populations and to a more rational distribution of their political and social rights. Rights to political participation and to full welfare inclusion would still remain tied to nationality, but access to nationality through eased mobility would be rationalized.

It might be objected that more-mobile immigrants could be tempted by inclusion-shopping behavior and move to more permissive EU countries. That in turn might trigger a "race to the top" and prompt member states to adopt restrictive inclusion regimes. Too many factors, however, play a role in immigrants' choices of where to live and work to give them the freedom to simply pursue favorable naturalization regimes.[36] And immigrants who show through their aspiration to citizenship a willingness to integrate into the host society are likely to be desirable for many member states whose natural population is gradually shrinking.

From a different point of view, mutual recognition with respect to nationality requirements can be seen as colliding with the fundamental interest of the member states in defining their own community. Discourses of European citizenship have always met with the reluctance of the member states to renounce any fraction of their sovereignty on the subject of nationality. For instance, a declaration attached to the Treaty of Maastricht, which had established a European citizenship for the first time, clarified that each member state remained free to determine who would be a national for European Community purposes.[37] Introducing a European law requirement that each member state must recognize the residence time and the proofs of integration that an immigrant has collected in other member states interferes at least indirectly with each nation's desire to "select" its own citizens. However, current law already limits each member state's freedom to define its own community. Free movement and corollary nondiscrimination rights stand in contrast with the right to national self-definition: they are a way of extending to EU citizens the entitlements enjoyed by national citizens. Each member state identifies its own citizens and thus its portion of European citizens. As these EU citizens are increasingly able to claim rights comparable to those of nationals in other member states, this means that each member state is delegating part of its definitional powers to all other member states.[38] As the rights entailed by free movement expand, the residual power of community self-definition shrinks. At the apex, where free-movement rights allow EU citizens to do anything national citizens can do and to claim anything national citizens can claim, the member states' power of self-definition is effectively annulled.

Member states may still legitimately claim that they are willing to extend to EU citizens certain benefits that they are unwilling to extend to immigrants who are not EU nationals. France could say for instance that it is willing to accommodate Germans, who are EU citizens, but not Turks, who are not. But what if Germany one day decided to grant citizenship to its entire resident foreign population, including 1.8 million resident Turks? The very next day all these Turks could move to France as EU citizens and there claim their rights. How different would they be, though, in terms of Europeanness from the Turks of the day before?

For a more realistic example, consider the case of illegal immigrants. Here, too, one state's choice affects all others. Many member states, particularly in southern Europe, have opted in the last two decades for generous amnesty programs, which promised legal pardon and legal status to undocumented immigrants. (In Italy, this happened in 1986, 1990, 1995, 1998, and 2002.[39]) The legalized immigrants obtain legal residence and are thus put on a potential pathway to national citizenship. They become part of the pool of candidate European citizens, to which other member states might be called to give residence and rights, even if they maintain a much stricter policy toward their own illegal immigrants.

In short, the power of self-definition of each national community in the EU has become increasingly subject to the immigration and nationality policy decisions of other member states. The effectiveness of any claimed intention by any member state to maintain a legitimate distinction of treatment between European nationals and TCNs within its borders must be tested against these considerations. European citizenship, which seems not to define, steals much definitional power undetected. Extending elements of mutual recognition to the experience of inclusion of TCNs in the various member states would not compromise definitional powers that have not already been compromised by European citizenship and free movement.

Conclusion

European citizenship makes for two Europes, a mobile and an immobile one. As an extension of nationality, however, it uses no independent criterion to distinguish mobile Europeans and immobile non-Europeans, to the detriment of a comprehensive notion of European belonging. Grounding effective mobility options in both nationality and residence, by extending principles of mutual recognition to the employment, residence, and cultural assimilation experiences of immigrants in the various member states, could be a way to mitigate the immobility of immigrants and at the same time to rethink the notion of European belonging and European citizenship. In an encompassing notion of "belonging to Europe," one open to both immigrants and natives, both national and external diversities of the European population might be reconciled. And once the EU has found ways to handle layers of diversity in its society, it probably will also have found answers to issues of identity and legitimacy.

Notes

1. *See* Lars-Erik Cederman, *Nationalism and Bounded Integration: What It Would Take to Construct a European* Demos, 7 Eur. J. Int'l Rel. 139 (2001) for an overview of various approaches in the literature on European integration to issues of democratic deficit and the prospects for a European *demos*.

2. For a sample of approaches to the issues of European identity in relevant interdisciplinary literature, *see* Europeanization, National Identities and Migration: Changes in Boundaries Construction between Western and Eastern Europe (Willfried Spohn and Anna Triandafyllidou eds., 2003); Transnational Identities: Becoming European in the EU (Richard K. Herrmann, Thomas Risse, and Marilynn B. Brewer eds., 2004); Changing European Identities: Social Psychological Analyses of Social Change (Glynis M. Breakwell and Evanthia Lyons eds., 1996); European Identity: Theoretical Perspectives and Empirical Insights (Ireneusz Pawel Karolewski and Viktoria Kaina eds., 2006); Neil Fligstein, Euroclash: The EU, European Identity, and the Future of Europe (2008).

3. Eurostat, *Population and Social Conditions*, http://epp.eurostat.ec.europa.eu/portal/page?_pageid=0,1136184,0_45572595&_dad=portal&_schema=PORTAL (accessed Sept. 12, 2008).

4. For the idea that European provisions on citizenship and free movement are not grounded in a solid idea of supranational belonging, *see* Lisa Conant, *Contested Boundaries: Citizens, States and Supranational Belonging in the European Union*, in Boundaries and Belonging: States and Societies in the Struggle to Shape Identities and Local Practices (Joel S. Migdal ed., 2004).

5. By bringing a young workforce to the EU, immigration offers solutions to the welfare problems posed by the decline in birthrates; on the other hand it contributes to the problem, as most immigrant workers remain employed in low-paying activities and thus enlarge the class of workers who contribute less than they receive to national welfare systems. *See* Craig A. Parsons and Timothy M. Smeeding, *What's Unique about Immigration in Europe?* in Immigration and the Transformation of Europe (Craig A. Parsons and Timothy M. Smeeding eds., 2006).

6. The definition of European citizenship and the main rights connected to it are contained in Articles 17 to 21 of the European Community treaty.

7. For the features of policies of access to nationality in European countries, *see* Italian Ministry of Interior, *Primo Rapporto sugli Immigrati in Italia* (Dec. 2007), http://www.interno.it/mininterno/export/sites/default/it/assets/files/15/0673_Rapporto_immigrazione_BARB AGLI.pdf, 164–66; *see also* Acquisition and Loss of Nationality: Policies and Trends in 15 European Countries (R. Bauböck, E. Ersboll, K. Groenendijk, & H. Waldrauch eds., 2006).

8. Nationals of twelve countries in Europe have experienced this transition in the last four years, and nationals of three more are set to experience something similar in a not-too-distant future. The twelve most recent entrants into the EU include Cyprus, the Czech Republic, Estonia, Hungary, Latvia, Lithuania, Malta, Poland, Slovakia, Slovenia, Bulgaria,

and Romania. Turkey, Croatia, and the Former Yugoslav Republic of Macedonia are currently candidate countries for accession to the EU.

9. *See, e.g.,* Case C-85/96, Martínez Sala v. Freistaat Bayern, 1998 E.C.R. 2691; Case C-413/99, Baumbast and R. v. Secretary of State for the Home Department, 2002 E.C.R. 7091; Case C-456/02, Michel Trojani v. Centre public d'aide sociale de Bruxelles (CPAS); 2004 E.C.R. 0; Case C-224/98, Marie-Nathalie D'Hoop v. Office national de l'emploi, 2002 E.C.R. 6191; Case C-184/99, Rudy Grzelczyk v. Centre Public d'Aide Sociale d'Ottignies-Louvain-La-Neuve, 2001 E.C.R. 6193; Case C-209/03, The Queen v. London Borough of Ealing, Secretary of State for Education and Skills 2005 E.C.R. I-2119. On the transformation of the right to free movement into a right of citizenship in the EU *see* Francesca Strumia, *Citizenship and Free Movement: European and American Features of a Judicial Formula for Increased Comity*, 12 Colum. J. Eur. Law 713, 731–32 (2006). In more recent judgments, the court has continued to support the mobility of citizens on the social side by opposing fiscal and social legislation in the member states that directly or indirectly created disadvantages for intra-community migrants (*see, e.g.,* Case 520/04, Turpeinen, 2006 E.C.R. I-10685); on the other hand, the court has also accepted challenges to member-state legislation that made the availability of study subsidies more difficult for intracommunity migrants (Case Morgan C-11 &12/06, 2007 E.C.R. I-9161).

10. Case C-413/99, Baumbast and R. v. Secretary of State for the Home Department, 2002 E.C.R. 7091.

11. Case C-456/02, Michel Trojani v. Centre public d'aide sociale de Bruxelles (CPAS), 2004 E.C.R. 0.

12. Parliament and Council Directive 2004/38, 2004 O.J. (L 158) 77 (EC).

13. *Id.* at arts. 6, 7, 16, 24.

14. *See* Alain Lamassoure, Député européen, Le Citoyen et l'Application du Droit Communautaire, Rapport au Président de la République (June 2008), http://lesrapports.ladocumentationfrancaise.fr/BRP/084000379/0000.pdf.

15. The Schengen system has its origin in a 1985 agreement and a 1990 convention among several EU countries. *See* Agreement Between the Governments of the States of the Benelux Economic Union, the Federal Republic of Germany and the French Republic on the Gradual Abolition of Checks at their Common Borders, June 14, 1985, 2000 O.J. (L 239) 43, at 13; Convention Implementing the Schengen Agreement of 14 June 1985, June 19, 1990, 2000 O.J. (L 239) 43, at 19. The Schengen instruments and subsequent regulations have been incorporated in the 1997 Treaty of Amsterdam and have thus become full-blown European law, which binds all member states with the exception of the United Kingdom, Ireland, Norway, and Iceland. The countries that TCNs are free to visit on a Schengen visa also include those that are party to the Schengen Agreement even if they are not members of the EU. They do not yet include all the countries that entered the EU as a result of the 2004 and 2007 enlargements. As of June 2008, the Czech Republic, Estonia, Hungary, Latvia, Lithuania, Malta, Poland, Slovakia, and Slovenia are part of the control-free area.

16. *Legal* resettlement, that is. Among the Schengen-participating EU countries, border controls have been abolished. This opens up easy opportunities for de facto resettlement in

the shade of the law. Many undocumented immigrants enter at particularly convenient spots along the external borders of the EU (such as the Strait of Gibraltar) and then move undetected across the Schengen borders.

17. Council Directive 2003/109, 2003, O.J. (L 16) 44 (EC). This directive has been adopted on the basis of Title IV of the EC treaty, and as a result it does not apply to the United Kingdom, Ireland, and Denmark, which have opted out of this part of the treaty. A proposal for a directive on TCNs' right to travel within the community had been previously adopted by the European Commission but never made it into law. *See* Commission Proposal for a Council Directive on the right of third-country nationals to travel in the community, COM (1995) 346 final.

18. Once they have entered a second member state, TCNs are also covered by an equal treatment guarantee for purposes of access to the labor markets, education, and related grants and social security. *See* Council Directive 2003/109, art. 21.

19. "A more vigorous integration policy should aim at granting them rights and obligations *comparable* to those of EU citizens." Presidency Conclusions, European Council, Oct. 18, 1999, 4; "The legal status of third country nationals should be approximated to that of Member State nationals." *Id.* at 21.

20. For Italian nationality law, *see* Law no. 91 of 1992 of February 5, 1992, Nuove Norme sulla Cittadinanza, in 1992 O.J. 38, *available at* http://www.giustizia.it/cassazione/leggi/l91_92.html. For French nationality law, *see* C. Civ., art. 21-7 to 21-18, *available at* http://www.legifrance.gouv.fr/html/codes_traduits/code_civil_textA.htm (in English). For Austrian nationality law, *see* Bundesgesetz über die österreichische Staatsbürgerschaft (Staatsbürgerschaftgesetz 1985, last modified 2006); *see also* http://www.wien.gv.at/english/administration/civilstatus/citizenship/claim.html. For Danish nationality law, *see* Consolidated Act on Danish Nationality no. 422 of 7 June 2004, http://www.nyidamark.dk/NR/rdonlyres/52136BD4-FA62-4818-AABB-5709AABAC6A6/0/consolidation_act_no_422_7_june_2004.pdf.

21. Yasemin Nuhoglu Soysal, Limits of Citizenship: Migrants and Postnational Membership in Europe (1994). But *see* Irene Bloemraad, *Citizenship and Pluralism: Multiculturalism in a World of Global Migration*, in Citizenship and Immigrant Incorporation: Comparative Perspectives on North America and Western Europe (Gokce Yurdakul & Michal Bodemann eds., 2007) at 58 (observing that citizenship remains the main avenue to obtain all government-sourced benefits).

22. The external validity of European citizenship still faces important limits. Most countries which benefit from visa-free travel to the EU have recognized visa-free access by reciprocity only to the nationals of some of the member states of the EU, even if the European Commission is negotiating with third countries for the extension of the reciprocity regime to *all* the nationals of the EU. The commission has recently suggested the adoption of retaliatory measures against those third countries which resist these extensions. Countries which resist the expansion of visa-free travel to all European citizens are Japan, Singapore, Panama, and the United States. Citizens of twelve EU member states (Bulgaria, the Czech Republic, Estonia, Greece, Cyprus, Latvia, Lithuania, Hungary, Malta, Poland, Romania, and Slovakia)

must still obtain visas to travel to the United States. Canada and Australia have proved more cooperative, even if conditions of full reciprocity with them remain undefined. *See* Press Release, Europa, The European Commission Adopts Its Fourth Report on Visa-Waiver Non-Reciprocity with Third Countries (July 23, 2008), http://europa.eu/rapid/press ReleasesAction.do?reference=IP/08/1189&format=HTML&aged=0&language=EN&guiLa nguage=en; *see also* EurActiv.com, EU threatens to slap visa sanctions on US, July 24, 2008, http://www.euractiv.com/en/transport/eu-threatens-slap-visa-sanctions-us/article-174461.

23. Council Directive 2004/114, 2004 O.J. (L 375) 12 (EC); Council Directive 2005/71, 2005 O.J. (L 289) 15 (EC); *Commission Proposal for a Council Directive on the Conditions for Entry and Residence of Third Country Nationals for the Purposes of Highly Qualified Employment*, COM (2007) 637 final (Oct. 23, 2007).

24. Source of U.S. data: Department of Homeland Security, Office of Immigration Statistics, Annual Flow Report, Naturalizations in the United States 2006, May 2007, *available at* http://www.dhs.gov/xlibrary/assets/statistics/publications/Natz_01_Sec508Compliant.pdf (accessed June 3, 2009); Source of EU data: Eurostat, access to citizenship in 2006, *available at* http://epp.eurostat.ec.europa.eu/tgm/table.do?tab=table&init=1&language=en&pcode= tps00024&plugin=1 (accessed June 3, 2009). Seven hundred thousand people were naturalized in the United States in 2006 out of an estimated legal permanent resident population of approximately 12 million. About 1.2 million people obtained legal permanent resident status in the United States in 2006, 60 percent by adjustment of status, while the rest were new entrants. Total admissions in the United States in the same year amounted to 33 million people, but this number includes about 29 million tourists and travelers on business.

25. Some data suggest that there are phenomena of secondary migration among the states in the U.S., ignited in part by diverging supplementary integration policies in different states. *See* Nathan Glazer, *Governmental and Nongovernmental Roles in the Absorption of Immigrants*, in Paths to Inclusion: The Integration of Migrants in the United States and Germany (Peter H. Schuck ed., 1998), 70–72.

26. This applies to naturalized citizens of Cyprus and Malta. The shortest residence requirement for naturalization is found in Belgium, while the longest requirements are found in Greece, Italy, Lithuania, Slovenia, and Spain. Austria, Bulgaria, Denmark, Estonia, Finland, Germany, Hungary, Latvia, Lithuania, Romania, and Slovenia impose financial requirements for the grant of citizenship. Release of previous citizenships is required in Austria, Bulgaria, the Czech Republic, Denmark, Estonia, Germany, Latvia, Luxembourg, the Netherlands, Poland, Slovenia, and Spain. With regard to children of immigrants, the most liberal states in the EU are Ireland, Belgium, Germany, Estonia, Latvia, Portugal, and the UK, which under some conditions grant citizenship to local-born children of foreign parents who have resided on their territory for a certain time before the children's birth. Spain allows local-born children of foreigners to naturalize after only one year of residence.

27. A direct reference to Europe can be found only in Austrian legislation, which states: "To evaluate the integration of a foreigner into Austria, her attitude towards social, economic and cultural life in Austria should be taken into account together with the basic values of a European democratic state and its society." *See* Bundesgesetz, Über die österreichische

Staatsbürgerschaft (Staatsbürgerschaftgesetz 1985, last modified 2006) *available at* http://www.unhcr.de/fileadmin/unhcr_data/pdfs/rechtsinformationen/5.1.A-Gesetze/A_Stb_02_Staatsbuergerschaftsgesetz.pdf, par. 11

28. For the Lithuanian pledge, *see* Law on Citizenship, art. 3 para. 17, September 2002, No. IX 1078, as amended by law 18 July 2006, No. X-768, *available at* http://www3.lrs.lt/pls/inter3/dokpaieska.showdoc_l?p_id=285786 (in English). For the Hungarian pledge, *see* Act LV of the Hungarian Parliament, 1993 on Hungarian Citizenship, sect. 7; available in unofficial English translation at http://www.coe.int/T/E/Legal_Affairs/Legal_co-operation/Foreigners_and_citizens/Nationality/Documents/National_legislation/Hungary% 20Act% 20LV%20of%201993.asp. For the Latvian pledge, *see* Citizenship Law, 1994 (amended 1998) sect. 18, *available in unofficial translation at* http://unpan1.un.org/intradoc/groups/public/documents/untc/unpan018407.pdf. For the Romanian pledge, *see* Romanian Citizenship Act of 1 March 1991, at art. 20; an unofficial English translation of the act is *available at* http://www.romanianpassport.co.il/english/ romanian-citizenship-law/.

29. *Compare* Parliament and Council Directive 2004/38, 2004 O.J. (L 158) 77, at 5, 12, 13, 17, 20 (FC) *with* Council Directive 2003/109, 2004 O.J. (L 16) 44 (EC). TCNs face some waiting periods to sponsor their TCN family members; integration requirements may be imposed on their entering family members; if a family member loses a qualifying relationship with his sponsor, his status in the EU becomes less secure than the status of an EU citizen's family member in similar conditions; and finally, family members of TCNs might face waiting periods before being given access to the labor market.

30. Albanian immigration into Italy intensified in the first half of the 1990s, while Romanians began to represent a dominant component of the immigration flux in the second half of the 1990s. *See* Italian Ministry of Interior, Primo Rapporto sugli Immigrati in Italia (Dec. 2007), at 69. Romanians and Albanians are the immigrants most likely to be accused of and arrested for a range of crimes in Italy, including murder and robbery. The percentage of foreigners among people accused of a crime in Italy increased from 6 percent in 1988 to about 30 percent in 2006, while the percentage of foreigners as a component of the population increased from 0.8 percent to 5 percent. Many of the accused foreigners are illegal immigrants, which alters the proportion between foreigners as a percentage of the population and foreigners accused of crimes. *See* Ministero dell'Interno Italiano, Rapporto sulla Criminalità (June 20, 2007), http://www.interno.it/mininterno/export/sites/default/it/assets/files/14/0900_r apporto_criminalita.pdf.

31. Under the provisions of the accession treaties, member states may introduce or maintain restrictions on potential entrant workers from the new member states. The free movement rights of these groups of workers may be limited for a maximum total period of seven years from the date of accession, a period that thus expires in the case of Romania on December 31, 2013.

32. The Lisbon Treaty, now of uncertain destiny after the Irish rejection, codifies the principle of conferral as the rule informing the division of competences between the member states and the EU. *See* Treaty of Lisbon, amending the Treaty on European Union and the Treaty establishing the European Community, art. 1, introducing art. 3a and 3b in the

Treaty on European Union, Dec. 13, 2007, 2007 O.J. (C 306) 01, *available at* http://eur-lex.europa.eu/JOHtml.do?uri=OJ:C:2007:306:SOM:EN:HTML.

33. In this respect, this proposal leans toward a territorially based conception of entitlement. For the virtues and limits of models of inclusion based on territoriality, *see* Linda Bosniak, *Being Here: Ethical Territoriality and the Rights of Immigrants*, 8 Theoretical Inquiries in Law 389 (2007), available at SSRN: http://ssrn.com/abstract=1126427. *See also* A. Aleinikoff, *Between Principles and Politics: U.S. Citizenship Policy*, in From Migrants to Citizens: Membership in a Changing World 119 (Thomas Alexander Aleinikoff & Douglas Klusmeyer eds., 2000) for the idea that lawful settlement should be at the basis of membership claims.

34. *See* Case 120/78, Rewe-Zentral v. Bundesmonopolverwaltung für Branntwein, 1979 E.C.R. 649.

35. *See* Peter H. Schuck, *The Devaluation of American Citizenship*, in Citizens, Strangers and In-Betweens: Essays on Immigration and Citizenship 163 (1998), on how weakening the difference between the status of citizen and noncitizen in the United States may devalue American citizenship, and on the problems connected with this devaluation.

36. A recent study on immigration in the European Union found that one of the main factors driving immigration flows is existing networks with people who already reside in the destination country. While the study focuses on immigration of TCNs to European countries, it suggests in more general terms that factors other than the availability of legal and social benefits play the bigger part in immigrants' choice of a destination country. *See* Peder J. Pedersen, Mariola Pytlikova, & Nina Smith, *Migration into OECD Countries, 1990–2000*, in Immigration and the Transformation of Europe, *supra* note 5, at 43.

37. Member states are also allowed to deposit declarations indicating who is to be considered a national of their state for community purposes; *see* Declaration on Nationality of a Member State annexed to the 1992 Treaty on European Union, 1992 O.J. (C 191), at 98, *available at* http://eur-lex.europa.eu/en/treaties/dat/11992M/htm/11992M.html#0098000022; *see also* Gerard Rene de Groot, *The Relationship between the Nationality Legislation of the Member States of the European Union and European Citizenship*, in European Citizenship: An Institutional Challenge, 115, 120 (Massimo La Torre ed., 1998). The attitude of the European Court of Justice when dealing with issues of nationality and political rights is much more restrained than when the court considers social rights issues; for instance, the court has insisted that member states are free to designate the criteria according to which their citizens are entitled to vote for the European Parliament. (*See, e.g.,* Case 145/04, Spain v. United Kingdom of 12 September 2006, 2006 E.C.R. I-7917).

38. Also, member states are prevented from imposing any additional requirement on a national of an EU member state in order for him to benefit from European Community law rights on their territory: the European Court of Justice set a clear rule in this respect in the 1992 Micheletti case. Spain had refused the right of establishment to a dual national Italian-Argentinian who had previously resided in Argentina. Spain had demanded that a dual national—a national of both a member state and a nonmember country—have his last habitual residence in a member state before being permitted to establish his activity in Spain. The court held that requirements of this kind are not admissible. Nationality of a member state

remains the only requirement for a person to be a fully entitled European citizen. *See Case* C-369-90, Mario Vicente Micheletti v. Delegación del Gobierno en Cantabria, 1992 E.C.R. I-04239.

39. *See* Report of the European Migration Network, Illegally Resident Third Country Nationals in Italy: State Approaches Towards Them and their Profile and Social Situation (Dec. 2005), http://emn.sarenet.es/Downloads/prepareShowFiles.do;jsessionid=B9698E F8D7790D7EC84E49C82A3A0299?directoryID=17. In 1986, 105,000 applications were accepted; the figure was 222,000 in 1990, 246,000 in 1995, 217,000 in 1998, and 650,000 in 2002.

4

"We, the Citizens of Europe": European Union Citizenship

Markus Kotzur

The decision of the American people "to form a more perfect Union" was, in Alexander Hamilton's words, an "act of reflection and choice."[1] As outlined in the preamble of the Maastricht Treaty (1992), the decision to "mark a new stage in the process of European Integration" was also an act of reflection and choice. The decision was made by (inter)governmental actors and political elites, not (primarily) by a European people desiring constitutional unity. Still, the Maastricht Treaty (or EU treaty) enshrined and formalized the concept of European Union citizenship. That concept reflects the more-than-symbolic move from the European Economic Community to the European Political Community, and it embodies the constitutional quality of the post-Maastricht integration process. "Resolved to establish a citizenship common to the nationals of their countries," the Maastricht signatories conceptualized union citizenship as based on, and complementary to, member state nationality. They also linked citizenship to the constitutional "principles of liberty, democracy and respect for human rights," to fundamental freedoms and the rule of law, and to "social rights" and "solidarity between peoples."[2] The Reform Treaty of Lisbon abandoned the ambitious and programmatic term "constitution," as well as symbols of identity such as a European flag or a European anthem. However, it did *not* give up the constitutional quality of its baseline provisions. The newly shaped three-part treaty complex, including the normatively binding EU Charter on Fundamental Rights, reintroduces a constitutional scheme for the union.[3]

The phrase "constitutional scheme," though, suggests one of the fundamental tensions in the concept of union citizenship, especially in light of Europe's political confession of faith as encapsulated more than fifty years ago

71

in the first preamble clause to the Treaty of Rome. The historical foundation of the European Community is not the creation of one European people, but "an ever closer union of the peoples of Europe."[4] The Union is not and does not aim to become a sovereign state, akin to the federal systems in the United States, Germany, Australia, or India. A multiplicity of *demoi*, not a single *demos*, stand behind European democracy. Closely linked to the missing "We, the People of Europe" is a question: what is the "added value" of union citizenship, if the associated rights, duties, chances, and responsibilities do not extend far beyond the status which the nationals of the member states already enjoy?

Legal scholars have discussed the citizenship questions intensively, and from a wide range of perspectives. Some doubt that the legacy of the market citizen can be the basis for political citizenship, which constitutes more than ambitious-but-vague symbolism. Others, relying on the tradition of the American and French revolutions, affirm that citizenship is essentially linked to statehood. Some complain about the paucity of rights under the EU treaty. Others emphasize that citizenship is not constituted only by rights but also by duties (taxes, military service, etc.)—a feature widely missing on the European level. For some, the potential of Article 17 (on union citizenship) and subsequent articles of the treaty establishing the European Community (the EC treaty) outweighs these concerns; for others these concerns outweigh the articles' potential.[5] Some believe that citizenship requires a preexistent set of commonalities which already have created a common identity.[6] Others believe that citizenship can be created by legal means, through political integration.[7] These last two perspectives suggest the paradox of forming a political community. This "formation" is based upon prerequisites which, at least to some extent, are first created during the very process of formation. A political community is thus a continuing process. That is also true of the constitution and the citizenship of the community.[8] The process cannot be determined by a homogenous people. Heterogeneous citizens are diversified process-actors and participants. The citizen qualifies as the nucleus of a polity—whether the nation-state or a transnational political entity.

The Constitutional Architecture: Multilevel Constitutionalism

An inquiry into European citizenship must start with the constitutional architecture of the European Union. The traditional vocabulary of citizenship is that of the state, nation, and peoplehood. Such vocabulary might seem anachronistic in an age when sovereignty has become fragmented and when formerly closed nation-states must accept some degree of supranational integration in order to address the challenges of globalization. However, while the notion of an *international, transnational,* or *supranational* order suggests a narrative of the *nation,* the narrative of European integration is based on the common tradition of constitutional statehood (*Verfassungsstaatlichkeit*), which encompasses a democratic form of government, a rule-of-law orientation, and human rights guarantees.[9] Thus, the supranational European Community and, in the future, the supranational European Union do not replace the nation-state, but are instead a prefederal integrative mechanism to transform the nation-state from a self-contained into a cooperatively open political entity. During this transformation, the peoples— as citizens—exercise the power of sovereign self-determination and self-organization by giving up sovereign rights. Due to the dynamics of transformation and integration, the national political entities are not the exclusive "masters of the treaty."[10] Neither, though, is the European Community or the European Union. The "masters," if the term should remain in use, are the citizens as nationals *and* as citizens of the union. The instrument to master this double role is the principle of conferral, which restricts both national and "European" sovereignty.

The most commonly used metaphor for this multilayered structure is "multilevel constitutionalism" or "constitutional pluralism," meaning an "ongoing process of establishing new structures of government complementary to and building upon—while also changing—existing forms of self-organization of the people or society."[11] Among the most important parameters of that process are the extent to which voluntary sovereignty is forfeited to international organizations or intergovernmental bodies, the rise and growing influence of non–state actors (such as non-government organizations [NGOs] and transnational enterprises) and finally, the continued viability of the national state. Multilevel constitutionalism does not surrender nationhood or statehood, but rather encapsulates the essential elements of belonging embodied in those notions: affinity, empathy, loyalty, shared fate, and common history. Belonging, however, has other applications: the individual belongs to his or her family, neighborhood, municipality, region, state, nation, and transnational entity. Belonging to one entity enables a person to create another.

Multilevel constitutionalism is not meant to evoke a picture of hierarchically stacked constitutional levels but rather one of intertwining, interdependent elements within both national and European constitutional ensembles (national constitutions, constitutional elements within the EU treaty, the EC treaty, the European Convention on Human Rights, or the Charter of Fundamental Rights of the European Union). Human relationships, especially in the economic sphere, no longer depend on a single legal system. A model of multiple intertwined legal systems offers a normative response to the internal effects and external dimensions of globalization. These theories draw attention to "the possibility that within the same social order, or social or geographical space, more than one body of law, pertaining to more or less the same set of activities, may co-exist." The individual citizen is still confronted with and subject to "rules and principles generated and used by the state organisation," but they appear as only one variation "besides law generated and maintained by other organisations and authorities with different legitimation such as religion or tradition."[12] Global legal pluralism, moreover, must take into account the different and differentiated sets of norms existing on the subnational, the national, the regional, and the international levels.

Multilevel constitutionalism represents a tremendous shift from the early stage of European integration, when it was generally assumed that traditional models of international law principles would apply to the European Community. The member states were held to be the only "masters of the treaties," so that democratic legitimization within the member states sufficed. However, in its *Van Gend en Loos*[13] and *Costa v. ENEL*[14] decisions, the European Court of Justice (ECJ) overturned these assumptions, and instead described the treaties as "a new legal order of international law for the benefit of which the states have limited their sovereign rights."[15] The court's *Costa* doctrine is even more radical, as it holds that EC regulations are directly applicable in all member states. Thus, EC law enjoys some degree of sovereignty and supremacy vis-à-vis domestic law. The European Community's powers cannot be seen as originating exclusively from the member states but rather require autonomous and original democratic legitimacy. Put differently, European treaties are more than ordinary international treaties. What makes them "more" is the transformation of formerly closed nation-states into an integrated union, along with the ensuing creation of shared sovereignties between the union and its member states. [16]

This transformation raises two interrelated issues. First, the diversity multiplies beyond what even a politically aware and cosmopolitan citizen can comprehend, let alone experience, as a meaningful legal foundation for his daily life.[17] (The continuing debates regarding the universality or cultural relativity of human rights do not make things easier.[18]) The citizen who wants to know which rights he can exercise, where and in which way he can most effectively exercise them, and, most importantly, to which legal regimes and political communities he belongs, faces serious challenges and insecurities. Citizenship must not become the playing field of multilevel governance, but instead must correspond to the real-world conditions of that order in Europe and elsewhere.

Second, these shared sovereignties need a specific form of common legitimacy in shared legitimizing moments.[19] They require a European analogy of "government of the people, by the people, for the people." The European Union enjoys powers unparalleled by any other international organization or transnational entity, but only members of its Parliament—not the European Council, not the European Commission, and not the ECJ—are directly and democratically elected. This "democratic deficit" looms large in light of the Union's power to create rights and obligations for member states and their nationals; to establish norms that have direct effect and enjoy supremacy, even over national constitutions;[20] to make major decisions regarding the economy and policy in the member states and in Europe, including public funding; and to engage its member states in international agreements. All these powers should be exercised by democratically accountable institutions. The more complex the multilevel form of democratic governance, though, the more complex the infrastructure of democratic accountability. European democratic legitimacy is created by the interplay of personal, material, and functional mechanisms to guarantee a government of, by, and for the citizens. It requires that input and output legitimacy be combined, and that direct and indirect forms of participation and control be interconnected. Transparency, control, procedural justice, and fair processes or participation constitute additional factors in legitimacy.[21] At bottom, the citizen is the source of legitimacy; democracy is rooted in the political substance of citizenship.[22]

European Citizenship: Fundamentals

Because the formerly self-sustained nation-state is now integrated in regional political entities or international organizations with an independent constitutional quality, it is essential to step back from the formal treaty provisions on citizenship and to examine whether the idea(l) of the citizen can be effectively reconceptualized in light of multilevel governance structures.[23] Two distinctions provide a basis for that assessment: the distinction between *citoyen* and bourgeois, and the distinction between nationality and citizenship.

Citoyen and Bourgeois. "There is no more dynamic social figure in modern history than the Citizen," Ralf Dahrendorf wrote in a famous 1974 article.[24] The modern *citoyen* is to a very important extent the common child of the American and the French revolutions. Both sought to create what can be described as the substance of citizenship and participatory democracy: "the equilibrium of equality and liberty."[25]

The Declaration of Independence illustrates the political notion of active citizenship in the democratic principle: "Governments are instituted among Men, deriving their just powers from the consent of the governed." Despite its title, the 1789 Declaration of the Rights of Man and the Citizen does not explicitly define a concept of the citizen. However, it refers to citizens as those "who participate in the formation of the general will," "who form the Nation, in the sense of being the moral title holders of sovereignty."[26] The august title of "*citoyen*," an "active citizen," was bestowed on enlightened and emancipated individuals endowed with civil as well as political rights. The right to vote became the most important means of political participation.[27] The ideal citizen did not only possess this right but was obligated to participate in "a system of government from the roots."[28]

To this day, the *citoyen* is defined by the ability (and the corresponding responsibility) to take part in the political decision-making processes of his or her political community, whereas the bourgeois is characterized by his or her "autonomy as a private subject (especially as owner of the means of production and entrepreneur), free from any State intervention."[29] The bourgeois enjoys the "right to be let alone"; the *citoyen* is expected to serve the common good. It might be tempting—and of some heuristic value—to equate the "market citizen" of the European community with the bourgeois, and the post-Maastricht "union citizen" with the *citoyen*.[30] However, such a black-and-white picture would fail to capture the nuances of the integration process and the complexity of the "old" as well as the "new" European citizen. The right to elect the European Parliament was already granted to the "market citizen" (former Art. 138, sec. 3 of the EC treaty), who was expected to exercise this right. The market citizen was vested with human rights, was the beneficiary of social guarantees, and enjoyed—at least when engaging in economic activity—the right of free movement.

When conceptualized as a responsible political participant, as a *homo politicus*, the *citoyen* becomes the institutional counterpart of rationality—the "crystallization of rationality into a social role."[31] However, modernity and postmodernity have lost the Enlightenment's confidence in rationality. This crisis is reflected in the fragmented picture of the twenty-first-century citizen. The Hobbesian "*homo homini lupus*," whose evil nature needs to be restrained by public authority, encounters and counteracts the Lockean rationalist, who may enter into the social contract with his free and equal fellow citizens. The citizen can be a self-interested consumer taking for granted an "area of freedom, security, and justice,"[32] or a political actor—even the missionary activist—concerned about freedom, security, and justice (that is to say, about political unity.) The citizen might be a private egoist or a public-spirited altruist; he might be educated and responsible, or ignorant and irresponsible. Most likely, the real citizen is a bit of all these. He comprises fragmented political, religious, cultural, and social identities.

What follows from this real-world picture for the *citoyen* as nucleus of political unity? H. Heller, in his 1927 treatise on sovereignty, gave a still-valid answer. Even though only a small minority of citizens participates in the daily plebiscite, the completely indifferent individual, the "sleeping citizen," still has his share in order-building: whatever he does or fails to do is regulated by the laws of the political community.[33] All actions or nonactions test, confirm, or question those laws. Such tests are more challenging in more heterogeneous bodies of citizens. Regardless of all its aberrations, the heterogeneous nation-state, "the greatest constitutional achievement in history,"[34] has provided for a firm legal and political framework to endure these challenges. So, too, will the European Union—not by replacing, but by encompassing, the nation-states.

Nationality and Citizenship. Though often used synonymously, citizenship and nationality are different concepts. "Citizenship" provides for "a positive legal prescription" of belonging to a state.[35] Nationality can be defined as a legally established link connecting the state and the people building that state. The individual, as a national, is subject to the public authority and legal order of his state. In principle, each state is free to grant nationality according to its own laws, and nationality questions fall within its domestic jurisdiction. Article 1 of the 1930 Hague Convention on the Conflict of Nationality Laws states that "it is for each state to determine under its own law who are its nationals." Prior to the introduction of EU citizenship, the Court of Justice confirmed this notion regarding the EC in holding that rules of nationality rest within the member states' exclusive competence. The court added, however, that the member states must exercise their power with due regard to the requirements of European Community law.[36]

Public international law sets only one limit, famously elaborated by the International Court of Justice (ICJ) in its *Nottebohm* case. The ICJ held that nationality is dependent on "a legal bond having as its basis a social attachment, a genuine connection of existence, interests and sentiments, together with the existence of reciprocal rights and duties."[37] What qualifies as this "genuine link" goes beyond the purely formal legal relationship between individual and state and refers to the moments of "existence, interests and sentiments" upon which citizenship is built.

Citizenship involves "numerous political, historical, social and cultural overtones" that engender significant "diversity in the make-up" of citizen-based legal entities.[38] From a jurisprudential point of view, what these entities have in common is the transformation of political ideas into a legal status that substantially defines the bond between the individual and the political community.[39] The status, however, need not be static; it qualifies as the foundation of a legally structured *process* of community building. Citizenship thus creates a *Rechtsgemeinschaft*, a community under law. As Dahrendorf remarked, citizenship "makes those who belong a part of the system of rules which protects them from each other and (from) outsiders."[40] Belonging is expressed in the legal language of rights and duties. But it is also expressed by the perception of the self and the other—individually and collectively—that is to say, by identity, and as a presupposition of identity consciousness.[41]

One important reference point for the political pattern of identity is societal self-organization (in a democratic society, the self-organization of the free and the equal). At its core are interdependent patterns of participation and communication, of cultural practices and religious beliefs, of "national consciousness" and "multicultural sensibility."[42] It is often said that a citizen perceives the identity of the polity as part of his own identity. This equation, however, must not be mistaken for a holistic or totalitarian concept of citizenship. The community is a heterogeneous amalgamation of imaginations, institutionalizations, and organizations with multiple and fragmented identities. The growing internal and external complexity of communities is paralleled by a growing number of referents for identity—among them, the nation and the union.[43] The consequent distinction between a national and a citizen amounts to a "conceptual decoupling of nationality from citizenship" and to the "conception of a polity the *demos* of which, its membership, is understood in the first place in civic and political rather than ethno-cultural terms."[44] These political terms can be described by means of commitments, shared values, responsibility for the public good, and mutual rights, duties, and social responsibility. All these means work on different levels—for example, those of the family, the workplace, local municipalities, regional communities, federal states, the nation-state, and the European Community.[45] The relevant identities as "a member of" are shared, and so is belonging itself.

All the aforementioned identities are in a permanent state of flux. And so are social roles, standards of inclusion and exclusion, and balances between rights and duties. Among the most obvious changes is migration, which not only has led to the creation of different political statuses (such as citizens, permanent residents, visitors, or live-in caregivers),[46] but also has brought about a more accurate and insightful view of the intrinsic pluralism of all societies, including relatively homogenous national societies. The European culture is a culture of "unity in diversity," as the EU's motto states. Accordingly, citizenship—as an emanation of culture, as a cultural process, as participation in culture, and participation in sociocultural standards[47]—is as diversified as European unity itself. Citizenship is the process of forming civic unity in diversity. Ernest Renan famously defined a nation's existence as "*a daily plebiscite*, just as an individual's existence is a perpetual affirmation of life."[48] In the same way, citizenship beyond the nation is a daily affirmation of belonging and thus of "unity in diversity."

European Union Citizenship

Before its enshrinement in the Treaty of Maastricht, the rhetoric of community citizenship corresponding to a "People's Europe" had long been in use.[49] But the treaty not only created a new legal quality; it also gave rise to the question of whether this new legal quality had any practical significance and, even more importantly, whether it put the former centrality of national citizenship in a new light. The dependency of union citizenship on the nationality of a member state is the crucial point. Contrary to the United States or comparable federal systems, where federal citizenship is supreme and state citizenship is subordinate, union citizenship is based upon member state nationality.[50] The conditions under which member states confer nationality are not regulated by EU law. Member states retain the constitutional power to decide on their own citizenship and naturalization laws, limited only by the public-law principle of a "genuine link" and the obligation under union law to recognize nationality granted by fellow member states.[51]

The rights that stem from union citizenship are not as complete as those flowing from national citizenship. For example, under European Community law, a union citizen who is not a national may be expelled from the territory of a member state for reasons of public policy, public safety, or public health.[52] Such an expulsion would not be available to the state if the person concerned were a national. The levels of belonging differ, as do the mutual rights and obligations of the individual toward the community.

Multilevel constitutionalism requires a corresponding concept of multilevel citizenship. On the national as well as the union level, the citizen is the constituent of his political community. Union citizens participate in the process of creating a European constitution, emotionally and rationally. The different means of citizen-based constitution building range from "imagining Europe" to filing a claim before the European Court of Justice.[53] The status of a European citizen may be somewhere in between a privileged alien and a real citizen, but some substantive elements of (European) citizenship on the national and union levels supplement each other. While the form and intensity of belonging and participation differ, the goal of union citizenship is the establishment of a "direct bond between the individual and the Union, devoid of the Member State."[54] This bond of an originally European citizenship must be seen as a symbolic political reaction to a crisis of legitimacy. Many observers (not only critics) believe that the creation of the European Union reflects an angst typical of modernity and post-modernity. The union appears a giant, overly complex, and dauntingly fragmented political entity, incapable of addressing the challenges of daily local and national life, which is lost in bureaucracy; able to make law without sufficient democratic input; able to engage itself and member states in military activities; committed to a socially blind market culture; and adhering to a neomaterialist ethos of consumerism. The old Leviathan seems to be reborn in European shape.[55]

As a response to these fears, European citizenship can be seen as a promise and a process. The promise is to define the role of the citizen within multilevel governance structures and to build a European constitution with the citizen as the democratic sovereign. The process is the continuous formation of a body of European citizens, which takes place by granting them rights, encouraging their political participation, and seeing them as the constituents of a European public sphere. In other words, the union's legitimation as a political union rests with its citizens. The formation of an "ever closer union" is not exclusively left to the member state, but is a common opportunity for and a common responsibility of citizens. The objectives of union citizenship can thus be summarized as follows: citizenship shall strengthen the protection of all relevant rights and interests of member state nationals; it shall especially guarantee a suitable degree of legal protection to mobile member state nationals in mobile societies; more generally, it shall help to reduce the democratic deficit and to develop a European identity; it shall make the individual a part of European constitution building and accordingly define the scope of Europe's political union as a citizens' Europe.[56]

Three Dimensions of Citizenship. According to Article 6, Section 2 of the EU treaty, "the Union shall respect fundamental rights, as guaranteed by the European Convention for the Protection of Human Rights and Fundamental Freedoms . . . and as they result from the constitutional traditions common to the member states, as general principles of Community law."[57] The EU Charter on Human Rights, not yet binding and thus soft law, offers a means of finding and interpreting the law. Of course, universal human rights are not limited to citizens, and the aforementioned human rights provisions would be effective even without union citizenship.[58] However, union citizenship supports human rights awareness and enforcement. The interdependent dimensions of human rights can be defined as a *status negativus, status positivus*, and *status activus*. Union citizenship is based on that threefold status. Fundamental (and thus universal) human rights should be enjoyed by man as such, whereas citizenship rights are selectively granted to those who belong to a particular political community. Connecting both categories will show that the threefold status of citizenship is to strengthen the threefold status of basic human rights.[59] The privileged status of citizenship is a status of inclusion and exclusion as to a specific political community. At the same time, citizenship, due to its implicit reference to humanity and a human rights universe, offers a means of overcoming the inclusion/exclusion dichotomy.

The *status negativus* is particularly pronounced in European law. The freedoms of the common market (e.g., Articles 23 and following as well as Articles 43 and following of the EC treaty) are the most obvious codifications of "negative" freedom. So are freedoms of religion and expression, freedom of assembly, freedom of the arts and sciences, property rights, privacy or due process rights, and many other rights "to be let alone" developed by the European Court of Justice. The *status positivus* creates an entitlement to social participation and active political protection. Article 34 of the EC treaty refers to social rights and social support, and the Human Rights Charter speaks of social as well as cultural participation.[60] Article 20 of the EC treaty requires effective political guardianship when providing for an entitlement to diplomatic and consular protection. It is only a small step from effective political protection to active political participation. Article 19, Section 2 of the EC treaty reflects the *status activus* in the right to vote and to stand as a candidate in elections to the European Parliament in the citizen's home state. Article 19, Section 1 is an innovative, much-discussed provision: the right to vote and to stand as a candidate at municipal elections in the member state in which the citizen resides.[61] Articles 21, 194, and 195, encompassing the right to petition either the European Parliament or the European Ombudsman, complete the picture.

The European Court of Justice has actively considered and developed the substantive and procedural status of citizenship. When the court protects human rights, it refers not only to principles that are common to the legal cultures of all member states or expressed in international conventions, but also to the structures and objectives of the community.[62] Citizenship is a new structure giving rise to a new human rights dimension. That can particularly be seen in the areas of free movement and residence.

Rights of Free Movement and Residence. The original European Economic Community provided mainly for economic rights—foremost, the "Four Freedoms" of the Common Market, including the free movement of persons, goods, services, and capital. These essential freedoms were supplemented with the principle of nondiscrimination and social rights, such as equal pay for men and women, while this market-based functional approach was insufficient for the creation of a supranational civil society.[63] The breakdown of domestic markets' barriers had a clear political dimension. In the very early days the right to move might have been conceived as a right for the "economically active: those in work, the self-employed, and those delivering services."[64] Because of the European Court of Justice's active role, however, the free movement of persons quickly transcended the Common Market logic and became a fundamental principle for the political community.[65] The pertinent treaty provisions were broadly interpreted and progressively expanded by the Luxemburg justices.[66] The scope of "*ratione personae*" was first limited to "market actors," namely workers and self-employed persons. It has since expanded to family members, recipients of services, tourists, consumers, and even students.[67]

Acting on the dynamic jurisprudence of the court, the European Parliament and the European Council echoed recent judgments in a 2004 Residence Directive:

> Union citizenship should be the fundamental status of nationals of the Member States when they exercise their right of free movement and residence. It is therefore necessary to codify and review the existing Community instruments dealing separately with workers, self-employed persons, as well as students and other inactive persons in order to simplify and strengthen the right of free movement and residence of all Union citizens.[68]

There is a clear tendency to establish a liberalized system of immigration, especially regarding the countries that participate in the Schengen accords. Economic activity no longer provides the decisive momentum to trigger the right of free movement and residence in the member state of one's own choice. This constitutional novelty is expressed in the ECJ's *Baumbast* ruling, which gave direct effect to EC treaty Article 18: "a citizen of the European Union who no longer enjoys a right of residence as a migrant worker in the host Member State can, as a citizen of the Union, enjoy there a right of residence by direct application of Art. 18 (I) EC."[69] The rights contained in Article 18 fill the gaps left by the free-movement guarantees within, and functionally restricted to, the Common Market. In the words of Advocate General Cosmos: "Art. 18 EC enshrines a true right of movement, stemming from the status as citizen of the Union, which is not subordinate in relation to European unification, whether economic or not."[70]

The Social Dimension of Union Citizenship. On the national level, the social welfare state constitutes a key element of political legitimacy. Especially after the Lisbon Reform Treaty, the concept of social market economy and notions of social justice and solidarity form a paradigm of both European constitutionalism and European citizenship.[71] Vertically, ties of mutual solidarity bind the political community to its citizens and in return require citizens' public-oriented loyalty. Horizontally, ties of solidarity structure relations between citizens. Social citizenship results from social responsibility.

This, however, is an idealistic picture in many regards. Political communities possess limited financial resources of which they must make sustainable use, and self-responsibility and self-sustainability are other central features of the liberal democratic paradigm of European constitutionalism and citizenship. Moreover, individuals may act irresponsibly and may selfishly rely on their right not to participate in processes conducive to the public good. A constitutional scheme of governance must counterbalance the freedom (or *liberté*) and the solidarity (or *"fraternité*) momentum of citizenship.

The European Court of Justice has greatly strengthened the solidarity dimension of union citizenship.[72] In *Martinez-Sala*,[73] the court created a new right for foreigners—that they be treated no differently from nationals with respect to their entitlement to social assistance. In a subsequent case (2001) concerning social assistance for students, the court stated: "Union citizenship is designed to be the fundamental status of nationals of the Member States, enabling those who find themselves in the same situation to enjoy the same treatment in law irrespective of their nationality, subject to such exceptions as are expressly provided for." Nothing, said the court, "suggest[s] that students who are citizens of the Union, when they move to another Member State to study there, lose the rights which the treaty confers on the citizens of the Union."[74] In *Trojani*, the court pointed out that the status of a citizen was a status of equality conferring directly effective rights of equal treatment.[75] In *Bidar*, the scope of the nondiscrimination clause in Article 12 of the EC treaty was broadened with respect to student loans and grants.[76] Thus union citizenship is used to consolidate both social and educational rights.

As progressive and promising as the social and educational rights aspect of union citizenship might be, the court's approach risks an ill-balanced concept of membership.[77] Fears of "welfare tourism" run counter to an "ever closer union." The consequence of an excessive emphasis on social rights would be (and to some extent already is) a "political debate as well as popular discourse in which unlimited socioeconomic rights of aliens are perceived as a factor contributing to erosion both of liberal democracy and the national welfare state."[78] What is intended to guarantee social inclusion might result in exclusion. The nonnational seeking social benefits might be seen as an unwelcome foreigner, rather than a fellow citizen, if social solidarity trumps legitimate interests of the member states. Aware of the risks of a judicially activist exercise in "social engineering," the ECJ has referred to the "principle of proportionality" as a useful tool for balancing social rights as prerequisite of belonging, and belonging as prerequisite for social rights. Applicants for financial support must have a "genuine link with the host country"—so to say, the *Nottebohm* principle Europeanized—and may not unreasonably burden the host member state's social system.[79] Solidarity is a corrective where self-sustainability fails, but it is not a substitute for personal responsibility.

Duties, Responsibilities, and Obligations of Union Citizens. Citizenship entails not only rights and freedoms but also duties, responsibilities, and obligations. In modern constitutional terms, the vertical dimension of duties toward the political community is most prominently expressed by the obligation to serve on juries, to pay taxes, and to perform military or social service. (Few constitutions mandate that citizens vote.) The horizontal dimension of duties toward fellow citizens is chiefly expressed by balancing human rights and freedoms, by the horizontal effect of human rights provisions, and by implicit social dimensions of human rights.

Regarding vertical duties, an obvious gap exists in the scheme of union citizenship. This gap, however, is filled by the mechanisms of multilevel constitutionalism. Since it cannot raise taxes, the European Community is financed by its member states. The national taxpayer's obligation qualifies— to the extent to which the union is entitled to financial support by the relevant member state—as an indirect European obligation. A parallel argument could be made for the military.

In the horizontal dimension, the states as well as the union hold that citizens must accept the limits of their human rights in correlation to the human rights of others. National constitutional courts and the European Court of Justice apply comparable balancing approaches. Regarding both the vertical and the horizontal dimension, the European treaties may not define explicit duties, but they contain implicit expectations of loyalty and respect; of awareness for safety and security; of support for the well-being of others and the prosperity of the community; and of engagement for peace and coexistence with neighbors. Since the European Union is in the process of being constitutionalized, this is a constitutional reading of constitutional expectations.

Conclusion

Kant's vision of *Weltbürgertum* or "cosmopolitan citizenship," expressed in his famous essay "The Idea of a General History with a Cosmopolitan Intention," conceptualized the citizen as being on his way from the city through the nation to a universal world-state and a universal federation of republics. While international legal structures are (fortunately) far away from forming a "world-state," the Kantian notion is somewhat evident in multilevel schemes of governance and citizenship, with two important qualifications.

First, the citizen "being on his way" does not imply a *transformation* of local or national citizenship into universal citizenship. Globalism and localism are not alternative but complementary principles.[80] The individual, as global economic actor, participant in political processes with global effect, or subject of universal human rights, can be a citizen of the world and at the same time of a region, a country, a federal state, or a municipality. All these relations describe multiple forms of belonging. Belonging, though, does not only require a legal framework; it needs to be a natural imagination and a day-to-day experience for those who belong. As K. Laenerts and E. De Smijter point out with reference to union citizenship, "democratic legitimation requires that the span between the politically wanted self-image of the citizens and their real self-image is not too wide."[81]

Second, when combined with universality, belonging may become meaningless. Universal belonging without inclusion and exclusion seems paradoxical. Universal rights belong to man as such, not as citizen or subject of a specific legal order. There is, however, an aspect of universal belonging: the belonging to a rational universe. The common assumption "that all men are endowed with certain basic qualities which enable them to be parts of a rational universe" refers to the "evident relationship between rationality, the implicit universality of the law, and citizenship."[82] The individual citizen is included in and excluded from different political entities; the citizen as universal political model or universal type is free, equal, and able to participate. Etymology invites attention to a related contextualization of rationality and citizenship: civilization. The term stems from the Latin word "*civilis*," the adjective form of "*civis*." Civilization is, etymologically and politically, to a significant extent the outcome of a universal process of citizenship building.

The obvious shortcomings of this rationality-based concept of global citizenship have already been mentioned. The individual does not, for many reasons, always feel that he or she belongs to the rational universe of humanity or behave as a rational actor. The nation-state—and the civil society forming it—has repeatedly proven that the enlightened, politically aware, and public-spirited *citoyen*, and thus the concept of active citizenship, sways between rhetoric and reality. The failures on the national level may appear on the regional, the European, and (especially) the transnational plane. A timely concept of citizenship must consider these "constitutive deficits": it must address *ratio* and *emotio*, and it must grapple with those who refuse responsible participation. Finally, citizenship is not a "goal in itself but a means toward enlarging the life chances of men."[83] The Kantian notion of *Weltbürgertum* provides the philosophical dimension for this process of enlargement. The "global village" of the twenty-first century creates the real-world parameter for this process, and public international law—especially human rights law—provides the legal framework.[84] Admittedly, even within the United Nations system, instruments of political participation are lacking. However, as a subject of human rights and complainant before international tribunals, as participant in international discourses, as NGO-activist—or simply as market actor, tourist, or Internet user, etc.—the individual has a chance to become more than a global player; he has the chance to become a global citizen.

European citizenship is a promise and a process. It is the promise to accept the "citizenship" of the other, and a process of disproving Carl Schmitt's "friend and foe" ideology by converting the closed national state into a polity composed of others—something present in the American experience.[85] Despite its shortcomings, it can be viewed "in terms of both its potential and its wider current meaning."[86] Its potential refers to the ongoing process of constitution and citizenship building; to the ever-changing parameters of belonging; to the aim of European integration, which is an ever-closer citizen-based unity in diversity. Its wider current meaning recalls the necessity to allow "narrowly defined Treaty provisions" as well as "other aspects of transnational civic engagement within the EU" to complete the picture.[87]

Basing union citizenship upon domicile or residence instead of member-state nationality might be a progressive means of European integration, heightening feelings of European belonging.[88] It might be easier to create a new European political identity without reference to national member states' political identities. It might be tempting to constitutionalize a citizens' Europe without member states as intermediary entities. But such far-reaching efforts to create a European federacy would not find member-state support. Nor would they correspond to the multilevel scheme of European constitutionalism. The union is neither a replacement for the nation-state nor a postnational entity. Rather, it is a new architecture composed of intertwined constitutional structures, each of which is as important for the larger European structure as a crossbeam is for a building. The image of "the House of Europe" pictures the richness of heterogenic, asymmetric political entities, assembled under a common roof.[89] What the completed European house will look like remains unclear. However, what should be engraved over the entrance is obvious: "We, the Citizens of Europe, have built it and will continuously rebuild it."

Notes

1. The Federalist No. 1 (Alexander Hamilton).

2. Maastricht Treaty on European Union, Feb. 7, 1992, 1992 O.J. (C 191) 1.

3. *See e.g.* Jörg Geerlings, *Der Europäische Verfassungsprozess nach den gescheiterten Referenden*, in Frankreich und den Niederlanden, 1 Deutsches Verwaltungsblatt 129 (2006); Hans M. Heinig, Europäisches Verfassungsrecht ohne Verfassung(svertrag)?, Juristenzeitung [JZ] 905 (2007); Franz C. Mayer, *Wege aus der Verfassungskrise—Zur Zukunft des Vertrages über eine Verfassung für Europa*, 62 JZ 593 (2007); Hans Jürgen Rabe, *Zur Metamorphose des Europäischen Verfassungsvertrages*, 44 Neue Juristische Wochenschrift [NJW] 3153 (2007); Thorsten S. Richter, *Die EU-Verfassung ist tot, es lebe der Reformvertrag!*, 20 Europaische Zeitschrift für Wirtschaftsrecht 631 (2007).

4. Joseph H. H. Weiler, *To Be a European Citizen: Eros und Civilization*, in The Constitution of Europe 324, 327 (1999).

5. For the relevant literature, *see* Paul Craig and Grainne de Búrca, EU Law 847 (4th ed. 2008); Damian Chalmers, Christos Hadjiemmanuil, Giorgio Monti, & Adam Tomkins, European Union Law 561 (2006).

6. Regarding that understanding, *see* Dieter Grimm, *Braucht Europa eine Verfassung?* in JZ 581, 587 (1995). For the linkage of identity and the nation-state on the one side, identity and the union on the other side, *see* Elspeth Guild, The Legal Elements of European Identity 9 (2004).

7. In that sense, *see, e.g.,* Christian Tomuschat and Stefan Kadelbach, *Staatsbürgerschaft—Unionsbürgerschaft—Weltbürgerschaft*, in Europäische Demokratie 73, 84, 89, 104 (Josef Drexl, Karl F. Kreuzer, & Dieter Scheuing eds., 1999).

8. The understanding of the "constitution as a public process" has been developed by Peter Häberle, Verfassung als öffentlicher Prozess (3d ed. 1998). The theory found widespread international reception, *see, e.g.,* Jörg Luther, *La Sciencia häberliana delle costituzioni*, in Analisi e diritto 2001 (a cura di Paolo Comanducci e. Riccardo Gustiano) 105 (2001); R. Caciado Amaral, Peter Häberle e a Hermeneutica Constitucional (2004). *See also* David O'Keefe, *Union Citizenship*, in Legal Issues of the Maastricht Treaty 106 (David O'Keefe & Patrick Twomey eds., 1994); he calls the concept of Union citizenship "a dynamic one, capable of being added to or strengthened, but not diminished." *Furthermore* Alina Domaradzka, Unionsbürger im Übergang (2006).

9. Peter Häberle, Verfassungslehre als Kulturwissenschaft 28 (2d ed. 1998).

10. Karen Alter, *Who Are the "Masters of the Treaty"?: European Governments and the European Court of Justice*, 52 Int. Org. 121 (1998)

11. Ingolf Pernice, *Multilevel Constitutionalism and the Treaty of Amsterdam: European Constitution-Making Revisited?* 36 Common Mkt. L. Rev. 703 (1999); *see also* Ingolf Pernice, *The Global Dimension of Multilevel Constitutionalism: A Legal Response to the Challenges of Globalisation*, in Völkerrecht als Wertordnung: Festschrift für Christian Tomuschat 973 (Pierre-Marie Dupuy, Bardo Fassbender, Malcolm N. Shaw, & Karl-Peter Sommermann eds., 2006); Jacques Vanderlinden, *Le pluralisme juridique: essai de*

synthèse, in Le Pluralisme Juridique 19 (John Gillissen ed., 1971); Jacques Vanderlinden, *Return to Legal Pluralism: Twenty Years Later*, 28 J. Leg. Pluralism 149 (1989); Keebet von Benda-Beckmann, *Transnational dimension of legal pluralsim*, in Begegnung und Konflikt—Eine kulturanthropologische Bestandsaufnahme (Wolfgang Fikentscher ed., 2001), 33; Franz von Benda-Beckmann, *Who's Afraid of Legal Pluralism?* 47 J. of Leg. Pluralism 37 (2002); Anne Griffiths and Neil Walker, *The Idea of Constitutional Pluralism*, 65 Modern Law Review 317 (2002); Miguel P. Maduro, *Contrapunctual Law: Europe's Constitutional Pluralism in Action*, in Sovereignty in Transition (Neil Walker ed., 2001); *Legal Pluralism*, in An Introduction to Law and Social Theory 289 (Reza Banakar and Max Travers eds., 2002).

12. Franz von Benda-Beckmann and Keebet von Benda-Beckmann, *The Dynamics of Change and Continuity in Plural Legal Orders*, 53–4 J. of Leg. Pluralism & Unofficial L. 14, 17 (2006).

13. Case 26/62, Van Gend en Loos, 1963 E.C.R. 1.

14. Case 6/64, Costa v. ENEL, 1964 E.C.R. 585.

15. Case 26/62, Van Gend en Loos, 1963 E.C.R. 1 at 47–8.

16. *See* Grainne de Búrca, *Sovereignty and the Supremacy Doctrine of the European Court of Justice*, in Sovereignty in Transition 449 (Neil Walker ed., 2003); Alexander Schmitt Glaeser, *Souveränität und Vorrang*, in Europäisches Verfassungsrecht 205 (Armin von Bogdandy ed., 2003). For an analysis of a parallel development in early U.S. constitutionalism shortly before and after 1787, *see* Jean-Paul Jaqué, *Der Vertrag über eine Verfassung für Europa: Konstitutionalisierung oder Vertragsrevision?* 2004 Europäische Grundrechte-Zeitschrift 551, 552–3 (2004). Important reference is made to The Federalist Nos. 15, 16 (Alexander Hamilton).

17. Jean-Phillipe Robé, *Multinational Enterprises: The Constitution of a Pluralistic Legal Order*, in Global Law Without a State 45 (Gunther Teubner ed., 1997); Gunther Teubner, *Global Bukowina: Legal Pluralism in the World Society*, in *id.* at 3; Gralf-Peter Calliess, *Reflective Transnational Law: On Definition of Transnational Law*, 23 Zeitschrift für Rechtssoziologie 185 (2002); Francis Snyder, *Governing Economic Globalization: Global Legal Pluralism and European Law*, in Law and Anthropology—A Reader 318 (Sally Moore ed., 2004).

18. Eva Brems, *Human Rights: Universality and Diversity* (2001); Eva Brems, *Enemies or Allies? Feminism and Cultural Relativism as Dissident Voices in Human Rights Discourse*, 19 Hum. Rts. Q. 136 (1997); Bonaventura De Sousa Santos, *Toward a Multicultural Conception of Human Rights*, 18 Zeitschrift für Rechtssoziologie 1 (1997); Abdoullahi An-Nacim, *Human Rights in Cross-Cultural Perspectives* (1992); Jack Donnelly, *Cultural Relativism and Universal Human Rights*, 6 Hum. Rts. Q. 400 (1984).

19. Arthur Benz, *Compounded Representation in EU Multilevel Governance*, in Linking EU and National Governance 82 (Beate Kohler-Koch ed., 2003); James Rosenau, *Governance and Democracy in a Globalizing World*, in Reimagining Political Community 28 (Daniele Archibugi, David Held, & Martin Köhler eds., 1998).

20. The dimension of this "constitutional supremacy" is disputed. From a German point of view *see* Maastricht, 89 Entscheidungen des Bundesverfassungsgerichtes

[BVerfGE] 155; Ulrich Everling, *The Maastricht Judgement of the German Federal Constitutional Court and Its Significance for the Development of the European Union*, 1994 Yearbook of Eur. L. 1 (1994); Manfred Zuleeg, *The European Constitution Under Constitutional Constraints: The German Scenario*, 22 Eur. L. Rev. 11 (1997); *see generally* Wojciech Sadurski, *"Solange Chapter 3": Constitutional Courts in Central Europe—Democracy—European Union* 14 Eur. L.J. 1 (2008).

21. Martin Nettesheim, *Demokratisierung der Europäischen Union und Europäisierung der Demokratietheorie—Wechselwirkungen bei der Herausbildung eines europäischen Demokratieprinzips*, in Demokratie in Europa 144, 176 (Harmut Bauer, Peter M. Huber and Karl Peter Sommermann eds., 2005); Benjamin Barber, Strong Democracy: Participatory Politics for a New Age (1984).

22. Daniel Thürer, *"Citizenship" und Demokratieprinzip: Föderative Ausgestaltung im innerstaatlichen, europäischen und globalen Rechtskreis*, in Globalisierung und Demokratie 177 (Hauke Brunkhorst & Matthias Kettner eds., 2000).

23. Jo Shaw, *European Union Citizenship: The IGC and Beyond*, 3 Eur. Pub. L. 413 (1997).

24. Ralf Dahrendorf, *Citizenship and Beyond: The Social Dynamics of an Idea*, in Citizenship: Critical Concepts, vol. II, 292 (Bryan S. Turner & Peter Hamiliton eds., 1994).

25. *Id.*

26. François Borella, *Nationalité et citoyenneté en droit français*, in L'Etat de droit. Travaux de la mission de la modernisation de l'Etat 35 (Dominique Colas ed., 1987); the English translation is provided by Benoit Guiguet, *Citizenship and Nationality: Tracing the French Roots of the Distinction*, in European Citizenship: An Institutional Challenge 95, 98 (Massimo La Torre ed., 1998).

27. Michel Troper, *The Concept of Citizenship in the Period of the French Revolution*, in European Citizenship: An Institutional Challenge, *supra* note 26, at 29.

28. Borella, *supra* note 26, at 99 (English translation).

29. Massimo La Torre, *Citizenship: A European Wager*, 8 Ratio Juris 113 (1995); Rudolf Smend, *Bürger und Bourgeois im deutschen Staatsrecht*, in Staatsrechtliche Abhandlungen (2d ed. 1968), distinguishing between the "sittlich an den Staat gebundenen Bürger" (*citoyen*) and the "rechenhafter Egoist der kapitalistischen Zeit" (bourgeois); *see also* Ulrich K. Preuß, *Der EU-Staatsbürger—Bourgeois oder Citoyen*, in Das Öffentliche Heute 179 (Gerd Winter ed., 2002).

30. Eberhard Grabitz, *Europäisches Bürgerrecht zwischen Marktbürgerschaft und Staatsbürgerschaft* (1970); Albrecht Randelzhofer, *Marktbürgerschaft, Unionsbürgerschaft, Staatsbürgerschaft*, in Gedächtnisschrift für Eberhard Grabitz 580 (E. Grabitz ed., 1995); J. Habermas, *Die postnationale Konstellation* 91, 142 (1998) speaks of a "funktionalistisch reduzierten Personenkonzept" (a functionalist thus limited concept of the human person).

31. Dahrendorf, *supra* note 24, at 294.

32. Gisbert Brinkmann, *An Area of Freedom, Security and Justice Five Years After its Creation: The Immigration and Asylum Agenda*, 10 Eur. L.J. 2 (2004); Matthias Ruffert,

Der Raum der Freiheit, der Sicherheit und des Rechts nach dem Reformvertrag—Kontinuierliche Verfassungsgebung in schwierigem Terrain, in Der Vertrag von Lissabon: Reform der EU ohne Verfassung 169 (Ingolf Pernice ed., 2008).

33. Hermann Heller, *Die Souveränität* (1927), reprinted in Gesammelte Schriften, vol. II 31, 108–9 (1971); *furthermore* W. Berka, Bürgerverantwortung im demokratischen Verfassungsstaat, 55 V. V. D. St. R. L. 48, 58 (1996).

34. Ralf Dahrendorf, *Cittadinanza: una nuova agenda per il cambiamneto*, in Sociologica del diritto 7, 16 (1993).

35. Siofra O'Leary, European Union Citizenship: The Options for Reform 12 (1996).

36. Case C-369/90, *Micheletti v. Delegacion del Gobierno Cantabriam*, 1992 E.C.R. I-4239. More recent rulings (after the introduction of union citizenship) with the same emphasis are Case C-192/99, R v. Secretary of State for the Home Department, *ex parte* Kaur, 2001 E.C.R. I-1169. *See* James D. Mather, *The Court of Justice and the Union Citizen*, 11 Eur. L.J. 722, 723–24 (2005).

37. I.C.J. Reports 4, 23 (1955).

38. O'Leary, *supra* note 35, at 12.

39. J. Donald Galloway, *Citizenship: A Jurisprudential Paradox*, in European Citizenship: An Institutional Challenge, *supra* note 26, at 68.

40. Dahrendorf, *supra* note 26, at 292.

41. *See* Peter Häberle, Europäische Verfassungslehre 354 (5th ed. 2008); *Verfassungslehre als Kulturwissenschaft*, *supra* note 8, at 624; Yasemin Nuhoglu Soysal, Limits of Citizenship: Migrants and Postnational Membership in Europe (1994); Ulrich Haltern, Euoparecht und das Politische 423 (2005).

42. *See also* Jürgen Habermas, *Citizenship and National Identity: Some Reflections on the Future of Europe*, 12 Praxis Int'l 1 (1992).

43. Weiler, *supra* note 4, at 324; and *see* Joseph H. H. Weiler, *Epilogue: The European Courts of Justice: Beyond "Beyond Doctrine" or the Legitimacy Crisis of European Constitutionalism*, in The European Courts and National Courts: Doctrine and Jurisprudence 365, 377 ff. (Ann-Marie Slaughter, Alec Stone Sweet, and Joseph H. H. Weiler eds., 1998); Joseph H. H. Weiler, *Fin-de-siècle Europe: Do the new clothes have an emperor?* in The Constitution of Europe 238 (1999).

44. Weiler, *supra* note 4, at 344.

45. *See* Vaclav Havel, *Die Herrschaft der Gesetze*, in Sommermeditationen 14, 26 (2d ed. 1994), combining the ideas of multiple sources of identity with universal human rights.

46. Galloway, *Citizenship: A Jurisprudential Paradox*, in European Citizenship, *supra* note 26, at 65, 66.

47. Valentin Petev, *Citizenship and Raison D'Etat: The Quest for Identity in Central and Eastern Europe*, in European Citizenship, *supra* note 26, at 83.

48. Ernest Renan, *What is a Nation?*, in Becoming National: A Reader 41, 41–55 (Geoff Eley & Ronald Grigor Suny eds., 1996); *see generally* Häberle, *supra* note 8.

49. Antje Wiener, *Assessing the Constructive Potential of Union Citizenship? A Socio-Historical Perspective*, 1 European Integration Online Papers 17 (1997); Craig and

de Búrca, *supra* note 5, at 847; S. Kadelbach, *Unionsbürgerschaft*, in Europäisches Verfassungs-recht, *supra* note 16, at 541. On "creating citizenship" before and after Maastricht, *see* Guild, *supra* note 6, at 35; Craig and de Búrca, *supra* note 5, at 848, 849.

50. Epaminondas A. Marias, *From Market Citizen to Union Citizen*, in European Citizenship 1, 13 (Epaminondas A. Marias ed., 1994) *with reference to* Carlos Closa, *The Concept of Citizenship in the Treaty on the European Union*, 29 Common Mkt. L. Rev. 1137, 1141 (1992).

51. Case C-369/90, Micheletti v. Delegación del Gobierno en Cantabria, 1992 E.C.R. I-4239; Case C-200/02, Chen v. Home Secretary, 2004 E.C.R. I-9925; *see also* Stephen Hall, *Determining the Scope Ratione Personae of European Citizenship: Customary International Law Prevails for Now*, 28; Kadelbach, *Unionsbürgerschaft*, in Europäisches Verfassungsrecht, *supra* note 16, at 539, 545.

52. *See, e.g.,* European Community treaty, art. 39 sec. 3, 45. Under international law, such an expulsion or exclusion would not be open to the state of which the person concerned is a national. Robin C. White, *The Citizen's Right to Free Movement*, in 16 European Business Law Review 547, 548 (2005). Particularly in migrant societies the relationship of third-country nationals and citizenship is of high importance; *see* Guild, *supra* note 6, at 82. A very critical perspective is offered by O'Leary, *supra* note 35, at iv: "Choosing Member State nationality as the means of access to citizenship suggests that a particular type of European identity is being fostered, one which bears little relation with the social reality in Member States which have been receiving immigrants from third countries for many years."

53. Häberle, *supra* note 41 at 354.

54. Mather, *supra* note 36, 722; Häberle, *supra* note 41, at 354: "Der Begriff Unionsbürgerschaft schiebt den Staatsbegriff beiseite, indem er ihn nicht verwendet." ("The term union citizenship puts aside the term of state by not using it.")

55. Weiler, *supra* note 4, at 332; O'Leary, *supra* note 35, at 7.

56. O'Leary, *supra* note 35, at 89.

57. Armin von Bogdandy, *The EU as Human Rights Organization*, 37 Common Mkt. L. Rev. 1307 (2000); Patrick M. Twomey, *European Citizenship and Human Rights: Actual Situation and Future Perspectives*, in European Citizenship 119 (Epaminondas A. Marias ed., 1994).

58. Joseph H. H. Weiler, *European Citizenship and Human Rights*, in Reforming the Treaty of the European Union: The Legal Debate 57 (Jan A. Winter ed., 1996).

59. The risk that a link between citizenship and the protection of human rights would be detrimental for human rights is relatively small. As to the controversial debate *see* O' Leary, *supra* note 35, at 69.

60. See Chapter IV, Article 22 of the charter, which treats diversity of cultures, religions, and languages. For further reference, *see* Markus Kotzur, *Die Soziale Marktwirtschaft nach dem Reformvertrag*, in Der Vertrag von Lissabon: Reform der EU ohne Verfassung, *supra* note 32, at 197.

61. Electoral rights on the basis of residence had already been suggested in 1986 by a commission report entitled *Voting Rights in Local Elections for Community Nationals*, COM (86) 487.

62. Jason Coppell and Aidan O'Neill, *The European Court of Justice: Taking Rights Seriously?* 12 Legal Stud. 227 (1992); Joseph H. H. Weiler and Nicolas Lockhart, *"Taking Rights Seriously" Seriously: The European Court and its Fundamental Rights Jurisprudence*, 32 Common Mkt. L. Rev. 51, 57–9 (1995).

63. Marias, *supra* note 50, at 2.

64. White, *supra* note 52, at 547.

65. Izolda Bulvinaite, *Union Citizenship and Its Role in the Free Movement of Persons Regimes* 5 Web J Current Legal Issues (2003).

66. Jan Wouters, *European Citizenship and the Case-Law of the Court of Justice of the European Communities and the Free Movement of Persons*, in European Citizenship *supra* note 50, at 25; O'Leary, *supra* note 35, at 26.

67. Case C-214/94, AG *Léger*, 1996 E.C.J. I-02253

68. Council Directive 2004/38, 2004 O.J. (L 158) 77 (EC). In 1974, the heads of state and government, meeting in Paris, had proposed that a working group should be instructed to "study the conditions and the timing" under which the citizens of the (at that time) nine member states "could be given special rights as Members of the Community" (Bull. E.C.12-1974, Point 111). In 1979 the European Commission had proposed a directive on a right of residence, followed by different reports regarding a possible status of union citizens. For detailed reference *see* O'Leary, *supra* note 35, at 35–36.

69. Case C-413/99, Baumbast and R v. Secretary of State for the Home Department, 2002 E.C.R. I-7091; for an analysis *see* Michael Dougan and Eleanor Spaventa, *Educating Rudy and the Non-English Patient: A Double Bill on Residency Rights Under Article 18 EC*, 28 Eur. L. Rev 699 (2003); White, *supra* note 52, at 549; Mather, *supra* note 36, at 725–26, *with reference to* the Cases *Adams, Phull, Mounciffe*, and *Wijensbeek*; Michael Dougan, *The Constitutional Dimension of the Case Law on Union Citizenship*, 31 Eur. L. Rev. 613 (2006).

70. Case C-378/97, Criminal Proceedings against Wijensbeek, 1999 E.C.R. I-6207, para. 5.

71. Roland Bieber, *Solidarität als Verfassungsprinzip der Europäischen Union*, in Solidarität und Europäische Integration 41 (Armin von Bogdandy & Stefan Kadelbach eds., 2002); Uwe Volkmann, *Solidarität—Programm und Prinzip der Verfassung* (1998); Christian Tomuschat, *Solidarität in Europa*, in Liber Amicorum P. Pescatore 729 (F. Capotorti *et al.* eds., 1987).

72. Michael Dougan, *The Constitutional Dimension of the Case Law on Union Citizenship*, 31 Eur. L. Rev. 613 (2006); Klaus-Dieter Borchardt, *Der sozialrechtliche Gehalt der Unionsbürgerschaft*, 29 Neue Juristische Wochenschrift 2057 (2000).

73. Case 85/96, Martinez-Sala v. Freistaat Bayern, 1998 E.C.R. I-2691; Siofra O'Leary, *Putting Flesh on the Bones of European Union Citizenship*, 24 Eur. L. Rev. 68 (1999); White, *supra* note 52, at 549; Mather, *supra* note 36, at 729.

74. Case C-184/99, Grzelczyk v. Centre Public d'Aide Sociale de Bruxelles (CPAS), 2001 E.C.R.

75. Case C-456/02 Trojani v. CPAS, 2004 E.C.R. I-7573; Case C-138/02, Collins v. Secretary of State for Work and Pensions, 2004 E.C.R. I-2703; Guild, *supra* note 6, at 51.

76. Case C-209/03 Bidar (on the application of Dany Bidar) v. Ealing LBC and Secretary of State for Education and Skills, 2005 E.C.R. I-2119; for an analysis *see* Oxana Golynker, *Student Loans: The European Concept of Social Justice According to Bidar*, 31 Eur. L. Rev. 390 (2006).

77. A very critical perspective is offered by Kay Hailbronner, *Union Citizenship and the Access to Social Benefits*, 42 Common Mkt. L. Rev. 1245 (2005).

78. Oxana Golynker, *Jobseekers' Rights in the European Union: Challenges of Changing the Paradigm of Social Solidarity*, 30 Eur. L. Rev. 111, 121; *furthermore* Kay Hailbronner, *Die Unionsbürgerschaft und das Ende rationaler Jurisprudenz durch den EuGH?* 31 Neue Juristische Wochenschrift 2185 (2004); Ulrich Becker, *Sozialrecht in der Europäischen Integration—Eine Zwischenbilanz*, 3 Zeitschrift für Sozialhilfe und Sozialgesetzbuch [ZFSH/SGB] 134 (2007).

79. Golynker, *supra* note 76, at 401; Golynker, *supra* note 78, at 111.

80. Vincenzo Ferrari, *Citizenship: Problems, Concepts and Policies*, in European Citizenship, *supra* note 26, at 51–52.

81. Koen Laenerts and Eddy De Smijter, *The Question of Democratic Representation*, Paper presented at the T. M. C. Asser Instituut conference, TEU: Suggestions for Revision (Sept. 14–16, 1995).

82. Dahrendorf, *supra* note 24, at 294.

83. *Id.* at 308.

84. For the interactions of public international and European Community law in the human rights field and the recent *Yusuf* decision of the European Court of First Instance, *see* Theodor Schilling, *Der Schutz der Menschenrechte gegen Beschlüsse des Sicherheitsrates*, 64 Zeitschrift für ausländisches öffentliches Recht und Völkerrecht 343 (2004); Christian Walter, *Grundrechtsschutz gegen Hoheitsakte internationaler Organisationen*, 129 Archiv des Öffentlichen Rechts 39 (2004); Markus Kotzur, *Eine Bewährungsprobe für die Europäische Grundrechtsgemeinschaft—Zur Entscheidung des EuG in der Rs. Yusuf u.a. gegen Rat*, 2006 Europaische Grundrechte Zeitschrift 19 (2006); Kirsten Schmalenbach, *Normtheorie vs. Terrorismus: Der Vorrang des UN-Rechts vor EU-Recht*, 7 JuristenZeitung 349 (2006); Christian Tietje and Sandy Hamelmann, *Gezielte Finanzsanktionen der Vereinten Nationen im Spannungsverhältnis zum Gemeinschaftsrecht und zu den Menschenrechten*, 4 Juristische Schulung 299 (2006); Christian Möllers, *Bezwingendes Recht*, Frankfurter Allgemeine Zeitung, Feb. 15, 2006, at 39.

85. Carl Schmitt, Der Begriff des Politischen: Text von 1932 mit einem Vorwort und drei Corollarien 29 (6th ed. 1996).

86. Paul Craig and Grainne de Búrca, *supra* note 5, at 873.

87. *Id.*

88. Mather, *supra* note 36, at 725 (2005).

89. Häberle, *supra* note 41, at 65, 102; *see also* Roy H. Ginsberg, Demystifying the European Union: The Enduring Logic of European Integration (2005).

5

A Conversation: The Public and Political Debate in Europe and the United States

Jürgen Kaube, Robert von Rimscha, Martin Klingst,
Ayaan Hirsi Ali, and Peter Skerry

Jürgen Kaube

In March 2006 teachers at a school in Berlin published an open letter announcing that they were no longer able to guarantee decent and effective classes. The reason was violence against teachers and students' resistance to any attempt to teach them. Eighty-one percent of the children at this school were the offspring of nonnative Germans. Among sixty youths leaving this school in 2005–06 with a *Hauptschulabschluß*, the lowest degree in the German secondary school system, not a single one managed to obtain an apprenticeship. Overall, 20 percent of foreign schoolchildren leave German schools without any degree.[1]

Some months earlier, another school in Berlin had decided that German should be the only language spoken not only in class but also in the schoolyard. That decision was made by teachers, parents, and schoolchildren. When a Green Party representative of Turkish ancestry denounced it as "discrimination," he was immediately supported by the Turkish press, left-wing politicians, and some teachers' lobbyists. They all voiced alarm over the unacceptable attempt to "Germanize" foreign cultures. The media hysteria stopped only when it became clear that most of the supposed "victims," namely the schoolchildren, themselves supported the initiative as the only means of preventing a segregation of the various ethnic communities in that school.

In December 2007, the governor of Hessen, Roland Koch (Christian Democratic Union), brought up the issue of criminal activity by immigrants. Days before, two young men, one from Turkey and the other from Greece, had been caught and charged with manslaughter; they had brutalized a German pensioner in the Munich subway for reminding them that smoking was not allowed. Koch used the intensive media coverage of this case to take a hard line on violent crime by youths, and to point out that a disproportionate share of such crime is committed by immigrants. His campaign for reelection was unsuccessful, not least because it came out that Koch himself had cut the expenditures for police and that the Hessian courts were among the slowest and most permissive with respect to crimes of this type. But Social Democrats called Koch *fremdenfeindlich* (xenophobic) and reminded the public that, in his first campaign in Hessen (1999), Koch had won the electorate by organizing a public protest against the liberalization of citizenship laws by the Red-Green coalition. In the debate which turned the expected winner of the Hessian election into a loser, moreover, arguments like this were made: violence is bad, whether committed by immigrants or German citizens; criminal activity is linked only to the "underclass," not to any specific ethnicity. These arguments did not acknowledge that young male non-Germans are prosecuted seven times more often for rape, 3.4 times more often for severe assault, and 3.6 times more often for highway robbery, than are young male Germans.

In Germany we have a highly emotional debate about the consequences of immigration, about what it means to be a German citizen or just to live in Germany, and about the adequate political response to the disproportionate incidence of criminal behavior among the foreign population. Our tendency is either to use euphemistic terms in describing our situation, or to exploit it in a rather simple-minded, populist way.

Let us establish some facts. Since World War II, Germany has had the highest immigration rate of any European country. By the end of 2007, 7.2 million German residents were foreigners (about 9 percent of the population). Of these, 1.7 million were of Turkish nationality and half a million were Italians, with smaller numbers of Poles, Serbs, Montenegrins, and Greeks. Since 1990 about 4.2 million people from Romania, Poland, Russia, and Kazakhstan have immigrated to Germany; their presence is not reflected in immigration statistics because they immigrated with German passports, having the status of "foreign Germans." During the last decade, about

120,000 people per year acquired German citizenship. Here, too, the Turkish minority was dominant (at approximately 45 percent).

Recently, Germany's immigration numbers have changed. Immigration has been overtaken by emigration. This trend was partly due to a stricter judicial administration of asylum laws (in 2005, only 10 percent of thirty thousand applicants were acknowledged as politically persecuted) and a tightening of German immigration laws, especially the rule for the *Familiennachzug* (that is, the rule permitting family members of foreign workers to follow their breadwinners). Fifty percent of the Turkish immigrants came to Germany via this "integration of families."

German immigration law is not very selective and, at the same time, it is rather complicated, with many rules and exceptions. We adopt no strict criteria with respect to applicants' education, profession, income, assets, age, or language abilities. A foreigner may be permitted to immigrate to Germany for one of four reasons: work, education at a German university, family relations, or humanitarian asylum.

After the 1999 reforms, a law was passed granting citizenship to children of foreigners, if born in Germany to at least one parent who has lived in Germany for at least eight years and has had the status of a permanent inhabitant for at least three years. Naturalization (*Einbürgerung*) can take place if the applicant has lived in Germany for eight years, earns his own income (unless he is in a "critical situation" [*Notlage*] or younger than twenty-three), has not been arrested, affirms the constitution, and has sufficient knowledge of German—a requirement that has never been subject to any proof or test. Children of foreigners may retain a dual citizenship up to their twenty-third birthday, after which they must decide between their parents' nationality and German nationality.

German demographic statistics give no realistic impression of how many of those living in Germany are immigrants, speak German, or define themselves as members of the national community. And the discussion of citizenship in Germany lacks sociological precision as well because we always mix up "foreigners," "immigrants with German passport," and "Germans with immigration background." We sometimes even lack a word for the groups our discussion deals with. Beyond any doubt, though, Germany is an *Einwanderungsland*—a country of immigration. The German population with some sort of "immigration background" rises annually, due not only to immigration but also to different birth rates between immigrants and non-immigrants.

Nevertheless, the term *Einwanderungsland* has been highly controversial in the political debate since the 1980s. (Before that time, it played no role at all.) Controversy stems from the fact that a huge share of the immigrants, especially those from southern and southeastern Europe and Turkey, were seen both by politicians and ordinary Germans as migrant laborers (guest workers) who would earn money in Germany and then return to their home countries. This illusion has been fostered by the fact that a lot of the immigrants shared it—indeed, many still do. Why call Germany a country of immigration, the thinking went, if the "immigrants" weren't planning to stay?

On the other hand, the Germans had always made a lot of fuss about their special "identity," defining it in a rather romantic way involving culture, deep roots, and language. For themselves and for others the impression was unavoidable that you had to *be* a German by upbringing; you could not simply become a German later in life. Or, at least, becoming a German was a very complicated and time-consuming process.

Over the years, Germany's immigration policy and the debate about it have been categorical and ideological rather than pragmatic. We talked principles but lived laissez-faire. Idealized notions of identity contradicted the rather down-to-earth questions of immigration, residence, and citizenship. Moreover, nobody could ever elaborate what exactly the cultural prerequisites of "being German" should be. The enduring demand that immigrants who seek German citizenship affirm a German "*Leitkultur*," a German canon of values and cultural patterns, lacks any specificity. Recently, some states have developed a "naturalization test," which is designed to check the applicant's knowledge about Germany; questions include "Name a German region of low mountains" and "Who elects the president of the federal republic?" In fact the test probably measures linguistic ability and the ability to memorize, but public discussion has focused on the fact that many German citizens find this exam quite difficult.

The question of what it means to be a German citizen is still open. Some foreigners live in Germany for a long time without becoming Germans. Some of them speak German; others don't. We have foreigners just arriving in Germany who are German citizens by heritage. Some of them speak German; some don't. And we have German citizens who possess another passport due to the law of dual citizenship. Some speak German; some don't; others speak only a little. They consider themselves Germans, or half-Germans, or only passport-Germans.

Why should it be a problem that a country has various mixtures of citizens and forms of citizenship? In the German case, there are two reasons: the German welfare system (*Sozialhilfe*), and the school system.

Germany's permissive immigration law, generous welfare system, and rather strict definition of "being a citizen," combined with the ill-founded belief that immigrants will return to their home countries someday, have worked to create an underclass. Not only does Germany refuse to discriminate between immigrants with respect to their qualifications; it exerts no pressure on them to assimilate, because it expects that they will eventually return to their home countries. It reserves the lower segment of the labor market for them, and makes welfare available to them. The result is not only passport-Germans lacking "strong civic convictions" and highly indifferent to a German *Leitkultur*, but also "welfare Germans," citizens who are citizens because of the social welfare system.

Schools, too, present serious problems. People who come to Germany because of its willingness to redistribute income have no incentive to integrate in a substantial way. Why try to achieve, if achievement is not necessary for subsistence? Why learn German if the population of your home country is large enough to create a self-sustaining community? If one compares the school certificates of foreigners and Germans, there is an enormous difference between the two groups: in 2000–01, more than 40 percent of the foreigners got only a basic degree, compared to 25 percent of the German school population. Twenty percent of the foreign population achieves no degree at all, compared to only 8 percent of the German population. The unemployment rate for citizens of foreign countries living in Germany is 25 percent, and 9 percent of these foreign citizens are dependent on welfare, compared to 2.5 percent of German citizens.

The German debate on immigration is centered on the concept of "integration." It poses questions like these: Do we make citizens out of people who are not willing to participate in German society in a more than superficial way, and who show their indifference toward our country by not learning our language? Have we blurred the status of citizenship? And have we done this for fear that clear rules could be interpreted as measures of exclusion?

One reason for the debate is the supposed existence of "parallel societies" or "ethnic colonies," the colloquial expression for spatially segregated ethnic subcommunities that are fully equipped with a whole infrastructure—an ethnic labor market, ethnic media, ethnic medical and financial services, even informal ethnic law. In some larger German cities (such as Frankfurt, Hamburg, and Berlin) such self-sustaining communities are already a reality. Eighty percent of all foreigners in Germany live in cities with more than a hundred thousand inhabitants (compared to 60 percent of the German population). Members of the foreign population who have jobs and sufficient economic resources tend to leave such colonies, and Germans living near them do, too, especially when they have young children (in Germany, children must attend the school closest to their residence). New immigrants, in contrast, tend to settle in such colonies. All this creates a self-reinforcing dynamic of ethnic segregation.

The German debate on immigration involves three basic concepts: assimilation, multiculturalism, and integration. Assimilation has a bad odor in German political discourse. It is sometimes considered discrimination to suggest that immigrants should learn German, adopt cultural norms, or seek to be successful if they want to be integrated into the national community of their new home country. When state governments recently established a citizenship test, many newspapers and politicians mocked the idea. The idea of shared cultural knowledge, shared norms, and shared social practices is denounced as "forcible Germanization" (*Zwangsgermanisierung*) or even racism. The failure of immigrants to integrate into the larger society is attributed to Germans' failure to accept and respect them. If a young citizen with Turkish background remains jobless, that is attributed to an ethnic bias on the part of employers and a failure of the welfare state and schools to support ethnic minorities and to eradicate social inequalities. The discourse is deeply paternalistic. The expectation that elementary education of children is supported by the family—one of the principles of the German school system—is criticized for ignoring the fact that in many families, such support would be impossible. But is there a need to change this situation? Or is it possible to substitute integration via the welfare state for integration via family life?

Many participants in the German debate on citizenship and immigration seem to think so—without any empirical evidence—and are insistent in their demands for more money and welfare programs. They are still inclined to the ideal of multiculturalism—a society in which all forms of ethnic belonging ("identities") can coexist without altering anybody's way of life, "a horizontal side-by-side of groups without cultural assimilation" as the German sociologist Hartmut Esser, highly critical of this ideal, has put it. According to Esser, there is no durable "indifferent ethnic cohabitation" in modern societies. There is, if assimilation is denied, only ethnic stratification.[2]

In 1979, the Berlin Senate declared its support for activities that made it possible for foreigners both to keep their cultural identity and to share that identity with German society as a whole. This type of identity-talk is responsible for the complete failure of German immigration policy to establish basic requirements—the requirement that immigrants, especially those becoming citizens, value educational and professional achievement and reject the myth of living in exile or even in resistance to a dominant culture or political system. This does not mean that immigrants have to give up every feature of their past. No population is homogenous in every respect. Even the "traditional" German citizen is a very mixed and locally determined person. But with respect to key issues of social integration—language, values, behavior in schools, law—assimilation is the only means to integration.

Sociological realism, then, could help make the German debate on citizenship less euphemistic, less utopian, and less dependent on crossed fingers. I think that no one in Germany believes that we are *not* a country of immigration. The question is if some groups of immigrants themselves believe the opposite.

Consider the following: when President Abdullah Gul of Turkey went to Cologne this year and gave a talk before a huge audience of Turkish background (including Turks with a second passport), he addressed them as his people—and nobody objected. Incidents of this kind suggest that the feeling of being German is not very widely distributed among immigrants with German passports, among those holding two passports, and even among children of immigrants who have grown up in Germany.

Children attending German schools may have good reason for a reluctance to feel German. History classes focus on the subject of the Third Reich in the seventh grade, the ninth grade, the eleventh grade, and the thirteenth grade. That is history in Germany. It is not a very inviting gesture toward applicants for citizenship. Who wants to belong to a community whose self-understanding is so problematic?

We seem to deal with this problem in two ways: we deny it, and we throw money at it. It was the welfare state whose subsidies financed this whole structure to begin with. No wonder there is so little pressure on immigrants to assimilate. That is the issue we should talk about—not about Beethoven, but also not about multiculturalism, which is just the leftist version of the Beethoven story.

Robert von Rimscha

First, two anecdotal remarks on the relativity of citizenship and on the accessability of *Leitkultur*. Ten years ago, when I married and needed some legal papers, I found out that I had not been born a German. My grandfather was born in Riga, now Latvia; he went to Germany in 1939 and then obtained German citizenship, but that status did not extend to his children. My father discovered that he had not become a German at that time only in early 1964, when he married. Later that year, I was born. Once my father discovered that he had never been appropriately naturalized, he retroactively obtained citizenship. But for the first six weeks of my life, I was stateless.

Ten days ago, my uncle turned seventy. Our whole family came together. Among my many nieces and nephews, one has a wife from Cameroon, one has a wife from Cuba, and one has a husband from Indonesia. The former Indonesian came to Germany in January 2001, at age thirty. He spent his first year in Germany learning German; worked as of January 2002, one year after stepping into the country; and was a German citizen by May 2004. So the process *can* work.

He went to the *Staatsbibliothek* in Berlin to prepare for his citizenship test and studied German history. In one conversation, I overheard him say—and remember this is a new arrival to Germany, an Asian young man, Muslim— "when we killed the Jews." That was one of the effects of his studies of German history. Regardless of whether there is too big a dose of historical guilt in the German self-image and in the German identity, that little episode suggests that an embrace even of the darkest chapters of German history is possible. That fact in turn sheds a little light on the issue of *Leitkultur*.

If *Leitkultur* is supposed to mean that you value Beethoven as better than Rachmaninoff, Goethe as better than Shakespeare, and Caspar David

Friedrich as better than Monet, it is obviously stupid. If *Leitkultur* means that you are aware of the existence of Beethoven, Goethe, and Caspar David Friedrich, its importance is something one can debate. At any rate, this understanding offers a more realistic frame for talking about *Leitkultur*. *Leitkultur* should mean knowledge, not superiority.

My second remark has to do with integration of immigrants. Significant parts of the German immigrant population are self-segregating and are failing to adopt the country's norms of behavior. Turkish unemployment in Berlin is a staggering 47 percent. The dropout rate in schools for Turks is eight times what it is for ethnic Germans. Seventy percent of juvenile criminals are Turks, Lebanese, and Arabs, whereas these groups make up 12 percent of the population. These problems, caused by a confluence of socioeconomic, cultural, ethnic, and other factors, are less common with first- and second-generation immigrants and more common with the third generation.

The most contested issue involving immigration and citizenship in Germany today is import brides. For decades, families in the Turkish and Kurdish immigrant community have selected very young brides—sometimes underage—from back home for their sons. There is a new law in Germany which stipulates that immigrants from a specific set of countries who come to Germany to marry must pass a German test before entering the country. So a Turk coming to Germany as an import bride would come under this law.

The Turkish government and Turkish organizations in Germany vehemently oppose the law because it selectively targets countries like Turkey, given that its purpose is to curb the immigration of import brides—meaning girls as young as fourteen or fifteen, who come from eastern Anatolia, have never lived in a big city, have no cultural connection to Germany, do not speak the language, and are basically a means of perpetuating a particular family structure and culture.

My third remark has to do with the German government, and mainly with the German judiciary. We can debate whether one ramification of self-rule is a deification of representative government, specifically a deification of Parliament. In Germany, we have a so-called grand coalition, meaning that more than two-thirds of the representatives in the Parliament come from the three parties running the administration: the CDU, SPD, and CSU; in the second chamber, the *Bundesrat*, all sixteen governors are from the

CDU, SPD, or CSU. In such a situation, the deification of Parliament does not work.

Like the Supreme Court in the United States, the German Constitutional Court—our supreme court in Karlsruhe—very carefully selects the cases it will hear. Within the last two years, the German Constitutional Court handed down the following decisions: It struck down a law which had allowed the acoustic monitoring of private residences. It struck down a law by the earlier Red-Green coalition that had permitted airplanes in the hands of terrorists to be shot down. It struck down online searches. It struck down automated highway license-plate screening. It struck down a law that requires telephone companies to keep data on phone and email conversations for half a year. It struck down the supposed rights of the customs police to screen mail and phone connections secretly. It struck down the police law of Lower Saxony. It struck down the *Rasterfahndung*, a dragnet approach used to identify possible criminal suspects by examining socio-economic data. It struck down parts of the European search warrant. It struck down the search and warrant rights of the police vis-à-vis journalists.

All in all these are ten cases within a good two years—ten instances where the German Constitutional Court felt called upon to remedy what a Parliament dominated by the so-called grand coalition lacked in democratic control, and to limit the powers that a huge majority in Parliament had given to the executive branch. "Legislation from the bench" takes on a whole new—and positive—meaning under such circumstances.

I am not a constitutional historian, but I am not aware of any other phase in recent German history that produced such a barrage, such an avalanche, of decisions intended to protect the rights of individuals from excessive public security measures.

I begin my fourth remark with an anecdote. A few days ago at Dulles Airport, I spoke with a functionary of the Pakistani Cab Association, which represents four hundred Muslim Pakistani cab drivers. He emphatically endorses Obama, and he hates Bush. He likes Obama because he is for peace, and Bush was bad because Bush was for war. He also very much liked Al Gore, but in 2000, he voted for Bush. I asked him why, and he said, "We all supported Al Gore but then he named Lieberman as vice president. And then, of course, we voted Bush." It was utterly unacceptable for this person and his organization to even entertain the notion of voting for a Jew.

Can we live with such collectivizations, with such a willingness to let a single issue determine a political decision? Is it fundamentally different from a member of the religious Right deciding that he is going to vote on a single issue like abortion? Do we find it acceptable that a collective entity would categorically rule out voting for a Jewish candidate in this country?

My last remark concerns the debate over whether constitutional loyalty is sufficient in the absence of a national loyalty. It has been mentioned, not incorrectly, that constitutional lawyers for the last two and a half thousand years have not really come up with revolutionary new concepts. The basic ideas—separation of powers, individual rights, rule of law, due process— have been around for a long time.

Think of an experiment. Give first-year law students a selection of written constitutions. Give them the South African constitution (just erase site-specific language like that about the eleven official languages). Take the Namibian constitution. Take some Western European constitutions; take some Eastern European constitutions. Let the students match countries with the respective constitutions. My prediction is that they will be unable to identify which constitution belongs to which country.

The point is this: If constitutions are more and more universal in their focus on universal rights, then such constitutions cannot logically create a sense of loyalty to a nation-state.

Martin Klingst

My father was born in Freiburg, Saxony, which is near the Czech border. He was a POW in Great Britain and stayed in the West, while his parents stayed in the East and became citizens of the German Democratic Republic. As a child, I visited every year. My mother was born in Königsberg, East Prussia, which is now part of Russia; the town is now called Kaliningrad. Being of Jewish descent, she fled to England in 1936, was raised and educated there, became a British subject, moved back to Germany after she met my father, and then became one of the first Germans with a dual nationality. Generally, Germany insists on single nationality: if you want to become German, you must surrender any other nationality. This is still a rule today, even though there are quite a number of exceptions. But being of Jewish descent, my mother was allowed to keep her British nationality. All the Jews who had left Germany lost their German nationality. The German government did not want that to happen again, so German Jews with a foreign nationality got back their German citizenship, if they wanted it, and could keep both nationalities.

I have observed two very different approaches looking at immigration in the United States and looking at immigration in Europe. Here, you have a more pragmatic view of immigrants. In Europe, especially in Germany, we have a more ideological approach. We always want to know, where do we come from, where are our roots? Where do we go? What is our identity? This discussion also takes place in the United States, especially in relation to the immigration waves from the Hispanic countries. But overall the approach here is more pragmatic.

In Germany, we do not look at our country as being a country of immigrants, although we have been one at least since the '60s. First, millions of foreign "guest workers" moved to Germany. We needed them to keep our economy running, but they were never regarded as immigrants. Initially, we had something called the rotation principle: guest workers should come for six years and then go back. The idea was to calm any fears that there might be an immigration wave. But employers were not satisfied with this solution because they had trained those people and didn't want to lose them. So the rotation principle was abandoned. When the economic crisis started in the early '70s, we stopped letting in any new foreign guest workers. Resident workers, however, got permission to stay and also to move their families to Germany—children, wives, in many cases uncles and parents. The biggest immigration wave we had in the '70s and '80s was called "family reunification." But we still did not look at them as immigrants. They still had the status of guest workers and foreigners, and everyone thought their presence was temporary. But we fooled ourselves.

The second wave of immigration involved a large influx of asylum seekers in the '90s. Under our constitution, anyone reaching German territory and asking for asylum automatically goes through the judicial procedure, which may accept or deny his request for asylum. But denial was in practice a difficult thing. Many of those denied were not actually sent back, perhaps because of civil wars, or perhaps because the authorities did not know precisely where an applicant—especially one from Africa—had come from. Countries were not willing to take them back, because there was no proof of nationality and origin. So the whole asylum system collapsed. We changed the constitution and made it more difficult to apply for asylum. Now anyone fleeing to Germany must ask for asylum where this is first possible during this journey. That means, someone passing through neighboring countries such as Poland or the Czech Republic must apply there, because they also grant asylum. The German Constitutional Court ruled this matter constitutional and the number of asylum seekers to Germany declined dramatically over the years. We are much more pragmatic now. We have changed our citizenship law, and now a child born in Germany will automatically be German if one parent has been living in Germany legally and as a permanent resident for at least eight years. We also introduced an integration law and for the first time allow people with certain professions and skills to apply for immigration. This law is a gateway to Germany, although those gates are still very, very narrow.

In the United States, you look at immigrants mainly as contributing to the wealth of society. They can come and get a green card, and they have the opportunity to stay and to become citizens. We have viewed them very differently in Germany. We looked at guest workers as only temporary immigrants, and we did not want to give them any further rights. This led to schizophrenic results. Millions of foreigners passed on their foreign legal status to their children and grandchildren because the German law did not offer them automatic citizenship. Children of foreigners remained foreigners, and suddenly we had a third generation of (for example) Turkish immigrants who still were Turks, even though they had never lived in Turkey.

In 1999, the citizenship law was changed. As I have already explained: if a foreigner has lived legally in Germany for eight years and has a child in Germany, that child automatically becomes a German citizen. This child may also keep a dual nationality because he is also a Turk by Turkish law. At age eighteen, the child has the option to decide whether he wants to remain a German or a Turk.

Still, the legal framework and the philosophy in the United States are very different from those in Europe, and especially in Germany, where immigrants until recently were mainly guest workers and asylum seekers. The asylum law especially complicated the situation. We had a huge influx of refugees in Germany in the '90s, during the Balkan wars, and quite a number remain today. Because asylum seekers were not allowed to work during their application procedure, which could last for years, they became part of the welfare system. The state had to cover their needs. They lived in homes for asylum seekers or in flats downtown, and the government and the German taxpayers paid. The German government was afraid that if they were permitted to work, others would come. In fact many asylum seekers were not political refugees or fleeing wars. Many came because they sought better economic opportunities.

In one year during the '90s, we had almost half a million asylum seekers from Romania. This led to riots and to discussions of how to handle such situations, and (as I have pointed out) to a change in the law. But the consequence of this change is that we have now built an invisible wall around Germany—and indeed around Europe. Because European countries had similar problems, they tried to find common ground to tackle the problems. We secured the outer borders of the European Union and thus put some of the asylum burden on the shoulders of our neighbors in Eastern Europe and in North Africa.

But the members of the EU also tried to find common ground inside the union: the EU now has something like burden sharing, which started with the influx of Balkan refugees in the '90s. Most of them came to Germany because few other countries were willing to take them. Eventually, though, the Scandinavians and the French started to take refugees. The European Union is now trying to tackle this problem in a common way, but as I have just said, it has also built a common wall. Europe is becoming something like a fortress: we control our outer borders, and we have common standards for laws governing integration and citizenship for asylum seekers.

What do we expect of immigrants? How do they have to adapt and integrate themselves? What do we offer them? In Europe, especially in Germany, the debate on this question remains very ideological. We want cultural assimilation. But what does that mean? Do immigrants have to drink beer and eat German sausage to become Germans? Do they have to know German writers like Goethe, Schiller, and Lessing, whom many Germans probably don't know? Or is it enough to say, I accept the German laws and the constitution, and will learn the German language? Some conservatives have asked immigrants to adapt to something they call "*Deutsche Leitkultur*," meaning the German leading culture. But they never explain what this really means, and it will probably be difficult even for Germans to agree on common cultural standards. This discussion has not ended yet. I must say that I like the very pragmatic American approach. It means accepting the laws and the constitution but being able to live culturally as you like.

I do not believe that a specific loyalty to the German culture can exist in a multicultural society. I do not even like the word "loyalty," because I'm a strict constitutionalist. As long as everyone learns German and accepts German as our common languange, as long as everyone also accepts our laws and the rule of law and the constitution—equality of rights, gender equality, freedom of expression, democracy, human rights and dignity—this all, as far as I am concerned, is proof enough of being a good citizen.

In Germany there was a court ruling involving an Afghan woman who wears a head scarf and wanted to become a schoolteacher. She was allowed to be trained as a teacher wearing the scarf, but she was not allowed to work as a teacher and a public servant if she wore the scarf. There were no doubts about her being a loyal citizen. She was loyal to the constitution; she wanted to wear the scarf only for religious reasons, not for political reasons. She believed in equal rights for men and women. But in Germany there ensued a huge discussion over the scarf as a symbol of religious intolerance, and the denial of equal rights, and so forth. My position is that it's not what is *on* your head, but what is *in* your head, that's important. I would vigorously defend women's right to wear the scarf as long as they accept the constitution and all basic laws our society is built on.

We tend to be very aware of whether immigrants have acquired a cultural identity that goes beyond just accepting the law. We seem to want them to become more German than the Germans. We have a test for immigrants which they have to pass if they want to become German citizens. When I look at some of the questions, I realize that if you asked Germans the same questions to become citizens again, many would fail.

The immigration and assimilation debate in Europe is now circling around the Muslim immigrants. In Germany, we have a large population of Turkish Muslims; they are the largest immigrant group, about three million. Most of them have more moderate religious views than the North Africans in France and Holland or the Pakistanis in Great Britain. So the debate varies across countries. But what is so often missed in this dispute is that the question of integration, assimilation, adaptation, and identity is also a social question. In the United States the Muslim question is not as urgent as it may be in Europe. As a matter of fact Muslim immigrants in the United States are often achievers and have a decent income; many of them belong to the middle and the upper-middle class. In Germany, in Holland, or in France, however, many Muslim immigrants are not well educated, work at unskilled jobs, depend on social welfare, and are therefore at the bottom of the social ladder. So the question of immigration really touches on our beliefs about society itself, for which jobs we need immigrants, on how we distribute wealth and opportunities.

To make my standpoint on immigration very clear: I have doubts about imposing cultural requirements. But I am an unwavering advocate of civil rights and the rule of law. I used to be a lawyer, and in that capacity I defended some Turkish girls against parents who forced them to wear a scarf or a veil or who wanted to force them into an arranged marriage. This is unlawful and violates fundamental rights. It is important for a free society to enforce its laws with all rigidity. The same applies to freedom of expression. When the debate and riots started over the decision of the Danish newspapers to print cartoons of the prophet Mohammed, the president of the United States sided with the Muslims. He scolded Europe, saying that we misunderstood Muslims and had insulted them. This partisanship was wrong. The cartoons might have been insulting, and publishing them might not have been smart. But freedom of press and freedom of expression are unalienable rights. They have to be vigorously defended.

Ayaan Hirsi Ali

In July 1992, when I first came to the Netherlands, I did not have a legal visa to the Netherlands but I had a three-month visa to Germany. In Germany, I would enter the immigration process designed to take me to Canada. But that visa also allowed me to take the train to the Netherlands.

On my way from Bonn to Amsterdam, I did not encounter any border controls. Once inside the Netherlands, I had two options: One, I could get a work permit. But I did not speak the language, and while I could cook and clean, there was not much more that I could do at the time. Two, I could ask for asylum. That was the better option.

When I asked for asylum I got a Legal Aid lawyer. I explained to her that I was running away from a forced marriage, and that I did not want to go to Canada. The Legal Aid lawyer said, "If you say that, you are not going to get in." "What do I need to do?" I asked. She said, "If you are from Somalia and you are persecuted by the government or a militia there, then you will meet some of the requirements for asylum."

So I changed my story. Now I was no longer running away from a forced marriage; I was pursued by some Somalia militia members whose name I invented. I changed my last name from Magan to Ali, and I made myself two years older so that my family could not track me down. Lo and behold, three weeks later, I was granted access to the Netherlands under an "A-status," which allows you into the country as a refugee.

The day that my refugee ID card was handed to me, I had an English translator because I did not speak Dutch. The translator was paid for by the Dutch Immigration and Naturalization Service (INS), and she gave me a long list of all the rights to which I was entitled under the A-status. I could get a roof over my head. I had access to health care and education. And I could find a job or start a business anywhere in the Netherlands. Having been granted only A-status and not full citizenship, then, I already had a long list of rights. My obligation was not to commit a crime for which the penalty is three or more years' imprisonment.

In 1997, I applied for citizenship. At the time, the application required legal residency in the Netherlands for five years, five hundred guilders, and two passport photos. The forms required my personalia, my home address, my INS number, and my social security number. Three weeks later I received a letter from the Queen telling me that I had become a citizen. All I had to do was to go to the municipality building and wait in line. When it was my turn—I spent about ten or fifteen minutes waiting—a blonde public servant handed me my file. I paid the five hundred guilders and got my passport. I became a Dutch citizen as of that moment.

By becoming a citizen, I acquired additional rights. I could vote, and I could also run for office. When traveling, I now could stand in the queue for European Union citizens. Again, as a holder of citizenship I received a range of benefits, including social security, welfare, home allowance, medical care, student grants, and family reunion and family formation assistance. That is, as an A-status holder, I could bring over my family, and

I could marry someone from outside the Netherlands and apply to bring him over.

The official to whom I handed over my money and paperwork did not tell me all of these rights. I knew them because I studied political science.

My motives for coming to the Netherlands were to enjoy freedom and to shape my own destiny. And I found those values realized. I got an education; I became independent. I had a wonderful time in Holland. But none of the values that bind that country together were explained to me, either as an asylum seeker or as an applicant for citizenship.

Between 1994 and 2001, I worked as a translator-interpreter for the Immigration and Naturalization Service of the Netherlands. During that period, I translated for Somalis who had applied for asylum and initially been rejected. Typically, they were rejected because they could not verify how they had come into the country, or prove that they were really being persecuted. Some of them obtained asylum on humanitarian grounds. If you were wretched enough and you could prove it, and you could prove that you had actually flown in from Somalia, then you would not be returned. You would get a permanent residence.

My next experience was as a member of Parliament in the Netherlands. At that time, issues of immigration and of naturalization suddenly became salient. Some people talked of national identity, common values, a shared language, a shared history. Those people and their concerns were often dismissed as xenophobic, petty, racist. And yet it does not seem inappropriate to ask who we are as Dutch people. Are we an ethnic community? Are we a community bound together by a common culture, language, and values? And can we demand political allegiance and some form of loyalty to our own values from immigrants who want to become citizens?

There is now a requirement saying that you have to speak the language in order to become a Dutch citizen. But you do not have to be fluent in Dutch; you merely need to have a vocabulary of about five hundred words. So the government is going to save money on translators, but knowing the language a little really does not make you more of a citizen. There is no agreement about what citizenship is.

After I was asked to join Parliament, my party leader asked me if I had any skeletons in the closet. "Yes, I do," I said. "When I came into the Netherlands I changed my name, I changed my year of birth and pretty much lied my way in." My party leader talked to some of the party's legal advisers and lawyers. (He was also good friends with the prime minister, Jan Peter Balkenende.) Everyone treated the whole affair as something insignificant, a small lie told years before.

In May 2006, the immigration and naturalization laws were being reviewed. A documentary maker asked me if I had lied and I said, as I had in many interviews, that yes, I had lied. The immigration minister at that time, Rita Verdonk, pretended that she had not known about the matter, and she took away my citizenship. Public outrage and several debates in Parliament followed. None of those debates was about the fact that I was assimilated; about my public service; about my being a citizen in the true sense of the word. Nor did anyone talk about national identity or language or anything of that kind. The concern was, did the relevant politicians, especially the minister of immigration, know about the lie? The conclusion was that she had to have known. No one was questioning my loyalty to the Crown.

So the prime minister, along with the other ministers and a majority of the members of Parliament, forced her to give me back my citizenship. She gave it back on the condition that I sign a letter saying that I had not lied. Signing that letter made me lie for a second time. But I had to sign; otherwise, the minister could not save face.

The Netherlands has no procedure for taking away someone's citizenship. This is a huge problem, and the government has now started to look into formal means of expelling or revoking the citizenship of (for example) certain imams. But in 1997, the process had to be arbitrary. The fact that I had lied in 1992 provided the minister with a way of saying that she was not taking away my citizenship. Her letter to me said, "You never received it." The D66 party, a member of the coalition government, deemed this outrageous—again, not because of anything related to the requirements for loyalty or citizenship, to national identity, to values, but because the minister had employed a method that reminded most Dutch politicians of a banana republic. And so the minister had to go, or D66 would go. D66 went, and the government fell.

The collapse of the government and the debate that ensued in Holland and in other European nations again did not lead to a substantial discussion of what it is to be a citizen, when and under what circumstances immigrants should be permitted into a country, and what their obligations are. It was all about whether I had lied, whether I was or was not a critic of Islam, was or was not a supporter of women's rights, was seeking fame, or was really sincere. It was all about trivialities, whether from the right wing or the left wing.

I came to the United States in 2006 after this debacle, and I did not have to lie my way in. I was very much aware of the fact that I came as a very privileged individual. I got immediate access to all levels of government, and everyone was willing to accommodate me. To get a visa and eventually a green card, I had to fill in endless forms. I had to prove that I really was coming to work for the American Enterprise Institute and that AEI could not find someone else in the United States who could do the same job.

I have had a green card now for one year, and I have started inquiring about how to become an American citizen. And I have to be, just as in Holland, a legal holder of the green card for five years, but I also have to know a great deal about the Constitution, speak the language and, in the ceremony itself, swear political allegiance to the United States.

In America it is possible to openly discuss this demand for loyalty. In Europe—not just among governments and politicians, but more generally—the issue is taboo. The issue of cultural loyalty is especially taboo. Can we expect that, when an immigrant's native culture collides with the culture of his host country, he will allow the culture of the host country to prevail? We do not ask that question in Europe.

In America, the demand for loyalty, the flag, and patriotism are everywhere. Yes, there is a cosmopolitan, liberal elite in New York and in Los Angeles that does not like to discuss the matter. But that is not how the American nation has its conversation on being an American and being loyal to America. Europeans, in contrast, display a paradoxical attitude. On the one hand, Europeans teach and feel that they are terribly bad people and any claim to any form of superiority will only lead to another world war or another Holocaust. But at the same time, the European attitude is also one of superiority. Europeans feel that they are too good, too generous, and too tolerant to demand that others look like them or take on their culture.

Martin Klingst said earlier that as long as people accept the constitution, he doesn't object to their cultural habits and way of life. Many of my European friends flee into formalities and focus on the constitution. What they forget, and this is the main blind spot in Europe today, is that the constitution is itself an outcome of culture. It is the outcome of a cultural tradition with its own intellectual discourse and its own education system behind it. The values embodied in the constitution may be so different from those of another culture that a collision of values is inevitable. There are, for example, Muslim immigrants who oppose and deplore the principles contained in the American Constitution and the various European constitutions.

Americans are much more comfortable than Europeans about telling immigrants that they must relinquish certain cultural practices: "Maybe where you come from, your wife obeys you. But in the United States, she is protected by the law." There is less of a tendency here to flee into abstractions and formalities.

I have not seen Americans asking immigrants to look like them, eat like them, sleep like them, fornicate like them. Americans want immigrants to learn the language and be loyal to the country. These are the same things Europeans ask for, except that in Europe you could be marginalized as a fascist, a right-winger, a xenophobe, a petty peasant, uncosmopolitan, for actually expecting these demands to be met. That inhibits the debate in Europe. (There is a debate in Germany on *Leitkultur*, but the debate is among Germans; it is not between Turkish Germans and German Germans.) But Europeans must have that debate.

Muslim immigrants bring to Europe a radically different value system. When Italians, Spanish, and Portuguese came to Holland, there were initial problems, but these were solved after a while, and the immigrants assimilated without question. The Muslim value system, on the other hand, is reinforced by self-segregation. Muslims from the same country of origin live in the same neighborhoods, send their children to the same schools, marry one another (or bring in brides from their orignal country to marry). The immigrant with dual citizenship has a kind of economic, instrumental loyalty to his new country, in part because of welfare-state benefits; but there is a cultural loyalty to, and a deeper identification with, the other, original citizenship.

That is a problem we cannot run away from.

The debates in Europe have shifted from the socioeconomic side of things to the sociocultural side of things. The discussion used to focus on the fact that immigrants come from poor countries to do work that Europeans don't want to do, and that by granting immigrants various welfare-state benefits and facilitating family reunification and family formation, Europe encourages even more immigration.

But starting around 1989, the focus of the discussion changed. First there were threats to freedom of expression, as governments banned works that might have been considered offensive or incendiary. Then came the terrorist attacks in New York, Madrid, and London, which most of the Muslim communities—including the educated, articulate, young, third-generation Muslims living in Europe—seemed to condone, and which seemed to encourage further limits on freedom of expression where criticism of Islam and the icons of Islam were concerned. Hence the sociocultural debate: Do we share the same values?

In the case of Holland, all of these debates are led by or subsidized by the government. In Amsterdam we have debating houses, places where neighbors, parents at school, and local politicians can come together. But you have to fill in forms and apply for money from the government in order to sit down together and debate. In the United States, philanthropy makes it possible for such debates to take place without reliance on government. In America, Muslims and non-Muslims are equally suspicious of government.

What is the outcome of the new debate on sociocultural values? I think it is too soon to tell. In countries where multiculturalism and political correctness have been ingrained for a long time, immigrants have participated in the values debate, but there has not been any institutional change. In Holland you can still open Muslim schools and Muslim universities, and you can hold on to your dual nationality. And if a Turkish leader or the Moroccan King comes to visit, the Dutch citizens of Turkish origin and of Moroccan origin will make clear that they consider this foreign leader their own. That is where their loyalty lies. That is not only a fault of the immigrants. It is also a fault of the policymakers in Holland.

After Theo van Gogh was murdered, the mayor of Amsterdam traveled to Morocco and got Moroccan diplomats and government leaders to come and talk to Dutch Moroccan citizens. That would be unthinkable in the United States. We have a passionate debate on immigration and immigrants, but we would not dream of getting foreign leaders to come and help us communicate with our own citizens.

Peter Skerry

In the United States today, the immigration debate is really a debate over Mexican immigrants. They are not the only immigrants here by any means. But a large group—almost a third of all foreign-born here—are of Mexican origin. Hispanics more generally (including from Central and South America) make up about 44 percent of all foreign-born.[3] In our history, a concentration of newcomers from one such linguistic-cultural background is unprecedented. It is clear from the opinion survey data that Americans today are much more concerned with Mexican day laborers hanging out on street corners looking for work than they are with Muslims or Muslim terrorists.

The United States does not really have much of a debate today about citizenship. To be sure, academics have been preoccupied with this issue for some time. But the explicit terms of the public debate in the United States have decidedly not been about citizenship. Noises about birthright citizenship bubble up every once in a while; but they are not central. Our debate has really been over *illegal* immigration. The McCain-Kennedy legislation that came to ignominious defeat in 2007 bears that out. Primarily, we debate whether illegal immigrants should be fined or penalized for being here. They should learn English: that demand has been emphasized by most participants. To an extent this reflects the belief that immigrants should accept American culture. But it is largely a practical concern. Americans want immigrants to learn English because that makes them easier to deal with.

Americans are also concerned about granting amnesty to illegal immigrants, who have committed the misdemeanor of living here without proper documents. This and similar concerns are all very mundane, procedural points. They all revolve around how and whether such immigrants are going to be brought into the system. Americans want to be assured that illegal immigrants will not benefit from breaking the rules. Very little of a real cultural dimension has figured in this debate.

To be sure, all these proposals make use of phrases such as "the path to citizenship" or "earned citizenship." But I submit that when politicians use the word "citizenship," they are talking less about any formal status immigrants may have and more about their behavior and demeanor.

Cultural anxieties do not figure much at all in the debate over immigration by Mexicans. Such concerns have in general shifted over to Muslims; we have lots of worries about whether Muslims are going to adapt to the culture of the United States. In American ethnic history this is a familiar dance. It is not a duel between racism and enlightenment; it is more like a game of hopscotch. Teddy Roosevelt and Woodrow Wilson were tough on the Germans. But Woodrow Wilson was easy on the Poles (and a free Poland was one of his Fourteen Points). Vis-à-vis Mexican immigrants, any cultural anxieties have been pushed to the background because they are now much more focused on Muslims.

But even here, I do not think Americans' anxieties go very deep. Americans have some fundamental sense that we can work out the cultural differences. Whether women wear the *hijab*, how Muslims worship or accommodate themselves to the requirements of their religion, how we accommodate the Muslims: the widespread understanding is that we've worked such difficulties out before and will work them out again.

The real difficulty for many Americans is political loyalty. The question I hear most often when people learn that I'm working on a book about Muslims in America is, why have "they" not apologized for 9/11? Or, how much influence do the Saudis have on Muslims in the United States? Concerns of this kind are what really trouble non-Muslim Americans.

Experts talk about competing loyalties, crosscutting loyalties, and nested loyalties. I do not have any quarrel with such categories. But I wonder if we are not at a crisis point when it comes to the issue of loyalty. In normal times, crosscutting or nested loyalties do not pose any particular problems. Besides, asking questions about a group's political loyalties is not a pleasant business, so we avoid those questions. But what happens when in an emergency there is suddenly no more slack in the system, and we want to know, "Are you with us or against us?" Then we have something to worry about. It is hardly inconceivable that such a day may come again, a day recalling the immediate aftermath of 9/11.

Muslim American leaders typically conclude that we are not at that point. One reason, I believe, is that they are being sustained by their newfound liberal allies in the media, in academia, and elsewhere in our political system. These allies are inculcating a particularly soft cosmopolitanism that tolerates ambiguous loyalties and that does not want to ask tough questions.

Meanwhile, Muslims themselves are reveling in our religious liberties and pluralism. They know better than anybody else how much religious liberty they enjoy in the United States, and they appreciate it. But as a result they are more easily brought into this kind of soft cosmopolitanism—a kind of middle-class live-and-let-live attitude about religion. At a dinner the other night, I happened to sit next to a middle-aged Indian woman from Hyderabad, whose husband works with Cisco Systems outside Boston. She sends her teenage daughter to a Catholic school in Worcester, Massachusetts. Many Muslims send their children to Catholic schools, but this woman went to some lengths to tell me that she thought one religion was as good as another. This practicing Muslim told me, "Those Catholics will teach my child some basic moral principles and I will fill in the blanks about Islam." That is not an unfamiliar or uncommon attitude among Muslims in the United States.

But along with this cosmopolitanism comes a political component—a problematic one, where nobody ever talks about saluting the flag or explicitly demonstrating loyalty to the United States. Cosmopolitans do talk about citizenship every once in a while, but it is typically citizenship in a small place—a localistic citizenship, where a good citizen volunteers at the local health clinic, visits an old age home, or participates in a blood drive. That is all very admirable, but it does not get to the heart of serious notions of citizenship and loyalty to the United States. Muslim Americans and their cosmopolitan allies manage to avoid such difficult topics.

What do the political adversaries or critics of Muslim Americans in the United States say? Are all these affiliations and ties and potentially competing loyalties benign, or do we have to be concerned? Certainly, many of the critics and would-be adversaries of Muslim Americans feel that we are close to a crisis point. They therefore ask those tough, sometimes nasty, questions: "Are you on our side, Muslim Americans?"

Yet those who are critical and eager to scrutinize the loyalty of Muslim Americans have too little appreciation of the ties that bind Muslim immigrants to their countrymen back home, to their coreligionists, and to their homelands. We have admitted large numbers of immigrants to this country for generations now. Certainly we must understand that they have continuing bonds to their homelands. Lincoln had a sense of the "mystic chords" that bind Americans to America—and Confederates to the Confederacy. This is why Lincoln did not want to try Robert E. Lee for treason: he appreciated that those mystic chords worked on both sides. That sort of generosity and wisdom seems lacking among the critics of Muslim Americans today.

To Muslims I would say, we are not at a crisis point yet, but we could be soon. And you should prepare for it. You should face up to the demands that may be put upon you by non-Muslim Americans who are going to want to know whether you are on their side—"on our side"—or not. And you had better think now, not after the fact, about what you have done to demonstrate your loyalty to America. That is not an easy question or an easy challenge, but it needs to be confronted now and not after the next terrorist attack.

Reliable Muslim interlocutors who represent the broad spectrum of Muslim America are critically needed. Yet we are not doing enough at this stage to bring them into the conversation. We are alienating them and pushing them to the margins by demanding of them more loyalty than is reasonable at this point. All of us need to think about what we might be up against when we are in much more grievous circumstances.

In earlier generations, there was probably a much greater preoccupation with the outward signs of political loyalty to the United States shown by immigrants. This change reflects a broader cosmopolitan culture that current immigrants are assimilating to. But this culture is undoubtedly more problematic for Muslims to decipher and negotiate than it is for non-Muslims.

Notes

1. For these and other empirical figures mentioned in the text, *see* Stefan Luft: Abschied von Multikulti. Wege aus der Integrationskrise (2007).

2. Hartmut Esser, *Strukturelle Assimilation und ethnische Schichtung*, in Interdisziplinäre Jugendforschung: Jugendliche zwischen Familie, Freunden und Feinden 89, 89–104 (Angela Ittel and Hans Merkens eds., 2006).

3. Figures are from the 2007 American Community Survey, tabluated by the Pew Hispanic Center, Statistical Portrait of Hispanics in the United States, 2007, http://pewhispanic.org/files/factsheets/hispanics2007/2007_Hispanic%20Profile_Final. pdf.

6

European Citizenship: Treaties and Case Law of the European Court of Justice

Jean-Claude Bonichot

Introduction, *François-Henri Briard*

European citizenship cannot be compared to traditional nation-state citizenship. It is not a concrete, well-established concept, but rather one that has yet to be clearly defined. And yet it is evident that the idea of European citizenship will increasingly influence the lives of individual citizens of member states. As the European Court of Justice has stated, European citizenship is "destined to be the fundamental status of nationals of the Member States."[1]

Currently, European citizenship is not an expression of common values or duties. Rather, it is mostly focused on the establishment and protection of individual rights.[2] Citizenship in a member state creates duties which bind that state's citizens; individuals in member states must respect the common goods, pay taxes, obey laws, and defend their nation's territory. European Union citizenship does not create similar binding obligations for European citizens; it is simply a legal status. The critical question implicit in the idea of any citizenship remains unanswered: would Europeans die for Europe? Would Italian, French, or Spanish citizens give their lives for the integrity of individual member states or even the European Union as a whole?

That question aside, one of the major challenges for the construction of European citizenship is to bring clarity and rigor to an unclear and

---

François-Henri Briard's remarks constitute an introduction to the more extensive reflections on the nature and development of European citizenship offered by Judge Jean-Claude Bonichot.

incoherent concept. Even with a flag, a territory, a hymn, and a motto ("united in diversity"), the content and understanding of citizenship remain problematic. Some scholars relate citizenship to the legal dimension of free movement,[3] while others relate it to civic behaviors that will lead to identification with the EU, and hence to political recognition for the EU.[4] The general European public, on the other hand, lacks a clear comprehension of any concept of European citizenship.

Like the European Union, which is a specific and *sui generis* postnational organization and cannot be compared to an individual nation, European citizenship cannot be compared to national citizenship. EU citizenship does not replace member-state citizenship. Rather, one must hold citizenship in a member state in order to acquire European citizenship. Article 17 of the EC treaty states: "Citizenship of the Union is hereby established. Every person holding the nationality of a Member State shall be a citizen of the Union. Citizenship of the Union shall complement and not replace national citizenship." Thus, with twenty-seven countries currently in the EU, there are twenty-seven ways to become an EU citizen. Moreover, as one must first belong to a member state in order to be a European citizen, EU citizenship remains based on exclusion: a third-country national has fewer rights than a European citizen.[5]

European citizenship serves several purposes for those who hold it. It provides effective rights to move[6] and reside with family in another member state,[7] to vote and to stand as a candidate in local elections,[8] to obtain diplomatic and consular protection in third countries, to petition before the European Parliament,[9] and to engage in public debate about the type of rights protected. It also extends some rights and protection to foreign residents who lack full citizenship in any particular member state. Finally, through the European Court of Justice, it promotes equality under EU laws regarding free movement and residence.[10]

But European citizenship should do more than protect citizens' rights. It should be made meaningful to individuals in member states. Citizens should receive civic education to encourage loyalty to Europe and should be taught the dangers of all kinds of fundamentalisms. European citizenship should also encourage more substantive political activity on the part of citizens, since European citizenship, like national citizenship, can act as a limit on public power and offer a means of participating in the political process. Finally, the idea of European citizenship should be publicized to a greater degree. The EU Commission is developing some special programs to foster a greater understanding of "active" citizenship, but much more can and should be done.

European citizenship must become more vertical—that is, it must strive to cultivate a greater understanding of citizens' relationship to the greater European Union. The horizontal dimension—that is, citizens' relationships with individuals residing in other EU member states—already exists as a result of free transnational movement. Only by strengthening the vertical dimension can the European Union create a real feeling of community among citizens of diverse national backgrounds.

To that end, European citizenship should be made to entail stronger political ties between the EU and individual citizens. Citizenship was introduced by the Maastricht Treaty in 1992 and then revised by the Amsterdam Treaty in 1997. However, the treaties did not establish any norms of political unity among citizens. There is also no corresponding decision-making process that allows citizens to express their political beliefs or achieve political goals. The EU Commission is taking steps to address this situation by encouraging the creation of "political foundations" to promote European consciousness and the expression of political will.[11] Yet EU citizens are still a long way from the traditional self-understanding of citizens—that is, they do not yet see themselves as belonging to a political community.

European citizenship has serious implications for all individuals in member states. Why, then, is the idea of citizenship almost completely absent from public debate? Academics and judges debate what EU citizenship means, but the public seems to ignore its critical ramifications. Perhaps Europeans believe that European citizenship does not affect their daily lives. It is commonly seen (incorrectly, I think) as too abstract. There is a widespread perception of a Brussels bureaucracy filled with official elites making economic decisions on which individuals can have no influence. Thus European citizenship remains unclear and problematic for the people of Europe.

Efforts to bring citizens closer to the European Union must overcome the obstacles posed by European integration, by globalization, and by multicultural societies. Europe enjoys no linguistic or cultural homogeneity that would provide a basis for shared values and duties. Perhaps European citizenship protects too many rights, or not the proper ones. I question whether social and economic rights can be a fruitful ground to inspire a feeling of community among Europeans. It is also not clear whether Europeans should even seek to build a common cultural identity that does not currently exist and that may be an impossible aspiration. But if it is possible to build a common identity on specific constitutional principles, I suggest that the relevant principles are individual freedom, free expression of opinions, federalism, separation of powers, strong but limited government, and an independent judiciary.

Europe was not born from thirteen colonies in the eighteenth century. It originated in a long succession of intellectual struggles, complicated national constructions, and continuous wars. A legally and economically unified Europe is still very young, and a Europe committed to common political ideals and shared duties of national and union defense is still to come. The transition from "soft" citizenship to real transnational citizenship may take many decades, but first the concept of European citizenship must be clearly defined with more substantive content. Making Europe a true federation might be the appropriate solution. Then the dream of Jean Monnet and Konrad Adenauer would be accomplished: EU citizens would be citizens of the United States of Europe.

European Citizenship: Treaties and Case Law of the European Court of Justice, *Jean-Claude Bonichot*

Does European citizenship really exist? The European Union is neither a state nor a federation. It is simply an international organization, and international organizations normally have no citizens.

The European Union is founded not on a constitution but rather on treaties. The first union treaty was the Paris Treaty, which was signed in 1951 by West Germany, Belgium, France, Italy, Luxembourg, and the Netherlands and which established the European Coal and Steel Community. This treaty is no longer in force. The Common Market was established under the Treaties of Rome, which were signed in 1957 by the six states that had also signed the 1951 treaty. The names given to the Common Market were the European Economic Community and European Atomic Energy Community. On January 1, 1973, the first enlargement took place: the United Kingdom,

Denmark, and Ireland entered the community. Greece followed in 1981; Spain and Portugal in 1986; Austria, Finland, and Sweden in 1995. The fall of the Berlin Wall led to the entry of eight Eastern European countries, along with Malta and Cyprus, in 2004. The union then consisted of twenty-five member-states. It reached twenty-seven with the entry of Romania and Bulgaria on January 1, 2007. Today one of the most difficult questions for Europe is how far it should expand. What should the limit of the union's borders be?

One must distinguish between the European Union, on the one hand, and the European Community on the other, even if, for the most part, their institutions are common to both.

In the framework of the *union*, the member states conduct common foreign and security policy. Or at least, they try to do so. The aim here is the creation of an area of "freedom, security, and justice."[12] For instance, under this framework, decisions relating to the fight against terrorism are taken. Member states also cooperate in the area of justice and criminal law and have now replaced extradition treaties with a European arrest warrant.

In the framework of the *community*, the member states have achieved, step by step, a single internal market. Since the origin of the community, this market has been based on four great freedoms: free movement of workers (including the right of establishment), of services, of goods, and of capital. In order to ensure the effective functioning of the Common Market, member states must conduct an efficient competition policy. With the passage of time, the number of common policies has increased. To the common agricultural and transportation policies, one must now add economic, monetary, social, and environmental policies.

Where is the citizen in all of this? The question is a difficult one, because for a long time the EU was mostly concerned with the economy and business. The community was an economic one and was named accordingly. The rights conferred by community law on the nationals of member states were given to them only as economic actors. The main idea was that a person or a business could move into another member state and settle, work, or operate there, free from discrimination on the grounds of nationality.

Today, the union is much more than that. The 495 million European citizens use the same form of passport. At airports, we have lines reserved for European citizens, just as in U.S. airports there are lines reserved for citizens of the United States. A large part of Europe shares the same currency—the Euro, which is in rather good health. Inside the union, people can move freely, without border controls. There is a European Parliament, which represents the peoples of the member states of the Union and which counts 785 elected representatives. There is even a president of the Union.

In recent years, the EU has had two main objectives: to enlarge the union to twenty-seven member states—achieved in 2007—and to give it much more political substance. The Treaty of Maastricht, which created the official European Union in 1992, was a step toward political substance. With the Maastricht Treaty, the EU created instruments of a common foreign and security policy and established very strong cooperation in the area of policing and criminal justice. The Treaty of Maastricht also created European citizenship. Another treaty, the Treaty of Amsterdam, created the "area of freedom, security and justice." It laid the foundations of a common immigration policy and of an approximation of civil law.

Of what does citizenship in this context consist?

European citizenship confers certain specific rights. It takes place in a wide framework called the "Europe of Citizens,"[13] which is based on the idea that the European Union must not only be a technocratic and economic union, but must also be close to its population and directly address its people. In its case law, as I will suggest below, the European Court of Justice has interpreted very broadly the rights conferred by European Union citizenship.

Who exactly are European citizens? Every person holding the nationality of a member state is a citizen of the Union. European citizenship complements national citizenship but does not replace it. A German or a French national has two citizenships: that of his country, and that of the Union. It must be noted, however, that in the EU the rules governing the attribution of nationality fall within the exclusive competence of the member states. As a result, the member states determine the concrete scope of European citizenship. Curiously, European citizenship does not determine who has the right to vote in the elections to the European Parliament. Member states can confer the right to vote to persons who are not their nationals, if they have a close link with them. So, for example, the United Kingdom has conferred the right to vote in elections for the European Parliament on Commonwealth citizens residing in Gibraltar who are not nationals of the United Kingdom.[14]

What are European citizens' real rights? There are four.

First, the European citizen has the right to move and reside freely within the whole territory of the member states. Prior to the Treaty of Maastricht, freedom of movement was conditioned on economic activity. A national of a member state could move to another member state as a tourist or in order to seek a job. But he did not have free access to a member state's territory only on the ground that he was a national of another member state. This economic requirement has disappeared. In 2004, the European Council and the European Parliament adopted a directive on freedom of movement.[15] This directive confers the right to reside for up to three months within the territory of another member state without the need for any formal permission. Any citizen is entitled to reside for more than three months if he has sufficient resources and if he is covered by medical insurance. Any citizen who has resided in a member state for five years has a permanent right to stay there.

The second right conferred by European citizenship is the right to vote and to stand as a candidate in municipal elections in the member state in which a person resides, even if he or she is not a national of this state. This hard-fought-for right is a major step forward, as it gives an individual the right to participate in the local political system where he or she lives. There are restrictions in some member states—for example, in Luxembourg, where 40 percent of the population is foreign born; and in France, where a national of another member state can be elected town councilor, but not mayor, because the French constitution forbids it. In France, the European citizens' right to vote required a revision of the constitution.

The third right of European citizens is the right to vote and to stand as candidates in elections to the European Parliament, in whatever member state they reside. Since 1999, the European Parliament has been elected by direct, universal suffrage. So, for example, an Italian living in France can vote and be elected as a European representative in France. However, he cannot vote twice, in both his home country and his country of residence. If he votes where he lives, he renounces his vote in his state of origin.

The last right is protection by diplomatic or consular authorities. Every citizen of the union who is abroad in a third country is entitled to the protection of the authorities of any member state, if his state has no representation in the country where the individual finds himself. This is not a mere theoretical possibility, because there are only five countries in which all member states are represented. Consular protection is extremely important in the event of difficulties such as accidents or problems with the police or judicial authorities of the host state.

There are other rights not reserved solely for European citizens that form part of the building of the Europe of Citizens.

First is the right to petition the European Parliament, which extends to any natural or legal person established in the union. The European Parliament received more than 1,500 petitions in 2007. The petitions concerned matters ranging from the environment to fundamental rights to social matters to discrimination. Petitions may result in legal proceedings by the European Commission against member states who have failed to implement European law.

Next is the right to bring a complaint before the European Ombudsman, who is appointed by the Parliament. Any citizen or person established in the union may apply to him in a case of maladministration by any European institution (such as the commission) or European body (such as the European Investment Bank). The ombudsman received more than three thousand complaints in 2007. Many of them were outside his mandate—only 16 percent were admissible—but more than three hundred (involving legal errors as well as negligence, delays, or unfairness) led to an inquiry.

A further right, that of any citizen or any person established in the union to access parliament, council, and commission documents, has effected in Europe a principle of transparency. This right is subject to specific conditions: it must not impinge on private life, defense and military secrecy, or industrial secrecy. In an important, much-debated judgment, the Court of Justice did not exempt from communication even advice offered by the European Council's Legal Service to council members considering a directive.[16]

Lastly, any citizen has the right to correspond with a European institution or body in any of the twenty-three official languages of the union and obtain an answer in that same language.

The case law of the Court of Justice has played a great role in building European citizenship. The court has always been an engine of Europe, and it has often made up for a lack of political power by interpreting the treaties in the specific spirit in which they were drafted. It was the Court of Justice, in an important 2001 judgment,[17] that established the concept of European Union citizenship. The court stated that "Union citizenship is destined to be the fundamental status of nationals of the member states, enabling those who find themselves in the same situation to enjoy the same treatment in law irrespective of their nationality, subject to such exceptions as are expressly provided for." This meant, the court explained, that a citizen of the union lawfully resident in another member state could avail himself of the principle of nondiscrimination on the ground of nationality in all situations which fall within the scope of European Community law. This covers the exercise of the different fundamental freedoms guaranteed by the Treaty establishing the European Community (EC treaty).

In the remainder of my discussion, I consider a number of recent cases heard by the European Court of Justice that suggest how an understanding of European citizenship is informing the court's rulings, and how these rulings may in turn help to deepen our understanding of European citizenship.

The right to move and to reside freely in another member state, guaranteed under the EC treaty, was at issue in *Grzelczyk*. In this case a French student studying in Belgium ran out of money and applied for the Belgian "minimex," a minimum subsistence allowance. The court stated that he could not be discriminated against purely on the ground of nationality, and was therefore entitled to receive the minimex. The court acknowledged that Belgium could withdraw the plaintiff's residency permit, because, according to community law, a student must have sufficient resources to avoid becoming an unreasonable burden on the finances of a host member state. But in a situation where need is temporary, the court stated, the burden should be considered a "reasonable" one.

Another important ruling concerning movement came in the *Baumbast* case, in which the court stated that Article 18 of the EC treaty, relating to the right of free movement and residence, directly conferred the right of residence on every union citizen.[18] The court pointed out that the right at issue was no longer dependent on economic activity, and hence that the plaintiff, who had worked for a number of years in the United Kingdom but had stopped working there, had a direct right to stay in the United Kingdom with his family.

Eman and Sevinger, a 2006 case, suggests the ways in which European citizenship has consequences for the right to vote in the European Parliament elections.[19] The law of the Netherlands provided that persons living in its overseas territories with dependent status (such as Aruba) could not participate in these elections. The court held that community law currently leaves to each member state the definition of persons entitled to vote. Still, it pointed out that nationals of the Netherlands living in third countries can vote and that the Dutch position could lead to discrimination between European citizens in comparable situations. Finally, the court noted that the Netherlands had not objectively justified such discrimination.

Recently, the court has drawn inferences from European citizenship to guide its decisions in the area of tax law.[20] German law recognizes taxpayers' right to deduct fees for education from their taxable income when they send their children to a private school established in Germany but not in another member state. A couple who lived in Germany and had sent their children to a school in Scotland were denied this right. The Court of Justice stated that by virtue of European citizenship, they should have the same benefit of reduced income tax, even if their children were being educated in another member state.

The court was also guided by an understanding of European citizenship in *Avello*.[21] A married couple—one a Spanish national and one a Belgian national—wanted to change the surname of their two children, who had dual nationality. Belgian law provides that children bear their father's surname, and the rules governing a person's surname fall within the competence of member states. Nevertheless, the court stated that these rules must comply with community law. It pointed out that persons having only Belgian nationality and those having dual nationality are not in the same situation. The latter may plead difficulties specific to their situation. The court concluded that refusing to grant an application for a change of surname in circumstances such as applied in this case was incompatible with European citizenship's commitment to the principle of nondiscrimination. This judgment is generally regarded as having given a very wide interpretation to European citizenship.

Another very important case is *Watts*,[22] in which the court stated that community law conferred the right to have hospital treatment in another member state reimbursed by the home state if, in the state where a person is domiciled (in this case the United Kingdom), the national health service is not able to provide timely care.

A final example of the way in which the concept of European citizenship is informing legal decisions—and in my opinion the most significant example—is the very recent *Huber* case.[23] It concerns an Austrian national who had moved to Germany and settled there in 1996. Before the national courts, he challenged the decision to enter his personal data in the national databases for foreign nationals, because he felt that to do so was discrimination against him on grounds of nationality.

German national law does, in fact, provide for two different databases which apply only to foreign nationals. One concerns the right of residence; the other tends to be used to fight crime. But the court viewed the two types of databases differently. It acknowledged that a member state may need certain data in order to ascertain whether the right of residence in its territory exists in relation to a national of another member state and to establish if there is a ground which would justify a restriction of that right. It also admitted the necessity of having a centralized register, even if local registers already exist. (Every person in Germany, national or not, has to inform the authorities when he settles in a new district and have his name added to the local register of population.) Thus, the court considered this database compatible with community law, inasmuch as it contained only the data which are necessary for the application of the law concerning foreign nationals. It also recognized that while a database was justified for statistical purposes, it ought not to contain individualized personal information.

In contrast, regarding the register for the purpose of fighting crime, the court held that as the database contained personal data on union citizens who are not nationals of that member state, it did not comply with the principle prohibiting discrimination on grounds of nationality. In fact, as the court pointed out, the fight against crime—in the general sense in which that term is used in German law—involves the prosecution of crimes committed irrespective of the nationality of their perpetrators. That being so, the situation of nationals and foreign nationals cannot be considered different. Therefore, the inequality of treatment vested in the German law constituted discrimination prohibited by treaty law.

What lies ahead for European citizenship? Alain Lamassoure, a former French minister and current member of the European Parliament, recently produced a detailed report on how European citizenship really affects people in their daily lives and how it could be improved—specifically, how citizens could be made to feel part of a wider community of nations, one which brings them greater benefits than citizenship in a single member state.[24] The report puts forward a raft of proposals, one of which is worthy of particular attention: the proposal to introduce a single social security card and a single

European identity card, which could be the basis for giving effect to the different rights conferred by community law.

Twenty-seven very old and very different countries, with twenty-three official languages and 495 million citizens among them, confront a true challenge in the effort to develop the status of the European citizen. But I have no doubt that European citizenship will come into its own in the coming years. Our children are already European citizens, roaming throughout the European Union without taking much account of regulations and directives. They see only the world in which they live, and build for themselves the future European citizen.

Notes

1. Case C-184/99, Grzelczyk v. Centre public d'aide sociale d'Ottignies-Louvain-la-Neuve, 2001 E.C.R. I-6193.

2. Council Decision 2007/252 O.J. (L110 and L141) (EC) (establishing the Fundamental Rights and Citizenship program of the EU Council); and Council Regulation 168/2007 O.J. (L 53) (EU) (establishing the European Union Agency for Fundamental Rights [focusing on discrimination racism, xenophobia, etc.]). Also relevant is the the Education for Democratic Citizenship project promoted by the Council of Europe.

3. Astrid Epiney, *The Scope of Article 12 EC: Some Remarks on the Influence of European Citizenship*, 13 Eur. L. J. 611 (2007).

4. Paul Magnette, *How Can One Be European? Reflections on the Pillars of European Civic Identity*, 13 Eur. L. J. 664 (2007).

5. *See* Francesca Strumia's essay in this volume.

6. The right to free circulation of persons inside the EU is found in Article 18 of the Treaty establishing the European Community, Nov. 10, 1997, 1997 O.J. (C340) 3 [hereinafter EC treaty]; Council Directive 2004/38/EC Citizenship, 2004 O. J. (L 158) 77; and EU court jurisprudence.

7. According to the fifth report of the European Commission, 8.2 million people were using their right to reside in a member state other than their country of birth. Report from the Commission, Fifth Report on Citizenship of the Union (1 May–30 June 2007), COM (2008) 85. The Luxemburg court has an extensive interpretation of free movement regarding family life and proportionality, going beyond treaties and related to other basic concepts: Case C-200/02, Zhu v. Secretary of State for the Home Department, 2004 E.C.R. I-9925; Case C-215/03, Oulane v. Minister voor Vreemdelingenzaken en Integratie, 2005 E.C.R. I-1215; Case C-157/03, Commission v. Spain, 2005 E.C.R. I-291; Case C-258/04, Office national de l'emploi v. Ioannidis, 2005 E.C.R. I-08275.

8. EC treaty, art. 19; Council Directive 2006/106/EC, 2006 O. J. (L 363) 409.

9. EC treaty, art. 20.

10. EC treaty, art. 12; Council Directive 2004/38/EC, 2004 O. J. (L 299) 35; Case C-456/02, Trojani v. CPAS, 2004 E.C.R. I-7573; Case C-209/03, Bidar v. London Borough of Ealing, 2005 E.C.R. I-2119.

11. Regulation (EC) 2004/2003 on the Regulations Governing Political Parties at European Level and the Rules Regarding their Funding, 2003 O. J. (L 297) 5; EC treaty, art. 191.

12. Treaty of Amsterdam Amending the Treaty on European Union, the Treaties Establishing the European Communities and Certain Related Acts, Oct. 2, 1997, art. K.1.

13. José Manuel Durão Barroso, "Building the Europe of the Future: A Europe of Citizens, Opportunities and Culture," Address Before the European Commission (May 24, 2008).

14. Case C-145/04, Spain v. United Kingdom 2006 E.C.R. I-07917.

15. Council Directive 2004/38, On the Right of Citizens of the Union and Their Family Members to Move and Reside Freely Within the Territory of the Member States, 2004 O.J. (L 229) 5 (EC).

16. Cases C 39/05 P and C 52/05 P, Kingdom of Sweden v. Council, 2008 E.C.R. I-0000.

17. Case C-184/99, Grzelczyk v. Centre public d'aide sociale d'Ottignies-Louvain-la-Neuve, 2001 E.C.R. I-06193, para. 77.

18. Case C-413/99, Baumbast v. Secretary of State for the Home Department, 2002 E.C.R. I-07091.

19. Case C-300/04, Eman and Sevinger v. College van Burgemeester en Wethouders van Den Haag, 2006 E.C.R. I-8005.

20. Case C-76/05, Schwarz and Gootjes-Schwarz v. Finanzamt Bergisch Gladbach, 2007 E.C.R. I-06849.

21. Case C-148/02, Avello v. Belgium, 2003 E.C.R. I-11613.

22. Case C-372/04, Watts v. Bedford Primary, 2006 E.C.R. I-4325.

23. Case C-524/06, Huber v. Germany, 2008 E.C.R. I-0000.

24. Alain Lamassoure, *Le Citoyen et l'Application du Droit Communitaire* [The Citizen and the Application of Community Law], Report to the President of France, June 8, 2008.

7

Citizenship, Alienage, and Personhood in the United States

Diane P. Wood

Imagine a world in which the idea of citizenship was, just for a time, entirely jettisoned. This world still has identifiable nation-states, but those nation-states have tossed out the window all laws, regulations, and restrictions on who may live within their physical boundaries, who may participate in local governance, and who is entitled to engage in the full range of life's activities. Although countries in this hypothetical world still guard their borders in order to ensure that dangerous materials do not enter the national space, no special measures exist either to keep dangerous people out or to permit them to stay within the country. Instead, the control of people is handled on a universal, nondiscriminatory basis. Whenever the police anywhere have adequate reason (consistent with national law and recognized constitutional norms) to believe that someone either has committed a crime within the country or poses a future risk to national security, they are entitled to arrest that person and have their suspicions tested somehow before a proper tribunal.

Could such a world survive for long? What would be missing that now exists in the present system? Why, in other words, do we find the need to draw lines between citizens and aliens? For what purpose do we restrict entry into and exit from the national territory, and why do we extend to aliens—even those who are lawfully present within the country, and even more so those whose presence is unauthorized—a diminished package of rights and entitlements? This is especially puzzling, given the fact that both Europe and the United States subscribe firmly to the proposition of equality among all persons. Why should the accident of someone's living in a country other than

137

the one of her birth (or the one to which her parents owe allegiance) have such great consequences?

These are big questions, and I do not pretend to give definitive answers to them. What I can do is offer some general thoughts about the modern justifications for citizenship (and its converse, alienage), with the goal of seeing which arguments hold up under scrutiny and which do not.

Let's begin with a look at the difference between "citizens" and "aliens." Professor Peter Schuck has said that "citizenship, conventionally understood, marks full and permanent membership in a political community; . . . it defines the circle of our greatest trust and of our most extensive common endeavors."[1] A popular casebook on immigration law defines "citizens" as "full members of the state, entitled to the basic rights and opportunities afforded by the state."[2] Who, then, are these outsiders who are not part of the community and who are either nonmembers or limited members? We call the outsiders "aliens"—a singularly unattractive term, in my opinion.[3]

At least since the Treaty of Westphalia of 1648, we have lived in a world divided up by nation-states, each of which presumptively has exclusive sovereignty over a particular defined piece of territory. I say "presumptively" because many exceptions or qualifications to the idea of neat and impenetrable territorial divisions have evolved over the last three and a half centuries, including the recognition that two or more nations may have overlapping jurisdiction to regulate certain matters and the existence of both subnational and supranational entities that may share competence over particular issues. But for present purposes, the Westphalian world is still the one that counts.

The American Law Institute's *Third Restatement of the Foreign Relations Law of the United States* offers a typical definition of the term "state," in the sense I am using it: "Under international law, a state is an entity that has a defined territory *and a permanent population*, under the control of its own government, and that engages in, or has the capacity to engage in, formal relations with other such entities."[4] It seems, from this definition, that some concept of "citizen" is essential to the modern understanding of the state. The population affiliated with a particular state must have some kind of permanent link with it. Those are the people who create the government and who engage in formal relations with other states or nations around the world. This immediately suggests one purpose that the status of citizenship might be performing: that is, it is one way of designating those whose commitment to, and affiliation with, a particular territorial state is deep enough, and permanent enough, that they can be relied upon to create a structured government and maintain an organized society. Casual visitors and those who come and go without any investment (physical or emotional) in the place would be too unreliable.

This does not explain, however, why there should be any particular barriers to the acquisition of citizenship. The vast majority of countries treat citizenship as a scarce commodity, not available to all who might wish to acquire it. Citizenship in today's world (as opposed, for example, to the world of the ancient Greeks and Romans) is not something that must invariably be earned. In the United States, two groups of people acquire citizenship by the simple act of being born: those who are born of a U.S. citizen parent, no matter where they are born in the world (that is, those who acquire citizenship by *jus sanguinis*); and those who are born on U.S. soil, no matter what the citizenship of their parents is (that is, those who qualify by *jus soli*). The latter route is not universally used in countries around the world, and its wisdom and implications have been debated within the United States over the years, but as of now it is part of U.S. law.

What about people without that initial link to a country? In the United States, naturalization has been recognized since the Constitution was written. Article I, Section 8, clause 4 empowers Congress "to establish [a] uniform Rule of Naturalization," and Congress has done so. The requirements for naturalization are not onerous for those who have already qualified as permanent residents of the United States and who have lived in the country without incident, and without significant absences, for a period of five years or more. As of 2005, according to the Pew Hispanic Center, there were more than 12.8 million naturalized citizens in the United States.[5] According to the U.S. Census, the current population of the United States is 305,411,324.[6] If we were to assume (counterfactually) that this number reflects only citizens, that suggests that naturalized citizens account for more than 4 percent of the population.

Naturalized citizenship is, however, more fragile than citizenship by birth. Unlike citizenship by birth, it can be lost. The government may bring an action to revoke the order admitting a person to citizenship if the naturalization order was "illegally procured or . . . procured by concealment of a material fact or by willful misrepresentation."[7] In a number of cases, the government has done just that with (for example) former Nazi concentration camp guards who concealed their past at the time they entered the United States and applied for citizenship.[8]

The path to naturalization illustrates the well-known fact that there are countless intermediate statuses between that of full citizen and true stranger to a country. Most of us have traveled to foreign countries as tourists; some of us may have lived, or may now live, for sustained periods of time in countries other than the one of our nationality. When we cross national boundaries, we experience first-hand the primary way in which nations seek to restrict their communities to citizens and others who are privileged to be there: border controls. In some instances, we must procure a visa before we even leave our native land. The visa memorializes the host country's decision to allow one to travel there and usually specifies the period of time during which one may stay. In other instances, the law itself provides for short-term visits. Americans who visit Europe as tourists normally simply stand in the "non-EU passport" line, get a stamp in their passports—sometimes not even that—and move on to enjoy their time there. These short-term visitors are called "nonresident aliens" in U.S. immigration parlance. Qualified people may also become permanent resident aliens and acquire the coveted "green card," if they can navigate the Byzantine set of immigration regulations we have created.

Problems arise in this scheme because people have an inconvenient habit of being people. A nonresident alien comes to the United States, falls in love, and wants to marry someone she met here. A pregnant woman comes to the United States, lawfully or otherwise, and gives birth to her child on American soil. A refugee fleeing torture and persecution in a foreign land comes to the United States, often using forged documents, and pleads for political asylum. People desperate for work slip across the U.S.-Mexican border and perform jobs in the shadow world of the "undocumented" aliens. Sometimes they stay for years.

Their stories can be truly harrowing, as was true in a recent case that came before the Seventh Circuit. In *United States v. Calimlim*,[9] the United States brought criminal charges against a wealthy Filipino family (permanent resident aliens themselves) living in Wisconsin, claiming that they violated the statute forbidding forced labor. The Calimlims had brought a sixteen-year-old girl over from the Philippines so that she could work as their live-in housekeeper. The girl, Irma Martinez, came from a very poor family and spoke no

English. As soon as she arrived, the Calimlims confiscated her passport and told her that she would have to reimburse them for her plane ticket. To make a long and sad story short, they compelled her to work from six in the morning until ten at night, seven days a week, caring for their home and children. She was forbidden to walk out of the house or to answer the telephone. On rare occasions when she was allowed to ride to the store, she had to keep her head down so that no one could see her. The Calimlims told her that they were keeping her money for her, but over a nineteen-year period they allowed her to send only $19,000 back to her family. They regularly threatened her with dire consequences if she revealed her existence. Finally, federal agents received an anonymous tip (later traced to the spouse of one of the then-grown children); the agents found Martinez huddling in the back of a closet, trembling with fear. In due time, the Calimlims were indicted, convicted by a jury, and sentenced to forty-eight months in prison. The court of appeals agreed with the government that further proceedings were required on the sentence, but it otherwise affirmed.

While it is unfortunately also possible to abuse a U.S. citizen in the way Martinez was treated, there can be no doubt that her status as an illegal alien strengthened her employers' hand considerably. Importantly, no one thought that the illegal nature of her extended presence in the United States somehow exonerated her employers. There are some instances in which a person's status—as a citizen, as a permanent resident alien, as a lawful visitor, or as an illegal or "undocumented" person—must be set aside. In other instances, it may be entirely appropriate for the government to draw these distinctions. The trick is figuring out which is which.

There is a troubling randomness to the way in which rights and status have been allocated in the United States. Aliens are entitled to many of the same rights as citizens, but in some instances their rights are qualified, and in still others they are severely restricted or absent. The table specifies the rights aliens share with citizens and the rights they are denied, whether in part or in full.

Thus, all aliens (regardless of the regularity of their presence) are entitled to all the protections the Constitution confers in criminal proceedings, including due process, trial by jury, right to counsel, and Fourth Amendment rights. The equal protection clause also protects all "persons" within the United States. The children of aliens—even illegal aliens—are entitled to a

TABLE 7-1
RIGHTS OF ALIENS IN THE UNITED STATES

Rights All Aliens Share with Citizens	Rights Restricted to Legal Aliens or Otherwise Qualified	Rights Severely Restricted or Absent
Constitutional criminal procedural rights, including right to due process, counsel, and trial by jury, and Fourth Amendment rights	Right to employment in government or federal civil service	Right to federal public benefits (e.g., Medicare, SSI, food stamps)
Right to free speech under First Amendment	Right to sit for bar	Right to certain public employment (e.g., police officer, parole officer, probation officer, public school teacher)
Right to equal protection (but note that standard of review may vary depending on legal status)	Right to serve as notary public	Right to vote
Right to public education (minors)	Right to receive state welfare benefits	Right to cross borders
	Right to be treated as state resident for purposes of (public) college tuition	Rights related to immigration procedures (i.e., right to an attorney; but note that many actions are not subject to judicial review)
	Right to protections of federal labor law	Right to public higher education

SOURCES: Various Supreme Court rulings; author's analysis.

free public education in the schools, and all aliens can invoke the rights set forth in federal labor laws such as the National Labor Relations Act and the Fair Labor Standards Act (if they dare). Legal aliens may sit for the bar or serve as a notary public; they are entitled to be treated as residents of the state where they live for purposes of college tuition. Finally, states are not entitled, as a matter of state law, to refuse to give them public welfare benefits.

On the other hand, nothing protects even legal aliens from state laws that restrict their ability to serve as parole or probation officers, public school teachers, or police officers. Although the Supreme Court found fault with a Civil Service Commission rule banning legal aliens from federal employment, the procedural flaws in that system were later corrected, and now legal aliens are severely restricted when it comes to public employment. (A federal judge is entitled to hire lawful permanent resident aliens as law clerks, as long as they come from a country with which the United States has a mutual defense treaty—I have thus had, over the years, one Italian clerk and one Australian clerk.) If the federal government chooses (and it has so chosen), it may refuse to all aliens, legal or otherwise, various public benefits such as Medicare, Supplemental Security Income payments, and food stamps. And of course, the classic restriction on aliens has to do with participation in governance: aliens are not entitled to vote.

It is possible to explain why some things are permitted and some forbidden by looking at our federal structure. Thus states are not supposed to deny public benefits to aliens, but the federal government may place restrictions on them as part of its broader power to condition their admission to the country. Nevertheless, it seems to me that systematic thinking has been sorely lacking in this area. Let's accept the idea that some distinctions between citizens and aliens are appropriate, and that some distinctions among permanent resident aliens, lawful visitors, and those who are here illegally should be drawn. It is not at all clear that we have settled on the *right* distinctions, for the right reasons.

Citizenship might be seen as a surrogate for many different things. One might think that it is a rough way of determining whose loyalty to the country is assured, and whose is not. The government often acts upon the assumption that U.S. citizens—both native-born and naturalized—are more likely to show unqualified commitment to the country than others. Thus, for example, only U.S. citizens are entitled to obtain security clearances to work in sensitive jobs. (Foreign nationals may, on special occasions, be granted a Limited Access Authorization, but this permits access only to materials classified up to the "secret" level; it does not extend to "top secret" or more sensitive materials.) It is reasonable to assume that citizens have spent most of their life in the United States (though we can all think of exceptions to this), and thus that it would be easier for the national security agencies to check on the background of a U.S. citizen. It is difficult to say, however, that citizenship is anything more than a rough proxy for who is likely to be reliable and discreet, and on the other side who is likely to be dangerous.

One might also argue that citizenship is a way of distinguishing the internal community of a country from all other external communities. It offers a form of national self-definition. As compared to those from other countries, citizens of one nation often share a common language, a common religion, and a common set of cultural values. Americans look back with nostalgia on the frontier tradition, and to this day cherish self-reliance and individuality. Perhaps in part because of that history, Americans have often been skeptical that government is able to provide the answers to the broad social problems facing the country. But there is nonetheless a sense of national identity that is hard to define in today's heterogeneous society. Classic criteria, like language, ethnicity, or religion, do not seem strong enough to do the job. English is without a doubt the dominant language in the United States, but we are becoming a bilingual nation more rapidly than we may think.

My personal view is that there is nothing to deplore in this trend—it will make Americans more competitive internationally and will demonstrate conclusively that we are just as capable of learning other languages as our friends in Europe have proven themselves to be. Religious homogeneity went the way of the Pilgrims; today's United States welcomes and nurtures a wide variety of religions. The CIA's *World Factbook* reports the following about the distribution of religions in the country, as of 2007: Protestant 51.3 percent, Roman Catholic 23.9 percent, Mormon 1.7 percent, other Christian 1.6 percent, Jewish 1.7 percent, Buddhist 0.7 percent, Muslim 0.6 percent, other or unspecified 2.5 percent, unaffiliated 12.1 percent, none 4 percent.[10] As for cultural values, while there is no doubt an important shared experience among Americans, it is worth asking whether Americans have more in common with one another than, for instance, urban Americans have with people from London, Toronto, or Sydney, and rural Americans with their counterparts in other countries.

Another reason for drawing sharp lines based on citizenship, and for imposing a strict policy with respect to admission of aliens at the border, is economic. As the story would have it, open borders would lead to a flood of immigrants who would take jobs from U.S. citizens, swamp public services, cram into substandard housing, and commit crimes. Indeed, we see a variant of this fear in the asylum cases that come before the federal appellate courts. Is it really true, some people ask, that we must give asylum to every single victim of China's notorious one-child policy? What are we to do with a failed society like Somalia, or an area like Darfur, when people show up at our borders with highly plausible stories of torture, persecution, and ruin? The fear of a flood of refugees is sometimes palpable. Yet somehow the flood does not materialize. Economics furnishes part of the answer why, and attachment to home the rest. However awful conditions may be in some places, it is exceedingly difficult and expensive for people to leave and make their way to Europe, to Australia, to Canada, or to the United States. It is unclear how many more immigrants from Central and South America would try their luck in the U.S. economy if the border were open. At some point, one suspects, an equilibrium would be reached—if there are no more jobs to be had in the United States, people will stay home.

The burden on social services imposed by immigrants is also a concern, although technically illegal immigrants are eligible for very few such services; indeed, even legal aliens have limited access. If the real problem is economic, then it would make sense to think of economic solutions for it. For example—and I do not mean to be frivolous in suggesting this—countries might even be able to arrange cross-payment systems for urgent medical care furnished to one another's citizens. We do this kind of thing for letters, through the international postal conventions, and the telecommunications companies have been doing it for years. Why not extend those practices to the care of people, rather than risking a repetition of the scene in which the undocumented alien lies suffering outside the hospital door? It is also worth recalling that aliens—both legal and illegal—pay the various indirect taxes that states and localities impose. And their work benefits the local communities in which they live, whether that work is in the traditional businesses of agriculture, restaurants, construction, and landscaping, or in less typical areas. The ultimate accounting of the costs and benefits of participation by noncitizens in the economy is much more complex than it appears at first blush.

Citizenship may seem important to some for a reason that is related to internal harmony but that is less noble: it is a way of defining both the insiders and the outsiders of a particular community. The definitions of citizenship that I mentioned earlier all use this metaphor of membership. Yet membership often entails an undercurrent of exclusion that is not always benign. The exclusive country club excludes people who are ethnically different, or who are economically in a different class, or who worship God in the wrong way. The gated community creates a lovely living environment for the members, but it keeps others out. Of course, not all membership organizations are like this. Some are expressly designed to facilitate the efforts of their members to reach out and help others. Some exist to help people pursue a common interest in something innocuous like music, art, gardening, or books. Citizenship conceived as membership in the latter type of group is, or should be, fully consistent with ideals of equal treatment and respect for all persons.

Lastly, citizenship as a concept might be surviving today for the simple reason that we cannot come up with anything better to serve the interests of administrative convenience. The organization of the world into the 192 nation-states recognized by the United Nations is a fact of life.[11] The option of a random assignment of people to territory is unattractive, to say the least. It is fair to ask for a precommitment to a place; a familiarity with one's neighbors; and a sustained willingness to participate in self-governance. It is hard to imagine nation-states without some form of border control, and with that comes a need to monitor who comes in for purposes of permanent residence and affiliation, and who is merely a visitor.

This brief overview reveals that the concept of citizenship is still an important one, but that, in the United States at least, the system for distinguishing between citizens and noncitizens needs serious work. Two different agencies within the Department of Homeland Security (DHS) are primarily responsible for this task, Citizenship and Immigration Services (CIS) and Immigration and Customs Enforcement (ICE). They were created from the old Immigration and Naturalization Service of the Department of Justice when the Department of Homeland Security was established. One vestige remains in the Department of Justice, the Executive Office of Immigration Review, where the immigration judges and the Board of Immigration Appeals (BIA) are lodged. Navigating the system we have created is not for the faint of heart. Sometimes papers need to be filed with CIS; sometimes ICE is in charge; sometimes it is an immigration judge or the BIA. Parallel proceedings abound, and the right hand frequently has no idea what the left is doing. Some matters lie clearly within the discretion of one of the agencies (either

DHS or the Attorney General); others do not. It is my hope that a hard look at the purposes that lie behind our concept of citizenship may lead to some clarification of the way that we treat our society's "insiders" and "outsiders." The maze of regulations and requirements that confronts people aspiring to come to the United States—for either a short stay or the long term—desperately needs attention. I hope that we can learn from our European friends how they handle similar problems, and that with a clearer goal in mind, we can sweep away as much of the underbrush as possible.

Notes

1.   Peter H. Schuck, *Citizenship in a Post-9/11 World: An Exchange Between Peter H. Schuck and David Cole* (The Meaning of American Citizenship in a Post-9/11 World), 75 Fordham L. Rev. 2531, 2534 (2007).

2 T. Alexander Aleinikoff, David A. Martin, Hiroshi Motomura, and Maryellen Fullerton, Immigration and Citizenship: Process and Policy 1 (6th ed. 2008).

3. Etymologically speaking, the term "alien" started out innocuously enough— it comes from the Latin word "*alius*," which just means "other one." Some people still use the Latin word in its original sense—especially in legal writing—when they use the phrase "*inter alia*" to mean "among other things." But the word "alien" has come to have less flattering secondary meanings in modern times—and not only in the world of science fiction.

4. Restatement (Third) of the Law of Foreign Relations § 201 (1987) (emphasis added).

5. Jeffrey S. Passel, *Growing Share of Immigrants Choosing Naturalization*, Pew Hispanic Center Report (Mar. 28, 2007), at http://pewhispanic.org/files/reports/74.pdf.

6. *See* U.S. Census Bureau Web site, http://www.census.gov.

7. *See* 8 U.S.C. § 1451.

8. *See, e.g.*, United States v. Dailide, 316 F.3d 611 (6th Cir. 2003); United States v. Szehinskyj, 277 F.3d 331 (3d Cir. 2002); United States v. Tittjung, 235 F.3d 330 (7th Cir. 2000).

9. 538 F.3d 706 (7th Cir. 2008).

10. *See* CIA World Factbook, at https://www.cia.gov/library/publications/the-world-factbook/print/us.html.

11. *See* United Nations, Member States, at http://www.un.org/members/list.shtml.

PART III
Rights

8

Three Models of Citizenship

Peter H. Schuck

By raising vital questions about membership and belonging, the notion of citizenship invites us to engage with a variety of normative visions of the good and just society, and of its borders (spatial or otherwise). Such visions are easier to defend when couched in the familiar and abstract language of citizenship than they are when advocated as specific social, political, and legal programs in their own right. This rhetorical stratagem is used by those who do not wish to speak of citizenship simply in its positive, legal-political sense—as a relationship between individuals and a polity that involves allegiance, obligations, and legal rights—but instead mean to invoke citizenship as a powerful aspiration. In this usage, citizenship is an open vessel into which we can pour personal, political, and social values—about our common public life and mutual rights and obligations. Decanting our values into this vessel in this way is seductive, because what we really want to assert are our most contestable ideas about distributive justice, the nature of the state, and its proper role in promoting those conceptions of justice.

It is this normative dimension of citizenship that I shall explore here.[1] I shall elaborate three models of citizenship that, although seldom presented as such, actually constitute core conceptions underlying our discourse about citizenship. I call them the *nationalistic*, *human rights*, and *Marshallian* models (the last named for the British sociologist and historian T. H. Marshall, whose lectures on citizenship remain influential[2]).

Thanks to Peter Spiro and to participants in the Yale Law School faculty workshop for comments on an earlier draft. Kate Heinzelman, Yale Law School class of 2009, ably assisted with some of the footnotes.

Each model includes claims about three dimensions of citizenship that are analytically distinct but conceptually, politically, and legally related. The first is *justification*: the principled reasons for conferring, withholding, or terminating citizenship. The second is the role of *territoriality*: the geographical basis for defining the rights and obligations of citizenship and the state's power to protect and enforce them. The third is *entitlement*: the bundle of legally enforceable rights that only the citizen can claim from the state, and the obligations that the state can demand only from its citizens.

Each model has its defenders and its detractors. Of course, the advocates of one or another of these models of citizenship are reluctant to acknowledge the costs that implementing them would entail; tradeoffs are the stuff of policy analysis, not of political rhetoric and mobilization. But the stakes in this debate over citizenship could hardly be higher. The outcome will not only shape a state's legal and social institutions and public policies, but will mark the boundaries dividing insiders, outsiders, and those in between.[3]

For each model, I shall develop the normative premises about justification, territoriality, and entitlement that characterize it and discuss some of the policy implications that may flow from those premises and from some empirical evidence bearing on them. My main purposes here are conceptual clarification and the sharpening of normative arguments. Accordingly, I shall discuss these premises and policy implications as if they were more categorical than their real-world applications would actually be.

I shall then pose what strikes me as the most urgent question to be raised about the model, and offer a tentative answer. The question about the nationalistic model concerns its relevance in a rapidly globalizing world. Is change rendering this traditional conception of citizenship anachronistic? The question about the human rights model concerns its seemingly limitless aspirations. Does it contain any limits on the obligations that it would impose on a state in its dealings with people who may be perfect strangers to that state (except perhaps in a universalistic, human rights sense)? The question about the Marshallian model concerns its fate and shape in advanced democratic states. Why, and in what respects, has it gained much less public support in the United States than in most Western European states and Japan? My conclusion briefly speculates about the Marshallian model's future in the United States and Europe.

Several further prefatory points are in order. First, for simplicity I shall speak of citizenship in general, as if it were an undifferentiated status. Historically, however, citizenship's availability and entailments in the United States and elsewhere have varied depending on characteristics such as race, gender, and ethnicity.[4] Decades after the civil rights revolution greatly expanded the domains of legal and actual equality among citizens, we continue to distinguish among Americans even with respect to their formal rights, not to mention their informal exercise. Felons, for example, are often denied voting rights; children are legally disabled from voting; and foreign-born Americans are ineligible to be president. Also for simplicity's sake, I speak of "Europe," although I recognize the differences among the nations that comprise the European Union, which a more fine-grained analysis would explore.

Second, my analysis focuses on citizenship in the United States. Nevertheless, I believe that its terms will be familiar, *mutatis mutandis*, to theoretically inclined participants in the debates over citizenship now raging in other economically advanced liberal democracies.

Third, I emphasize the rights of citizenship, not its obligations, because modern liberal democratic polities have steadily reduced the distinctive duties of citizenship to a bare minimum. In the United States, which does not mandate voting or compel military service, jury service is probably the only example of such a duty—and even this may more properly be viewed as a right of democratic participation in self-governance.

Finally, the Marshallian model differs from the nationalistic and human rights models in one important respect: it concerns the scope of equality among citizens within a state and says little about the treatment of immigrants or strangers. Territoriality plays no particular role, and in this sense the Marshallian model arguably should not be compared to the other models.

Nevertheless, I include the Marshallian model for several reasons. Like the other models, it provides a justification for allocating a particular ensemble of rights to some group. That Marshall took the identity of this group to be unproblematic limits the model's contemporary relevance only somewhat. Second, academic debates about citizenship often invoke Marshall's vision in order to compare it, almost always favorably, with a nationalistic model seen as less inclusive and egalitarian. But it is important to note that the differences among the models are only conceptual; they emphasize certain norms and justifications more than (not necessarily to the exclusion of) others. Thus, the

nationalistic model could, without illogic or offense to its underlying principles, yield policies that are just as inclusive or egalitarian as those produced
by the other two models.

The Nationalistic Model

The nationalistic model[5] is the long-standing, dominant view of citizenship—
the one most clearly institutionalized in the law of America and other nation-
states, although the more transcendent human rights model has made some
headway in international treaties, in international and domestic courts, in
elite opinion, and perhaps also in more popular attitudes.

The model is nationalistic in several senses. It embraces the idea that the
United States is a spatially bounded political community and a sovereign state
exercising plenary power over its territory, with the power and duty—constrained only by the federal Constitution and laws—to defend its physical
borders; to define for itself who are insiders, outsiders, and in-betweens; to
determine the rights of these individuals and their obligations to the state;
and to decide which, if any, international law limits (in addition to peremp-
tory *jus cogens* norms) on America's sovereignty it will accept. The model
invokes America's distinctive values, governing institutions, culture, and public policies—not abstract theories—to shape the law, practice, and meanings
of citizenship. The nationalistic model is often skeptical about whether governmental commitments to supranational legal orderings are consistent with
American values and institutions. A similar concern animates the current
debate within the U.S. Supreme Court and among academics about the validity of using foreign law to inform interpretations of the U.S. Constitution.[6]

Justification. According to Peter Spiro, an insightful critic, the nationalistic
model of citizenship comes in two distinct but incoherent forms:

> Conservative nationalists preach a hard-edged assimilationism,
> typically pressing cultural as well as political attributes of
> American nationality; they accept the class of Americans as a priv-
> ileged and exclusive group. Liberal nationalists . . . articulate a
> thinner, civic notion of American identity, and consider citizen-

ship a pillar of inclusiveness and equality. Both versions . . . have been defined at least in part in opposition to a third competing paradigm, that of multiculturalism.[7]

Spiro considers the conservative version, propounded by commentators such as Samuel Huntington, John Miller, Peter Brimelow, and Georgie Anne Geyer,[8] nostalgic in its yearning for a parochial, U.S.-centered, state-bounded world that no longer exists. The liberal version, advanced by Michael Walzer, Kenneth Karst, David Miller, Rogers Smith, and me,[9] among others, cannot in his view "reconcile its tenet of inclusiveness with the inherent exclusiveness of citizenship regimes," a failing that "becomes more pronounced as the civic conception of America itself becomes increasingly less distinctive, as democratic constitutional values take hold at the global level."[10]

The conservative nationalists must answer for themselves if they can,[11] but the liberal nationalist position (whether correct or not) is perfectly coherent: an inclusive citizenship need not (in logic) and cannot (in practice) mean a universal one. Coherence requires only that the principles of exclusion be justified and fairly applied—which are challenges enough.

Nationalistic citizenship is usually based on the liberal ideal of the *mutual consent* of the citizen and the polity. This consensual grounding, captured metaphorically in the idea of a social contract and inscribed ideologically in the Declaration of Independence, is most obviously true of citizenship that is enacted through putative citizens' preparation for their naturalization examination and the drama of the naturalization ceremony itself—*rites de passage* that many advocates of nationalistic citizenship want to make more demanding and meaningful.[12] The consent principle is also embodied in the statutes that confer U.S. citizenship by descent (*jus sanguinis*) and by legislative grace (as in the case of certain statutorily eligible categories of foreign-born soldiers who have served honorably in the military).

Birthright citizenship (*jus soli*), which is by far the largest source of American citizens, is also based on consent. But the consensual basis of birthright citizenship is problematic. First, few if any birthright citizens ever consent explicitly to their membership, as naturalized citizens do. Instead, as Peter Spiro observes, they "come to their status unthinkingly" at birth.[13] They simply take it for granted as the constitutional default, and their inertia then does the rest—save for the relative handful who choose to expatriate themselves. Second, the U.S.-born children of undocumented immigrants are treated as birthright citizens under the Constitution. It seems bizarre to suggest that the American people, through their government, have consented to the illegal presence of these children, much less to their automatic citizenship by the accident of their birth here.[14]

Political scientist Rogers M. Smith and I have explained these apparent anomalies as part of an effort to reconcile the law of American citizenship with its normative underpinnings. We maintained that the drafters of the Fourteenth Amendment's citizenship clause, the constitutional provenance for birthright citizenship, intended the clause to institutionalize a requirement of mutual consent (by both the individual and the polity).[15] Consistent with common law and common sense, the consent principle imputed the parents' nationality to their children at the time of birth, and this tacit consent of the children continued indefinitely, absent their voluntary expatriation.

The compatibility of the consent principle with the birthright citizenship status of the U.S.-born children of illegal immigrants is far more uncertain. The key lies in the citizenship clause's provision limiting birthright citizenship to people "subject to the jurisdiction" of the United States. As Smith and I demonstrated, the clause's drafters applied this limitation most explicitly to the members of Indian tribes, who were of course born on American soil but were largely subject to tribal jurisdiction, and who even today remain statutory, not constitutional, citizens. Although the drafters understandably did not consider how the consent principle would apply to the children of illegal immigrants—this now-immense category did not then exist—their sense of the consent principle and of the textual "subject to the jurisdiction" limitation would not have mandated birthright citizenship for this category, to whose presence Congress manifestly did *not* consent. Instead, the clause left it to Congress, if it wished, to confer citizenship on this category as a matter of policy. The Supreme Court has never squarely faced this issue, but has assumed (erroneously in our view) that the clause renders these U.S.-born children automatic birthright citizens as a matter of constitutional mandate, preempting Congress from limiting or regulating the status.[16] Consequently, America's version of birthright citizenship, unqualified by conditions concerning parental status or other ties to the United States, is probably the most categorical, liberal, and inclusive in the world.[17]

When it comes to the *termination* of U.S. citizenship, the justificatory primacy of the mutual consent principle is even clearer. Citizenship may be formally renounced in prescribed circumstances designed to assure this mutuality.[18] However, the constitutional principles governing putative expatriations that citizens effect through informal actions—for example, by voting in a foreign election, acquiring foreign nationality through a pledge of allegiance, or serving in a foreign army or government—were clarified only in the Supreme Court's 1967 decision in *Afroyim v. Rusk.*[19] In a series of earlier rulings, a sharply divided Court had interpreted a statute providing for loss of citizenship by one who performed certain expatriating acts. These decisions established that such acts must be committed voluntarily in order to be deemed expatriating, but other principles governing expatriation remained uncertain.

The most important open question was whether the actor must *intend* thereby to relinquish his or her citizenship.[20] In *Afroyim,* another sharply divided Court decided that question in the affirmative: the expatriating act must be voluntary, and the actor's intention must consist of a knowing desire to renounce his or her citizenship. *Afroyim's* reasoning was not altogether convincing; Congress had long defined certain voluntary acts as conclusively establishing the citizen's lack of allegiance and imputed his or her intent to renounce on that basis.[21] Even so, *Afroyim's* insistence that the Constitution requires the renunciation to be not only voluntary but knowing and intentional seems normatively desirable. It remains the rule and was subsequently codified in the statute.[22]

Role of Territoriality. The nationalistic model of citizenship, we have seen, is premised on a bounded state's sovereignty over particular territory, which fundamentally determines the state's power to confer citizenship and to execute the duties and rights associated with that status. This relationship between territory and status is most obvious in the realm of birthright citizenship, in the statutory rules governing citizenship by descent (which require that at least one parent purporting to transmit the citizenship be an American who has resided or been physically present in the United States[23]), and in the government's hostility to dual nationality.[24]

Recent scholarship has noted the traditional reasons for the nationalistic emphasis on territoriality while maintaining that this emphasis has become anachronistic in a swiftly globalizing world in which rights are, or at least should be, accessible on the basis of universal humanity and need, not on the happenstance of territorial location at a particular time. (This critique is the essence of the human rights model of citizenship.)

It is worthwhile to lay out the standard rationales for this territorial focus, which retain considerable support both in American and European political cultures—and also in the hard facts of geopolitical reality. First, the exercise of sovereign power over a defined, bounded physical space is the basis under international law for statehood itself, the basic unit of the Westphalian international system. Membership in such polities is rooted in physical attachment to the territory that purports to define and legitimate the state and within which all its citizens have resided at the moment of birth or naturalization, or (in the case of *jus sanguinis*) during some other pivotal period of their lives.

Second, territorial presence and control are a necessary, though not always sufficient, basis for the exercise of the state's power to coerce individuals, a power ultimately limited by the government's legal and effective authority. To be sure, the United States may be able to influence those outside its sovereign territory; and if its effective control is great enough, it may even have some obligations under domestic law to citizens there, as well as some obligations under international law or moral law to others adversely affected by its exercise of power there.[25] By and large, however, a state's extraterritorial control—even in the case of the American Goliath—is likely to impose only limited obligations of this kind.

Perhaps most important, the political and social connections that citizenship both apotheosizes as an ideological matter and nourishes in fact are rooted irreducibly in the national territory on which those connections are forged. This is why, as Spiro has explained, an assimilation-minded United States feels the primordial attraction of territoriality and of its most dramatic legal manifestation, *jus soli*: "The American system would not tolerate a subordinated group [by which he evidently means an alien and permanently unassimilated group] in its communal midst."[26] These civic ties are invigorated by more than the "mystic chords of memory stretching from every battlefield and patriot grave to every living heart and hearthstone all over this broad land" (in Lincoln's majestic phrase).[27] More prosaically, they are refreshed and extended by interactions, shared experiences, cultural patterns, and other commonalities that constitute an overarching national identity and, comparatively speaking, a remarkable patriotism.[28] These connections and this identity are based almost entirely on their construction on a national territory. This is why Kurds and Palestinians—probably the largest ethnic groups without any internationally recognized homeland—have struggled so long, violently, and tragically to gain control over such a territory.

Entitlements. Any model of citizenship associates that status with some set of entitlements, some ensemble of enforceable rights and obligations, in, from, and against the state. In principle, the nationalistic model is agnostic about the nature and scope of entitlements. It could, without illogic or offense to its underlying values, yield policies that are just as inclusive or egalitarian as those produced by the other two models.

In fact, the liberal, highly individualistic American polity takes a decidedly ambivalent view of entitlements. They are part of the *quid pro quo*, the social contract on which consensual membership rests, at least in developed societies; and most Americans believe that even (especially?) in a liberal polity, certain minimum entitlements are necessary to secure a dignified, participatory, independent life for their fellow citizens and for at least some of the noncitizens who reside and work among them. The specific configuration of the American welfare state, even after the Welfare Reform Act of 1996, is strong evidence of this belief. On the other hand, Americans also believe that additional entitlements, either in kind or amount, threaten these same values, especially independence, and would at the margin reduce the motivation to work and to take responsibility for oneself and one's family. Although all developed societies exhibit this ambivalence, different ones strike the balance among the benefits, costs, and risks of entitlements quite differently, with the United States being an outlier in limiting publicly funded welfare supports.

But the normative coherence of the nationalistic model is defined less by the type and magnitude of entitlements than by whether or to what extent only citizens may claim them. Here, too, the model evinces considerable ambivalence. The answer seems to be "it depends." Leading exponents of nationalistic citizenship would restrict most welfare-state entitlements to citizens,[29] a view embodied in the 1996 welfare reform law, which sharply limited noncitizens' access to cash and near-cash benefits. Congress, however, continued to accord them eligibility for certain other benefits such as disaster relief, emergency health care under Medicaid, and in some cases food stamps. Significantly, the leading immigrant-receiving states provided and even extended many public benefits to legal resident noncitizens and (in the case of certain benefits) undocumented immigrants.[30] The SSI Extension for Elderly and Disabled Refugees Act, signed by President Bush in 2008, lengthens the period during which refugees may receive a variety of cash welfare benefits in order to cover them during their administratively delayed process for obtaining citizenship.[31]

In the nationalistic conception of citizenship, then, public benefit entitlements are meant for citizens; yet this general commitment is sometimes compromised, particularly with respect to "affiliated" noncitizens and undocumented ones in the areas of public health, emergency conditions, food, and public education. Public funding for educating undocumented children is constitutionally required at the elementary and secondary levels under *Plyler v. Doe*, but many states have extended it to higher education tuition benefits as well.[32]

One might explain some of these exceptions as national self-interest: the entitlements protect the nation from long-term residents in our midst whose ignorance and illness could threaten the well-being of citizens. And while more altruistic and universalistic motives for granting these entitlements to the undocumented probably dominate the policy choice, these altruistic motives are at least consistent with the nationalistic model of citizenship. By the same token, the fact that the federal government permits states to enforce some rules against undocumented immigration (e.g., federal-state agreements; state-employer sanctions that are not pre-empted by federal law[33]) is consistent with an interest-based justification for entitlements.

"Due process of law" is the Constitution-level rationale for certain other nonwelfare entitlements extended to noncitizens, but the notorious indeterminacy of that phrase permits disagreement about the scope of such rights, who may claim them, and under what conditions and in which places. A recent example of this disagreement was a bitterly divided Supreme Court's extension of the right to file writs of habeas corpus not merely to noncitizens on U.S. territory but also to alleged enemy combatants detained at Guantanamo in Cuba.[34] This judicial struggle over which categories of noncitizens may exercise this right illustrates dramatically the perceived stakes, particularly after 9/11, in what is actually a fundamental debate over the appropriate boundaries between the nationalistic and human rights conceptions of citizenship.[35]

The Human Rights Model

While the nationalistic model of citizenship may explain existing practices, it may also appear anachronistic, ill-suited to the globalizing, interdependent world of the twenty-first century. A far more normatively appealing conception may be what I call the "human rights" model.[36] I characterize the model as "human rights" rather than "postnational" (a label often used to describe it) because the nation-state cannot accurately be characterized as a mere transition phase that is leading to a more universalistic international order. We are not yet "post" the nation-state. Indeed, I have argued elsewhere that with certain tenuous exceptions, the sovereignty of the state is here to stay. On balance, this is good for human rights. Even professional human rights advocates recognize (regretfully) the continuing centrality of the state's protective functions in the international system and the importance of the public attitudes that sustain its nationalistic projects, including its distinctive conception of citizenship.

Justification. If the raison d'être of nationalistic citizenship is to vindicate the liberal value of democratic consent, the purpose of the human rights model, simply stated, is to secure individual and group rights that will assure humane and protective conditions for persons who reside in cruel or despotic states, and for individuals outside their country of nationality and at risk of unequal and inhumane treatment in their new locations.[37] Unlike the nationalistic conception, the human rights model rejects any normative grounding in mutual consent. Rather, the model is based on a unilateral right of a non-member to affiliate with a state for certain purposes. Indeed, it is seen as a necessary complement to nationalistic citizenship precisely because of states' refusal to consent to protect needful individuals who are unaffiliated with these states.

Advocates of the human rights model emphasize numerous important changes in the world that they think render the nationalistic model a relic of an earlier, more nationalistic age. First, vastly increased global migration displaces immense populations from their traditional communities and often leaves them in states not their own. Their dislocation renders them exceedingly vulnerable—legally, economically, politically, culturally, linguistically, and in other respects—in the "host" country. This vulnerability, which is magnified by growing inequalities between the developed states and the undeveloped and even "de-developing" ones, is particularly great if the migrants are political or economic refugees, if they are members of already disadvantaged minorities, or if they are fleeing other intolerable conditions.

Second, advocates of the human rights model affirm that the migrants often confer substantial benefits on the receiving countries, such as labor value, cultural endowments, community vitality, and demographic fertility. Their remittances, technology transfers, and experiences and contacts abroad also foster development in their original countries,[38] which often serves the host countries' foreign and economic policy interests. All the more reason, it is argued, for according equal treatment to the migrants.

Third, the post–World War II elaboration of an extensive body of international human rights law has restricted state sovereignty in certain respects, while granting rights to states' own nationals and to migrants to be free of abuse, exploitation, unfair process, and other harms by the state.[39] This development has both reflected and contributed to the spread of democracy, creating a significant commonality of liberal political values among states.[40]

Fourth, dramatic changes in technology, trade, telecommunications, industrial practices, transportation, and cultural diffusion have fostered a system of global interdependence among states in which they have lost some of their traditional freedom of action, ceded more of it to supranational entities such as the General Agreement on Tariffs and Trade (GATT), and surrendered still more of it through various international agreements. The proliferation of nongovernmental organizations which transcend national borders helps to create an international civil society that provides important quasi-public services on a global scale.[41]

According to the human rights model, these important developments reduce the distinctiveness of national cultures and identities, constrain the autonomy of states, and increase their obligations to protect needful sojourners in their midst and even complete strangers who remain vulnerable to arbitrary exercises of state power. Such changes, the model assumes, justify a notion and institutionalization of citizenship that is more congruent with the scope of these interdependent relationships than is the nationalistic model. In short, it seeks a constitutional community whose inclusiveness is not limited to citizens as traditionally defined or to the arbitrarily fixed space within a nation's borders.[42]

Role of Territoriality. Because the locus of the human rights model is emphatically transnational, not territorially bounded,[43] the model sees birth in a particular state and to particular parents as adventitious, an accident too arbitrary to determine access to rights that, as a matter of distributive justice, should be enjoyed universally.[44] The model's hostility to territoriality as the basis for essential rights is tied to a historical claim (or hope) according to which a progressive dynamic, driven by a combination of increased globalism (especially migration), enlightened national self-interest, and a rising universalist-egalitarian zeitgeist, will drive the locus of citizenship (or at least its most essential rights elements) beyond the status quo of national territories to regional supranational bodies like the European Union, and then on to more universal governance regimes like the United Nations.[45] For it is only at this deterritorialized, universal level that equal access to certain rights and other goods will be possible.

Advocates of the human rights model presumably recognize that for the near future, territoriality and the traditional nation-state will continue to dominate the international system, and hence that citizenship will continue to be an essentially national project.[46] As such, it will inevitably be exclusionary, with clearly defined insiders and outsiders. And it is the harsh consequences of exclusion—and the territorially based inequalities and discrimination it entails—that the human rights movement is determined to challenge.

Entitlements. What, then, would a human rights–based citizenship look like? Which rights and duties would it entail and what political-legal regime would enforce them? The model's aspirational character and the vagueness of its academic expositions make these questions difficult to answer. Still, the literature on this model, augmented by the examples of the European Union and the United Nations regimes, suggest some of the individual rights that it would probably protect.

Because the main rationale for human rights citizenship is the expansion of individual rights, the model is keen to preserve the full panoply of civil and political rights already guaranteed (constitutionally or by statute) to nationals in the United States, European states, and other liberal democracies. These rights constitute the baseline for entitlements; the model's goal is to extend them to virtually all people who are located within the sovereign state and thus subject to its governmental authority.[47]

Human rights proponents typically demand for noncitizens certain rights that states have traditionally withheld from them. Perhaps the most important is the right to vote, especially in national elections—a right that is not granted even by those states that are otherwise relatively receptive to immigrant rights (if not always to the immigrants themselves). The EU, for example, grants the right to vote to resident nationals of EU member states, but only in municipal and local elections and for the European Parliament, not in national elections.[48] In the United States, only a handful of localities permit noncitizen voting today—and even there, such voting is usually allowed only in local school board or other special-purpose elections. The argument in favor of extending the franchise to resident noncitizens is a straightforward, if controversial, application of liberal democratic theory: all those who are subject to governmental authority should be able to participate in the elections that alone can legitimate that authority.[49] Substantially the same principle is deployed to argue for restoring voting rights to felons who have been disenfranchised, and for lowering the voting age. Campaigns to extend the franchise to felons have succeeded in some states and are under way in others, and the Twenty-sixth Amendment, ratified in 1971, lowered the voting age to 18. In contrast, most noncitizen voting proposals have failed, probably because most citizens fear that noncitizens lack adequate political knowledge or will tend to favor one party or the other, or because noncitizens simply are not yet deemed to be full members of the polity. The incomplete American citizenship of Puerto Ricans and residents of the District of Columbia may illustrate these inhibitions.[50]

A second entitlement that the human rights model presupposes is the right to hold plural citizenships. This feature is now well established in positive law in the United States and even more so in the law of our most important sending countries. Spiro has described its implications for national identity and the traditional notion of citizenship:

Just as a regime of mono-nationality reinforced thick national identity, the rise of plural citizenship both implies and facilitates its erosion. Acceptance of plural nationality suggests a less intensive competition among states, the accompanying decline in invocations of "loyalty" and "allegiance" further demonstrating that individuals need no longer throw in their lot with one and only one nation. Multiple, same-category attachments will on average be less meaningful than exclusive ones. Acceptance of multiple attachments also lowers the threshold for membership. It becomes cheaper, in effect, for the would-be member to acquire one tie where she doesn't have to give up another. . . . Plural citizenship is a fact of the new world and a reflection of citizenship's smaller place within it.[51]

A third entitlement in this model concerns the rights of migrants who are actually at the border of a state not their own, or are treated by the law as if they were. These entitlements include the right of *nonrefoulement*, as well as the right to apply for asylum; to be represented by counsel; to be free of any arbitrary detention (i.e., not clearly required to assure public safety or attendance at one's legal proceedings); to have due process in such proceedings, including translation services; to have access to the consular protections of one's own country; to receive special protective services for children and families while in the host country; to receive a reasonable level of other social services while there; and so forth. These rights are generally prescribed in various international conventions and instruments to which most states have subscribed.[52]

The fourth kind of entitlement that a system of human rights citizenship would confer on noncitizens is really an ensemble of what may loosely be called economic, social, family, labor, or welfare rights. These rights, *mutatis mutandis*, also constitute the distinctive endowment of Marshallian citizenship, the third and final model, to which I now turn.

The Marshallian Model

In the late 1940s, the British sociologist T. H. Marshall advanced a conception of citizenship that subsequently attracted immense interest among social

reformers, particularly liberals and social democrats, and exerted much influence in debates about social policy and full participation in social life. This
model, as just noted, bears a considerable resemblance to the human rights
model. Marshall's focus, however, was not on the rights of noncitizens but
rather on what he viewed as the incomplete rights accorded to those who are
already full citizens. In other words (mine, not his), he wanted to justify
"human rights in one (liberal democratic) country."

The late Seymour Martin Lipset aptly summarized Marshallian citizenship as

> a status that involves access to various rights and powers. . . . For
> Marshall, the concept of citizenship has three components: civil,
> political, and social. The civil aspects of citizenship . . . arose in
> the eighteenth century and involve a set of independent rights—
> liberty, freedom of speech, equality before the law, and the right to
> own property. Political rights, the access to the decision-making
> process through participation in the choice of parliament by uni-
> versal manhood suffrage . . . emerged in the nineteenth century
> and reflect in part the demands of the working classes for citizen-
> ship. Social rights—welfare, security, and education—have
> become a major component in the definition of citizenship in
> the twentieth century. Perhaps the most important aspect of the
> concept of citizenship in Marshall's view is its assumption of
> equality. Equality. . . . is a status bestowed on those who are
> full members of the community . . . But if citizenship rights, which
> arose with capitalism and industrialization, imply equality, the
> class structure is a system of inequality. Hence . . . citizenship and
> class create "a conflict between opposing principles."[53]

For Marshall, the development of citizenship is an evolving process,
shaped largely by economic, ideological, and other historical changes and
their legal and political consequences. In this process, the state has sequentially protected civil rights (e.g., the right to contract), then political rights
(e.g., voting and association), and now an expanding array of social rights
(e.g., education). It has done so directly (by enacting laws), and indirectly (by
empowering rights-demanding institutions like labor unions). In Marshall's
account, this gradual expansion of rights, the ever-greater inclusiveness of the

community of rights holders, is certainly progressive, driven by powerful logics of equality and participation. He does not claim, however, that this ascent is teleological; it is a process not of self-propelled inevitability but of contingent social and political struggle. And each stage, he insists, entails the curtailment of the free market and of the class inequalities that free markets characteristically engender.[54]

Justification. If the nationalistic model is grounded in a concern for demo-cratic consent, and the human rights model seeks to protect individuals, the Marshallian model aspires to social equality for all citizens, including their equal access to those resources that are essential for full and equal participa-tion in community life. For Marshall himself, equality is not the only good but it is certainly the greatest good, one to which other values—in particular, economic growth—must be subordinated.[55]

Role of Territoriality. As noted earlier, Marshall's discussion of citizenship has little to say about territoriality, perhaps because he assumes the autonomy of the nation-state and specifically his own, the United Kingdom. This assumption is important because, unlike the other models, Marshall's fails to discuss large-scale immigration and the consequent claims against the state by noncitizens, a phenomenon that is central today. He is concerned only with the rights of citizens against their conventional, territorially based state. It is striking, and odd, that he does not mention the massive displacements caused by refugee movements in Europe in the wake of World War II, much less consider their enormous—and problematic—implications for his thesis.

Entitlements. Marshall's specific focus is the evolution of rights in the UK, and his account is historically situated in a period of British social policy inno-vation centering on the construction of a new welfare state out of the ruins of World War II. Nevertheless, his analysis also applies, *mutatis mutandis*, to the United States and any other modern liberal or social democracy where, very broadly speaking, a similar evolution from civil to political to social rights has unfolded to the point where the nature and extent of those social rights are a major site of political conflict. In the remainder of this essay, I shall briefly consider how this vision has fared in the United States compared with Europe, and why it has fared so differently in the two places.[56]

Marshallian Social Entitlements in the United States and Europe

Marshall's vision of social entitlements reflects the time when he wrote—at an early stage in the development of the modern welfare state. Perhaps for that reason, he is very short on specifics. The rights that he does mention—legal aid, social insurance to reduce risk and insecurity, public education, housing, and a fair wage structure—were then being gradually introduced. Marshall did not favor equal outcomes, which he thought impracticable, given innate differences in abilities, the market's propensity to recreate inequality, and the practical impossibility of having the state perform the constant readjustment of incomes required to maintain equal results.[57] Instead, he favored equal opportunity, suggesting that the state would have to establish new or expanded social rights in order to ensure that these inequalities did not exceed an evolving level of social acceptability and thereby threaten his notion of full (and to this extent, equal) citizenship. By and large, these entitlements have become widely accepted.

In the United States—and in all other countries, for reasons to be explained below—the proper shape and magnitude of these entitlements remain matters of intense debate. The American welfare state has evolved in fits and starts. It began with very limited, targeted programs in the early nineteenth century for communities and individuals victimized by various kinds of catastrophes, such as floods and Indian raids.[58] After the Civil War, veterans' family pensions were established.[59] In the 1920s, many states, aided by federal matching funds, adopted programs to support the blind, maternal and child health, and some widows. The New Deal ushered in many new entitlements, especially under the Social Security Act of 1935 and farm subsidy programs, and other nonentitlement welfare programs such as public housing. In the 1950s, Congress funded state vocational education and rehabilitation programs and expanded disability benefits. In the 1960s, the Great Society programs such as Medicare, Medicaid, and the Food Stamp Program were created. In the 1970s, the Earned Income Tax Credit (EITC) and Supplemental Security Income (SSI) were adopted, as well as new special-education and job-training programs. The 1980s and 1990s saw major expansions of Medicare, Medicaid, food stamps, EITC, child care subsidies, and guaranteed loans. An enormous drug benefit subsidy under Medicare went into effect in 2006. Congress has steadily expanded entitlements for farmers, students, children, parents, minorities, and others.[60] Many states have done likewise. According to a recent government report, 16.2 percent of Americans' income consisted of federal and state safety-net payments, the highest percentage since the government began compiling records in 1929.[61]

There is always much talk, especially in Republican administrations, of rolling back the welfare state. In fact, actual retrenchment in nominal terms has occurred very rarely. Even the Welfare Reform Act of 1996, endorsed by President Clinton and widely denounced (and praised) as a significant cutback, actually increased the amount of federal funds going to the states for welfare-to-work support services. Welfare rolls have increased sharply during the current recession.[62] And as noted earlier, many states have restored welfare benefits for those immigrants whom the 1996 act had rendered ineligible, and Congress recently expanded such benefits for refugees and others.[63] Neither of these groups votes, of course, so it is difficult to explain these benefit expansions in terms of conventional interest-group politics.[64] Many entitlement programs help the poor (e.g., Medicaid and food stamps) and others help the working class (e.g., EITC). Still others, however, are regressive as a matter of distributive justice; they favor more fortunate and politically entrenched groups such as higher-income farmers, the elderly, college students, suburbanites, homeowners, and those accumulating tax-favored pensions.

The immensity of these entitlements overall might suggest that Marshallian citizenship is flourishing in the United States. Yet it is common to speak of the United States as a "welfare state laggard" compared to the European welfare states. As we shall see, the nature of the American welfare state is more complicated than the "laggard" label suggests.

The canonical work comparing the U.S. and European welfare states, published in 2004 by economists Alberto Alesina and Edward Glaeser, concludes that the U.S. system is "much less generous."[65] The authors show, for example, that government expenditures on social programs in 1998 were 15 percent of gross domestic product in the United States and 25.5 percent in Europe on average—an enormous difference that even the possibly greater target efficiency of American programs could not fully explain.[66]

One possible explanation for this difference—that Americans are less generous toward the poor—is clearly false. Americans are vastly more charitable toward the poor and more generally. Social scientist Arthur Brooks has addressed this comparison.[67] Brooks shows that the differences are mostly attributable to Americans' far greater religiosity; that most of this charity goes not to religious activities but to secular ones such as education, health, and social welfare; that low-income families give away a higher percentage of their incomes than do better-off families (especially if the former's income is from earned wages rather than government transfers); and that self-described "conservatives" are more likely to give, and give more generously, than self-described "liberals" with comparable incomes.[68] Alesina and Glaeser present additional data consistent with Brooks's claim that Americans are more charitable than Europeans, and speculate that "public provision of welfare (in Europe) in part crowds out private charity" and that "Europe's more generous provision of welfare does not stem from a greater innate endowment of altruism in Europe."[69]

If greater generosity toward the poor does not explain Europe's more extensive redistribution through the welfare state, what does? Alesina and Glaeser find little explanatory power for America's less extensive redistributive policies in purely economic variables (e.g., differences in the pretax distribution of income, in social mobility and income uncertainty, and in the costs of effectuating redistribution), but they do find differences in geography and political institutions to be important. They emphasize the absence of any devastating wars on U.S. soil since 1865; the barriers that a vast continent posed to an effective socialist movement and party; the lack of proportional representation; a form of federalism that leaves many redistributive functions to states and localities; and a system of checks and balances that hinders far-reaching changes in social policy in the absence of a national crisis.[70]

But the most powerful single factor, in their view, is racial hostility, which they say "can explain approximately one-half of the difference in the degree of redistribution between the United States and Europe."[71] They insist that the "importance of ethnic fractionalization cannot be overemphasized. The ethnic and racial fragmentation of the United States' working class interfered with the formation of a unified and powerful labor movement and Socialist Party. Racial fragmentation is correlated with income differences. . . . A less generous welfare state is in part due to the fact that the white majority does not want to redistribute in a way that would favor racial minorities." They further note, "In Sweden, say, where 95 percent of the population has the same race, ethnicity, and religion, it is much more difficult to identify the poor with some racial characteristics. Once again, racial conflicts can also be used strategically by political entrepreneurs interested not . . . in 'hating blacks' but in preventing redistribution."[72] In this way, they argue, Americans' racial hostility has led to an ideology profoundly skeptical of redistribution.

Finally, Alesina and Glaeser emphasize "huge" U.S.-European differences in popular attitudes toward individualism, the causes of poverty, and its remedies:[73]

> Europeans maintain a belief that birth determines status and the poor are trapped. Americans believe that they live in a land of opportunity where the people who stay poor are those who are too lazy to pull themselves up by their own bootstraps. . . . Across countries, places that believe that the poor are trapped are much more likely to redistribute than countries that do not have this belief. Across the United States, the states where more people believe that achievement is determined by family background are more likely to have more generous welfare payments.[74]

These distinctive American attitudes, the authors claim, persist in the face of certain realities that might seem to refute them. For example, they cite data indicating that the poor seem to work as hard in the United States as in Europe, and that, contrary to the Horatio Alger myth, social mobility in the United States has stalled and is no longer greater than in some European countries.

The Alesina and Glaeser analysis goes a long way toward explaining why the victory of Marshallian citizenship in Europe has been more complete than in the United States. Attitudinal, institutional, and political differences matter enormously, and they all seem to cut causally in the same direction: favoring a more limited welfare state in America than in Europe. Nevertheless, several complicating factors—particularly immigration, demographic trends, and the continuing economic crisis—will fundamentally shape the future of this vision in the United States and Europe.

Size. Alesina and Glaeser underestimate the size of the American welfare state by considering only national governmental budgets.[75] They therefore miss the most important feature of the American welfare state—its reliance on private provision of certain benefits through policy instruments whose costs are not wholly reflected in public budgets.[76] Tax credits, tax subsidies, loan guarantees, regulatory mandates, and other incentives to private employers and providers finance health insurance, retirement pensions, unemployment compensation, worker's compensation, educational tuition support, child subsidies, and many other benefits provided directly by government in Europe. In addition, many social programs in the United States, most notably Medicaid and many worker benefits, are joint federal-state programs in which the states finance much of the cost. Moreover, the largest and most important of these programs targeting the poor—particularly Medicaid, food stamps, Section 8 housing, and the EITC—have expanded significantly not only over the last two decades but even in recent years. If these off-budget "tax expenditures" and nonfederal payments were included in the tally, the American welfare state would be more comparable to its foreign counterparts.

Perhaps most important, when the U.S.-Europe comparison includes in-kind benefits and indirect taxes (e.g., sales, value-added, property taxes, and taxes on the benefits), the magnitude of the differences in transfers and inequality is substantially reduced, particularly at the lower end of the income distribution.[77] According to a recent comparative analysis:

> What distinguishes the United States from other rich nations is not so much our overall level of spending or the degree of inequality of tortal resources at the bottom of the income distribution, but rather the kinds of resources being transferred. Comparatively speaking, United States spending is very low on cash benefits and early childhood education, relatively high on education, and very high on health care. The United States spends enough on health care transfers to reduce the economic distance between low-income families and average-income families nearly as much as do other rich nations.[78]

Immigration. Alesina and Glaeser discuss immigration's effect on redistribution in the United States in a one-dimensional way, focusing largely on how ethnic heterogeneity impeded the kind of leftist solidarity that produced welfare states in the far more homogeneous Europe. While their account is correct as far as it goes, it is only part of the story.

First, the authors fail to note how the relatively high levels of immigration to the United States complicate their comparisons of inequality, poverty, and mobility levels in the two places. Immigrants, entering with much lower human capital than the American average, inevitably increase U.S. poverty and inequality measures. At the same time, immigrants vastly increase their incomes over their premigration levels. Yet general mobility measures ignore this dramatic improvement in immigrants' life prospects.[79]

Second, the American immigration mythos—the conviction that people who leave miserable conditions and come here with nothing but their determination to succeed can achieve the American dream—has profoundly affected Americans' beliefs about social mobility. The authors acknowledge that this "must play some role in the beliefs about the bounty of the American economy," but quickly add that the American belief in mobility is not true "either today or even in the past when the foundations of the welfare state were laid out."[80] But as just noted, whatever the current levels of mobility among the U.S.-born, it is very misleading for a mobility analysis to ignore immigrants' dramatic improvements over their premigration conditions, particularly when the foreign-born now constitute more than 12 percent of the population.

Third, the rapid increase of immigration to Europe in recent decades constitutes an enormous challenge to its welfare states. Alesina and Glaeser recognize this challenge, noting the rise of right-wing populist, xenophobic parties in Europe pursuing "exactly the same form of racist, anti-welfare demagoguery that worked so effectively in the United States. We shall see whether the generous European welfare state can really survive in a hetero-geneous society."[81] There are good reasons to believe that it cannot. European societies—in rather stark contrast with the United States—seem uncongenial, if not hostile, to the prospect of effectively integrating the growing racial, eth-nic, and religious diversity in their midst.[82] Absent such integration, the sol-idaristic feelings that underlay those welfare states in the past will likely be attenuated when applied to immigrants with whom Europeans feel they have little in common. This seems especially likely if the relatively slow economic growth, high unemployment, high tax rates, and rigidly regulated labor mar-kets that have been endemic in Europe continue. And unlike the United States, Europe lacks a tradition of extensive private charity to the poor that could help to fill the gap, probably because of its long-standing commitment to statism and, increasingly, secularism.

Demography. Even more threatening to European welfare states are the dire implications of their low fertility rates for the future fiscal viability of their social programs. Compounding this demographic problem are their already high tax rates, which cannot be raised to fund these programs without courting grave economic risks. These constraints contrast sharply with the American situation. Population trends in the United States—replacement fertility rates among natives, aided by high-fertility, revenue-generating immigration—are more favorable to its programs' fiscal viability. Moreover, individual marginal tax rates are generally much lower than in Europe (except perhaps in the highest-taxing American states and localities).[83]

Privatization. There are signs that European states are moving in the American direction of privatizing portions of their welfare states. Indeed, the pension systems in traditionally statist Sweden and some of the Baltic countries are being privatized more completely than in the United States. Despite fierce ideological pressures within their party, the Laborites under Tony Blair privatized some of the UK's previously sacrosanct health care and social services programs. France, Germany, Italy, and Denmark, under more market-friendly governments, have been experimenting with a greater role for private provision in social programs. Liberalizing labor markets has become a reform priority for even leftist governments in Europe.[84] This will certainly reduce the perceived gap between the U.S. and European welfare states.

Globalization. Increasing competition from low-wage countries will surely reduce the leeway within which states can continue to undertake economically inefficient welfare-program transfers without sacrificing some of their competitive edge in world markets. While not all such transfers are necessarily inefficient, any inefficiencies that redistribution causes will be harder to sustain as globalization proceeds. France's recent decision to retreat from its thirty-five-hour workweek reflects this inescapable reality, as does Germany's reconsideration of its generous vacation and disability benefits. Such international economic pressures on traditional welfare states seem likely to intensify in the future.

Intra-EU Dynamics. I speculate that the EU's massive subsidies to its relatively poor member states, particularly to the most recent entrants from Central and Eastern Europe, are pressing the limits of the union's altruism, especially in its remarkable project of internal (EU-to-states) redistribution. These limits, along with most EU states' fear of immigration and their concern that they may encourage even more of it by aiding economic development in the poorer states, partly explain the EU's hestiation in admitting other poor countries in the future (even aside from the special case of Turkey), as well as its paralysis on the issue of reducing EU farm subsidies within the GATT framework, a paralysis shared by the United States. If those altruistic limits have indeed been reached at the EU-to-states level, it may be that future intrastate redistributions through social welfare programs will be limited as well. At the very least, national politicians and their constituents may perceive a growing zero-sum conflict between internal and external redistributions.

But Europe has not only reached the limits of intrastate altruism and redistribution. The mechanism of political-constitutional integration at the EU level also seems to have stalled (and potentially reversed), as some arrogated EU powers devolve back to the member states and perhaps even to substate regions in a reassertion of the federalist and subsidiary principles. The prospects for ratification of the Lisbon Treaty seem quite dim at this time,[85] particularly given the recession-related intensification of pressures for more nationalistic economic policies. How these EU-wide dynamics will affect the members' domestic welfare-state commitments remains uncertain.

The Economic Crisis. The duration and long-term consequences of the deep recession that engulfed the world in 2008 are impossible to predict. Even so, it seems clear that programs to enlarge Mashallian rights will be constrained in the future by policies in both Europe and the United States seeking to reverse the decline, restore economic growth, and manage the immense burden of additional public debt undertaken to fund antirecession spending. In the United States, enactment of health insurance reform would narrow the Marshallian rights gap with Europe, but would also limit the political and fiscal space available for other forms of redistribution.

Conclusion

Not so long ago, many theoretically inclined observers believed that history was ineluctably leading modern liberal democracies toward ever-greater de-territorialized inclusiveness and expanding welfare-state citizenship. These predictions were made by some on both the left (prayerfully) and the right (mournfully). But like "the end of history" that some glimpsed in the Soviet Union's demise,[86] this prospect seems to be receding. In Europe, I suspect, the fiscal consequences of demographic change, the solidarity-reducing effects of immigration, and the efficiency-driven austerities induced by globalization will accelerate this recession.

In the less statist United States, perhaps paradoxically, Marshallian rights are likely to grow with a modest expansion of the welfare state. This expansion is dictated by an aging population that emphatically votes its interests and by pent-up demand for more social spending. Officials elected in November 2008 are already responding to these demands, now fortified by the hardships inflicted by high unemployment levels.[87] The beneficiaries of any such expansion, however, will likely be limited largely to the body of citizens, which is the site of the felt solidarities necessary to sustain such an expansion emotionally and politically.

At the same time, America's political culture, ideology, and institutions conspire to render most unlikely the extension of the franchise to noncitizens,[88] one of the paramount goals of proponents of human rights citizenship. This will remain true despite growing global interdependencies. Indeed, the frustrations engendered by this reduced sense of national autonomy could cause Americans—again, paradoxically—to respond in ways that are inimical to the human rights vision, as they seek the "kitchen comforts" of familiar tradition and conventional legal categories in a kind of retreat from bewildering complexity, uncertainty, and greater global dependency.[89] At the very least, the political, policy, and conceptual implications of global interconnectedness for how we do and should think about citizenship will remain deeply contested. Ultimately, this debate will be conducted largely on the basis of long-standing moral paradigms.

Thus the traditional notion of territoriality will continue to shape the nationalistic vision of American citizenship, yielding only at the margin to the human rights demands for more universalist duties to those currently viewed as strangers or in-betweens. To the moral question "To whom do we owe special duties of support and concern?" the answer (setting refugees and foreign policy responsibilities aside) will continue to be "Americans" and perhaps long-term legal residents. This enduring tension is complicated in interesting ways by the widespread belief among Americans that the United States is *already* the preeminent, if not only, "universal nation," one that both embodies and advances universal ideals such as individual freedom, tolerance, assimilation, the rule of law, and discharging universal duties such as maintenance of world order.[90]

America's stature in these respects compares very favorably with its competitor nations. Other ethnically diverse, immigrant-welcoming nations like Canada and Australia have very small populations in comparison and have no interest in an order-maintenance role. India has the population and extraordinary diversity, but its internal cohesion and tolerance are under constant, serious challenge.[91] Europe has a larger aggregate population than the United States, but its global influence is modest and its openness to diversity is very much in question. Despite enormous demographic pressures, Japan remains militantly homogeneous. China, while economically expansive, is politically and culturally inward-turning and repressive, at least for now.

America's religious, ethnic, and regional diversities and its political culture of individualism, decentralization, privatism, and suspicion of government have rendered the construction and maintenance of national solidarity a perennial challenge, but one that has been met with remarkable success, *comparatively speaking*.[92] The future will only deepen this challenge, with growing political polarization, Internet-driven social fragmentation, a deep economic crisis, and what seems to be the growing incompetence of federal government performance relative to the demands placed upon it. To many Americans, the government's remarkably maladroit response to Hurricane Katrina, its tragically incompetent administration of postinvasion Iraq, and its failure to solve the vote-counting problem even eight years after Florida's fiasco in the 2000 presidential election—performances denounced by liberals and conservatives alike—will tend to discredit new calls for government-led pursuit of "national greatness." This seems likely to deepen rather than disarm our ancient skepticisms.

In such an environment, a distinctively liberal, individualistic, privatistic form of nationalist citizenship will continue to flourish, although that will surely be chastened by the market (and governmental) failures that contributed to the economic meltdown. Our peculiar notions of citizenship, I suspect, will continue to bewilder Europeans even as they edge their way inexorably toward their own, more communitarian, version of it.

Notes

1. I have discussed the *positive* characteristics of citizenship law in the United States and elsewhere in earlier work. Peter H. Schuck, *Citizenship in Federal Systems*, 48 Am. J. Comp. L. 195 (2000); Peter H. Schuck, Citizens, Strangers, and In-Betweens: Essays on Immigration and Citizenship chs. 7–8 (1998). For a general survey of citizenship law, *see* Dual Nationality, Social Rights and Federal Citizenship in the U.S. and Europe: The Reinvention of Citizenship (Randall Hansen and Patrick Weil eds., 2002); From Migrants to Citizens: Membership in a Changing World (Alexander Aleinikoff and Douglas B. Klusmeyer eds., 2000).

2. T. H. Marshall, Citizenship and Social Class (1950).

3. For an elaboration of this trichotomy, *see* Schuck, Citizens, Strangers, and In-Betweens, *supra* note 1. One in-between status is that of denizen, which in some states is the highest status a foreigner can attain short of citizenship.

4. On the American case, *see* Rogers M. Smith, Civic Ideals: Conflict Visions of Citizenship in U.S. History (1997). On other nations' citizenship laws, *see* From Migrants to Citizens, *supra* note 1; Dual Nationality, *supra* note 1, and, more skeletally, Rita Simon & Alison Brooks, The Rights and Responsibilties of Citizenship the World Over (2008).

5. My choice of the term "nationalistic" to characterize the model calls for a clarification of the terms nation, state, and nation-state. A state is a legal-political entity that consists of a governmental apparatus exercising internationally recognized legal authority over a territory and the people within it. A nation is a self-conscious community of people who share (or in Benedict Anderson's classic formulation, *imagine* that they share) an identity based on culture, descent, ethnicity, language, religion, or other commonality. *See* Benedict Anderson, Imagined Communities (rev'd ed. 1991). A nation-state (such as Japan) is an entity in which statehood and nationhood are coterminous—although the term is often used more loosely to describe states that are not nations in this strict sense. From a nation's perspective, the legal boundaries of a state may seem arbitrary and, in cases where the state refuses to recognize nationhood, perhaps a provocation to violence. From the perspective of a state, the claim of nationhood by those within and without its borders may likewise seem arbitrary and may constitute either a threat (as with Turkey and its Kurds) or an opportunity (as with a revanchist Russia and the Russian speakers in South Ossetia). I use "nationalistic" to refer to a state's use of citizenship as an instrument of political self-definition, which may involve the assertion of a robust nationhood, albeit one (as in the American case) that is based on a civic rather than an ethno-cultural conception of national community.

6. *See, e.g.*, Roper v. Simmons, 543 U.S. 551 (2005).

7. Peter J. Spiro, Beyond Citizenship: American Identity After Globalization 109–10 (2008).

8. The relevant titles are Samuel P. Huntingon, Who Are We? The Challenges to America's National Identity (2004); John J. Miller, The Unmaking of Americans: How

Multiculturalism Has Undermined the Assimilation Ethic (1998); Peter Brimelow, Alien Nation: Common Sense about America's Immigration Disaster (1996); and Georgie Anne Geyer, Americans No More (1996).

9. The relevant titles are Michael Walzer, What It Means to Be an American (1996); Kenneth L. Karst, Belonging to America: Equal Citizenship and the Constitution (1989); David Miller, On Nationality (1995); Smith, Civic Ideals, *supra* note 4; and Schuck, Citizens, Strangers, and In-Betweens, *supra* note 1, at ch. 8. I discuss (and critique) the existing liberal approach to naturalization law in Peter H. Schuck, *Whose Membership Is It, Anyway? Comments on Gerald Neuman*, 35 Va. J. Int'l L. 321 (1994).

10. Spiro, *supra* note 7 at 115.

11. This is doubtful. *See, e.g.*, Andrew Hacker, *Patriot Games*, N.Y. Rev. Books, June 24, 2004 (critiquing Samuel P. Huntington, *supra* note 8); Louis Menand, *Patriot Games: The New Nativism of Samuel P. Huntington*, New Yorker, May 17, 2004 (same).

12. *See, e.g.*, Noah Pickus, True Faith and Allegiance: Immigration and American Civic Nationalism 175–78 (2005); Peter D. Salins, Assimilation, American-Style (1997). For a critique of this position, *see* Spiro, *supra* note 7, at 114. *See also* Kirk Semple, *Citizenship Seekers Told Not to Fear a New Test*, N.Y. Times, Sept. 24, 2008, at B3.

13. Spiro, *supra* note 7, at 9.

14. For a significant but unknown and probably unknowable number of immigrants, the birth of their children here is no accident. This is hardly surprising given the advantages of American citizenship to the children.

15. Peter H. Schuck and Rogers M. Smith, Citizenship Without Consent: Illegal Aliens in the American Polity (1985).

16. *Plyler v. Doe*, 457 U.S. 202, 211 n.10 (1982).

17. As a policy matter (not a constitutional one), birthright citizenship has many advantages in facilitating immigrant assimilation, advantages that some European states have begun to recognize, albeit in more restrictive versions than the American one.

18. Immigration and Nationality Act, sec. 349(a)(5) and (6), 8 U.S.C.A. §§ 1481(a)(5) and (6).

19. 387 U.S. 253 (1967).

20. For a summary of this jurisprudence, *see* Thomas Alexander Aleinikoff, David A. Martin, Hiroshi Motomura, and Maryellen Fullerton, Immigration and Citizenship: Process and Policy 115–26 (6th ed., 2008).

21. This history is summarized in Justice Harlan's dissenting opinion in *Afroyim*, 387 U.S. at 271–82 (Harlan, J., dissenting).

22. Immigration and Nationality Act sec. 349(a), 8 U.S.C.A. § 1481(a).

23. Immigration and Nationality Act, sec. 301, 8 U.S.C.A. § 1401.

24. On the history of dual nationality in American law, *see* Spiro, *supra* note 7, at ch. 3. *But see Schneider v. Rusk*, 377 U.S. 163 (1964) (invalidating statute that expatriated a naturalized citizen who then returned to his native country and resided there for three years).

25. *See Rasul v. Bush*, 542 U.S. 466 (2004) (habeas corpus available to those in U.S. custody in a place (Guantanamo Bay prison) over which the United States exercises

"complete jurisdiction and control," though not "ultimate sovereignty"). *See generally* Gerald L. Neuman, Strangers to the Constitution: Immigrants, Borders, and Fundamental Law (1996).

26. Spiro, *supra* note 7, at 18–19.

27. Abraham Lincoln, Second Inaugural Address, *reprinted in* This Fiery Trial: The Speeches and Writings of Abraham Lincoln 183 (William E. Gienapp ed., 2002).

28. Peter H. Schuck and James Q. Wilson, *Looking Back*, in Understanding America: The Anatomy of an Exceptional Nation 628–29 (Peter H. Schuck and James Q. Wilson eds., 2008).

29. *See, e.g.*, Salins, *supra* note 12, at 216; Miller, *supra* note 8.

30. Peter H. Schuck, *Taking Immigration Federalism Seriously*, 2007 U. Chi. L. F. 57, 60–64 . The most interesting example is in-state tuition benefits for the undocumented, which have been challenged in state and federal courts. *E.g.*, Martinez v. Univ. of Cal., 83 Cal. Rptr. 3d 518 (Cal. App. 3d), *cert. granted*, 198 P.3d 1 (Cal. 2008) (reversing dismissal of class action suit alleging that California's authorization of in-state higher education tuition for illegal aliens violates federal law); *see* Michael A. Olivas, *Lawmakers Gone Wild? College Residency and the Response to Professor Kobach*, 61 SMU L. Rev. 99, 108–29 (2008). Some states are also authorizing the issuance of drivers' licenses to the undocumented.

31. Pub. L. No. 110-328.

32. *See* Olivas, *supra* note 30.

33. A recent example is *Chicanos Por La Causa, Inc. v. Napolitano*, 544 F.3d 976 (9th Cir., Sept. 17, 2008) (upholding Arizona employer sanctions law against preemption challenge). For an extended argument in favor of a greater role for the states in immigration enforcement, *see* Schuck, *supra* note 30.

34. *Boumediene v. Bush*, 128 S. Ct. 2229 (2008).

35. For brief reflections on this debate, see Peter H. Schuck, *The Meaning of American Citizenship in a Post-9/11 World*, 75 Fordham L. Rev. 2531, 2531–40 (2007). Some other battlegrounds are the appropriate use of foreign law in American constitutional interpretation; *see, e.g.*, the majority and dissenting opinions in *Roper v. Simmons*, 543 U.S. 551 (2005) (capital punishment of minors), and America's stance toward participation in international bodies. *See* Jason Ralph, Defending the Society of States: Why America Opposes the International Criminal Court and its Vision of World Society (2007).

36. A new book refers to this as "global citizenship." Gender Equality: Dimensions of Women's Equal Citizenship 3 (Linda C. McClain and Joanna L. Grossman eds., 2009).

37. For present purposes, I put to one side notoriously difficult questions concerning what we mean by equal treatment, the characteristics of individuals or contexts that may justify differential treatment (notwithstanding a general commitment to equality), the tradeoffs that may attend an egalitarian program, the relationship between procedural and substantive equality, and the like.

38. *See* articles in *Symposium: A Tribute to the Work of Kim Barry*, 81 N.Y.U. L. Rev. 1 (2006). The current economic recession has substantially reduced this migration to,

and remittances from, the United States. Elizabeth Malkin, *Money Sent Home by Mexican Workers in U.S. Falls Sharply*, N.Y. Times, June 2, 2009, at A5.

39. *See, e.g.*, Stephen Gardbaum, *Human Rights as International Constitutional Rights*, 19 Eur. J. Int'l. L. 749 (2008).

40. For a list of published indices of freedom, see http://en.wikipedia.org/wiki/List_of_indices_of _freedom.

41. *See* Peter J. Spiro, *New Global Communities: Nongovernmental Organizations in International Decision-Making Institutions*, 18 Wash. Q. 45 (1995).

42. For the spirit and potential scope of this inclusiveness, see Kevin R. Johnson, Opening the Floodgates: Why America Needs to Rethink Its Borders and Immigration Laws (2007) (arguing for essentially unlimited immigration except for exclusion of criminals, potential terrorists, and so forth).

43. For the view that territoriality is more inclusive than status-based systems, *see* Linda S. Bosniak, 8 Theoretical Inquiries in Law 389 (2007).

44. Thus, Ayelet Shachar criticizes birthright citizenship as the legal equivalent of an inherited property right that reinforces and magnifies existing morally unacceptable global inequalities. *See* Ayelet Shachar, The Birthright Lottery: Citizenship and Global Inequality (2009); Ayelet Shachar and Ran Hirschl, *Citizenship as Inherited Property*, 35 Legal Theory 253 (2008).

45. As Linda Bosniak points out, "EU citizenship represents a dramatic reconstitution of citizenship in Europe. . . . Nevertheless, EU citizenship remains grounded in, and derivative of, the citizenships of the constituent national states, and . . . is still subordinate to those citizenships in important respects." *Supra* note 43, at 25.

46. *E.g.*, Spiro, *supra* note 7.

47. Hiroshi Motomura, Americans in Waiting: The Lost Story of Immigration and Citizenship in the United States 10 (2006) (on "territorial personhood"). Few of the model's expositors squarely address whether, and to what extent, the state may legitimately discriminate among noncitizens, and between them and citizens, in defining eligibility for entitlements according to the duration, purposes, or links created by their presence in the host country. Motomura is a limited exception. He would grant certain of these rights, notably welfare benefits, only until the migrant has had a full opportunity to naturalize and has failed to do so.

48. European Community Treaty, art. 19, sec. 8(b).

49. *Id.*

50. Jose A. Cabranes, *Citizenship and the American Empire*, 127 U. Pa. L. Rev. 391 (1978); Foreign in a Domestic Sense: Puerto Rico, American Expansion, and the Constitution (Christina Duffy Burnett & Burke Marshall eds., 2001).

51. Spiro, *supra* note 7, at 60. For a more cautious endorsement of plural citizenship, see Schuck, Citizens, Strangers, and In-Betweens, *supra* note 1, at ch. 10.

52. Convention on the Rights of the Child, Nov. 20, 1989, 1577 U.N.T.S. 3 (the United States has not ratified the convention); Convention Against Torture and Other Cruel, Inhuman, or Degrading Treatment or Punishment, Dec. 10, 1984, S. Treaty Doc.

No. 100-20 (1988), 1465 U.N.T.S. 85; U.S. Refugee Act of 1980, Pub. L. No. 96-212, 94 Stat. 102 (codified at 8 U.S.C. §§ 1101–1125 and 22 U.S.C. § 2601 (1980)) (codifying the Refugee Convention); Convention on the Elimination of All Forms of Discrimination Against Women, G.A. Res. 34/180/Annex, U.N. GAOR, 34th Sess., Supp. No. 46, U.N. Doc. 34/180-79 (Dec. 18, 1979) (the United States has not ratified the convention); International Covenant on Civil and Political Rights, Dec. 19, 1966, S. Exec. Doc. E, 95-2 (1978), 999 U.N.T.S. 171; International Covenant on Economic Social and Cultural Rights, Dec. 16, 1966, 993 U.N.T.S. 3 (the United States has not ratified the covenant).

53. Seymour Martin Lipset, *Introduction*, in Class, Citizenship, and Social Development: Essays by T. H. Marshall ix–x (1964).

54. Marshall does countenance inequalities "provided that they do not cut too deep, but occur within a population united in a single civilization; and provided they are not an expression of hereditary privilege." Marshall, *supra* note 2, at 116.

55. *Id.*

56. For a more extensive discussion, see Gary Burtless and Ron Haskins, *Inequality, Economic Mobility, and Social Policy*, in Understanding America, *supra* note 28, ch. 17.

57. Marshall, *supra* note 2, at 102–03, 109, 116.

58. Michele Landis Dauber, The Sympathetic State: Disaster Relief and the Origins of the American Welfare State (2004).

59. Theda Skocpol, Protecting Soldiers and Mothers: The Political Origins of Social Policy in the United States (1992).

60. Some of these entitlements take the form of tax expenditures. *See* Christopher Howard, The Hidden Welfare State: Tax Expenditures and Social Policy in the United States (2001).

61. Dennis Cauchon, *Benefit spending soars to new high*, USA Today, June 4, 2009, at 1.

62. Sara Murray, *Numbers on Welfare See Sharp Increase*, Wall St. J., June 22, 2009, at A1.

63. *See* text accompanying notes 30–31, *supra*.

64. *But see* Schuck, Citizens, Strangers, and In-Betweens, *supra* note 1, at ch. 4.

65. Alberto Alesina and Edward L. Glaeser, Fighting Poverty in the US and Europe: A World of Difference 219 (2004).

66. *Id.* at 18–20. The authors also note some differences in definitions and data points.

67. "No developed country approaches American giving and volunteering levels. For example, in 1995, Americans gave, per capita, three and a half times as much to causes and charities as the French, seven times as much as the Germans, and fourteen times as much as the Italians. Similarly, in 1998, Americans were 15 percentage points more likely to volunteer than the Dutch, 21 points more likely than the Swiss, and 32 points more likely than the Germans. These differences are not attributable to demographic characteristics such as education, income, age, sex, or marital status." Arthur C. Brooks, *Philanthropy and the Non-Profit Sector*, in Understanding America, *supra* note 28, at 539, 544.

68. *Id.* at 543, 550–53, 557.

69. Alesina and Glaeser, *supra* note 65, at 45. Americans may prefer private charity to public welfare for several reasons: they may believe private charity successfully

targets the "deserving poor" and promotes self-sufficiency and moral uplift, and that welfare by contrast is inefficient, bureaucratic, inflexible, and unaccountable; that it worsens poverty; and that it sends the wrong signals about the virtues of self-help and long-term independence. *See id.* at 44–45; Michael B. Katz, The Undeserving Poor: From the War on Poverty to the War on Welfare (1990); Marvin Olasky, The Tragedy of American Compassion (1992); and Charles A. Murray, Losing Ground: American Social Policy, 1950–1980 (1984). For an earlier version, *see* Alexis De Tocqueville, Memoir on Pauperism: Does Public Charity Produce an Idle and Dependent Class of Society? (1835).

70. Alesina and Glaeser, *supra* note 65, at chs. 4–5, and 219.

71. *Id.* at 181, and ch. 6 *generally*.

72. *Id.* at 218.

73. *Id.* at 216.

74. *Id.* at 184. They might have added that Americans are in fact experiencing more income volatility than in the 1970s, while having to bear more of that risk themselves because of reduced health insurance, reduced defined-benefit pensions, and other changes. *See generally* Jacob S. Hacker, The Great Risk Shift: The Assault on American Jobs, Families, Health Care, and Retirement and How You Can Fight Back (2006).

75. Alesina and Glaeser, *supra* note 65 at 49 ("All reported measures are for general government.").

76. *See generally* Howard, *supra* note 60.

77. Irwin Garfinkel, Lee Rainwater, and Timothy Smeeding, *A Re-examination of Welfare States and Inequality in Rich Nations: How In-kind Transfers and Indirect Taxes Change the Story*, 25 Journal of Policy Analysis and Management 897, 905–6 (2006).

78. *Id.* at 913.

79. *See* Burtless and Haskins, *supra* note 56, at 510–11. These statistical effects are less significant in Europe where immigration levels are generally much lower.

80. Alesina and Glaeser, *supra* note 65, at 191.

81. *Id.* at 181. *See also id.* at 175–77.

82. *See, e.g.*, John R. Bowen, Why the French Don't Like Headscarves: Islam, the State, and Public Space (2006).

83. *See* Nicholas Eberstadt, *Born in the USA*, Am. Int., May-June 2007, Edward C. Prescott, op-ed, *Are Europeans Lazy? No, Just Overtaxed*, Wall St. J., Oct. 24, 2004, at A21. To be sure, declining worker-to-beneficiary ratios in the United States do pose fiscal challenges to entitlement programs but the problem is far less serious than in Europe. And U.S. corporate tax rates are already relatively high. *America the Uncompetitive*, Wall St. J., Aug. 15, 2008, at A14.

84. *See* Mark Hyde et al., *Welfare Retrenchment or Collective Responsibility? The Privatisation of Public Pensions in Western Europe*, 2 Soc. Pol'y & Soc'y 189 (2003).

85. *See, e.g.*, Marc Champion and Charles Forelle, *Europe in Turmoil After Irish Vote*, Wall St. J., June 14, 2008, at A1 (explaining that Ireland's vote against the Lisbon Treaty "derailed plans aimed at making the European Union a stronger global player"). *See gen-*

erally Christoph Henkel, *The Allocation of Powers in the European Union: A Closer Look at the Principle of Subsidiarity*, 20 Berkeley J. Int'l L. 359, 371 (2002) (describing the adoption of the principle of subsidiarity as "a means to limit centralization").

86. The reference is to Francis Fukuyama, The End of History and the Last Man (1992). He was hardly alone in his heady optimism, which now seems tragicomically naive and mistaken.

87. Safety-net benefits paid in early 2009 were already at record levels. Cauchon, *supra* note 61.

88. This, despite the fact that many states allowed noncitizens to vote well into the twentieth century. *See* Jamin B. Raskin, *Legal Aliens, Local Citizens: The Historical, Constitutional and Theoretical Meanings of Alien Suffrage*, 141 U. Penn. L. Rev. 1452 (1993).

89. The phrase "kitchen comforts" comes from Kwame Anthony Appiah, *The Multiculturalist Misunderstanding*, N.Y. Rev. Books, Oct. 9, 2997, at 30, 32–33. Appiah himself favors a more inclusive zone of moral obligation. Appiah, Cosmopolitanism: Ethics in a World of Strangers ch. 10 (2006). On the notion of retreat, see Peter H. Schuck, *In Diversity We (Sorta) Trust*, Am. Lawyer, Dec. 2007, at 83–84 (discussing Robert Putnam's empirical findings on how diversity affects civic engagement in American communities).

90. *See, e.g.*, Michael Mandelbaum, The Case for Goliath: How America Acts as the World's Government in the 21st Century (2005). *See also* Josef Joffe, Überpower: America's Imperial Temptation (2006).

91. *E.g.*, Hari Kumar and Alan Cowell, *Dozens Die in Bomb Attacks in Northeast India*, N.Y. Times, A1 (Oct. 31, 2008); Somini Sengupta, *In World's Largest Democracy, Tolerance Is a Weak Pillar*, N.Y. Times (Oct. 28, 2008).

92. According to comparative survey data, Americans are far more patriotic than Europeans, with a deeper sense of nationhood and optimism. Schuck and Wilson, *supra* note 28, at 621–26, 628–29.

9

The Changing Nature of Citizenship in Britain: Constitutional and Legal Perspectives

Adam Tomkins

This paper explores the dynamics of citizenship in Britain. It commences by outlining the ways in which citizenship has been understood under the political constitution model, which has been dominant in British constitutional analysis for most of the twentieth century. It traces the origin of and the rationale for this model's understanding of "parliamentary citizenship." The paper then examines a recent review of citizenship commissioned by Prime Minister Gordon Brown, and explores some of its implications. It links this review of citizenship to broader, ongoing shifts in British constitutionalism away from the traditional model of the political constitution and toward a more legal or rights-based constitutionalism. The paper closes with some critical remarks about the implications of this shift for our understandings and practices of citizenship.

The Model of the Political Constitution

The British constitution has traditionally been seen as a political rather than a legal constitution.[1] It relies principally on political institutions, actors, and

I am grateful to Michael Greve and Bruce Smith for written comments on this paper in draft, and to Shep Melnick and all the conference participants who engaged in a lively and very useful discussion following the panel in which this paper was presented.

mechanisms to perform the core constitutional task of holding the government of the day accountable, rather than relying principally on legal institutions and mechanisms. This is a very unusual model of constitutionalism.[2] Almost all comparable constitutions in the United States, the Commonwealth, and Europe tend to privilege courts, judges, and constitutional adjudication over parliaments, politicians, and legislative scrutiny as the constitutional form of choice. After 1989, Eastern Europe famously looked to American and (West) German models, not to Britain.[3] Likewise, the dual "Europeanizations" of national constitutional law—under the European Union and its court, the European Court of Justice, and under the European Convention on Human Rights and its court, the European Court of Human Rights (ECHR)—have augmented legal constitutionalism at the expense of political constitutionalism.[4] The rule of law and the jurisprudence of fundamental, entrenched constitutional rights form the backbone of today's constitutional norm.[5] British parliamentarism has become the exception.

Courts, judges, and constitutional adjudication (even about constitutional rights) have not been unimportant in the British constitutional scheme. Likewise, even in the most committed "legal" constitution, political actors and mechanisms remain significant. At issue is the relationship, or balance, between the political and the legal—the question of which is privileged over the other. In Britain, the government of the day has owed its principal obligations of constitutional accountability and responsibility to Parliament rather than to the courts of law. While the rule of law in the British constitution has been relatively weak,[6] notions and practices of political responsibility have been strong. For example, it was decided as long ago as 1765 that all government actions require clear legal authorization; otherwise they are liable to be declared illegal by the courts.[7] While individuals may do anything not prohibited by law, the reverse is the case for the government: it is permitted to do nothing without clear legal authorization. This has not proved a difficult test for the government to meet.[8] If a minister wishes to act in a certain way and discovers that he lacks the requisite legal power, he must simply introduce a bill into Parliament which, when passed, confers that power on him. Because the government of the day generally controls Parliament's legislative agenda, this is not too bothersome an obstacle for a well-organized and successful government.

Similarly, for many years the primary standard for judicial review of administrative action in Britain was the doctrine of "*Wednesbury* unreasonableness," which allows the court to quash an administrative (or governmental) decision only if it is so unreasonable that no reasonable authority could have made it.[9] This tautological standard was expressly designed to limit judicial intervention in, and supervision of, public administration. In later case law, the test was refined such that the courts should intervene on this ground of review only where a decision maker had "taken leave of his senses," acted "perversely," or behaved in a way that was "outrageous in its defiance of logic or accepted moral standards."[10] Thus, if the government acts unreasonably, but not so unreasonably that its actions can be categorized as being perverse or illogical, its actions will be upheld as lawful. Citizens (or others: noncitizens may seek judicial review) aggrieved at the government's unreasonable actions are thereby encouraged to litigate only in the most extreme cases. In the ordinary course of events—where citizens disagree with the government and think it is acting unreasonably, but where the action is not so wrongheaded as to amount to a defiance of logic—citizens are encouraged to take their grievances elsewhere.[11]

Where, then, if not to the courts? The answer is, to Parliament. In the British constitutional scheme, Parliament, and in particular the House of Commons, has served as the people's representative—the "grand inquest of the nation" was the rather lofty term used in the nineteenth century.[12] The government has owed its principal constitutional obligations to Parliament and, in particular, to the House of Commons. Indeed, the very definition of "the government" suggests this. The British government is not directly elected. The House of Commons is directly elected. The government is formed (largely) out of the House of Commons,[13] and consists of members of Parliament (MPs) who, for the time being, enjoy the "confidence" of the House of Commons. (In contemporary practice, this normally means that the government enjoys majority support in the House.) The government may hold power for only as long as it continues to enjoy such confidence. The moment it loses the confidence of the Commons, it must resign. To my mind, this is the most fundamental rule of the British constitution. It is why the British constitution is described as a "political" or as a "parliamentary" constitution.

In the modern age, motions of "no confidence" are rare. The last British government to lose a formal vote of confidence was Prime Minister James Callaghan's Labor government of 1978–79. His government's loss of this vote led directly to the general election of 1979, won by Margaret Thatcher's

Conservative Party. The rarity of formal votes of confidence does not mean, however, that the government's constitutional accountability to Parliament is only an occasional occurrence. On the contrary, numerous parliamentary means have been developed to ensure the government's routine accountability. A core part of Parliament's daily business is to hold ministers to account. In the House of Commons, proceedings in the chamber and in committees work toward this end. Three of these proceedings merit mention: debates, questioning, and scrutiny by committees.

Debates in the chamber may deal with a particular legislative policy or with general scrutiny of the government's position on a certain issue. Such debates are, on the whole, well attended and of high quality. In Westminster, debates remain a significant part of what Parliament does. Debates of this type are likewise an extremely important function of the House of Lords.

The Commons also spends a considerable amount of time questioning ministers. About an hour of oral questions will be undertaken every parliamentary day, and the Prime Minister's Question Time (PMQT) occurs once each week for half an hour. While PMQT sometimes resembles a Punch and Judy show, or mere political pantomime, it can also be an extremely effective means of executing political judgment. Most parliamentary questions, though, are written rather than oral. Every day *Hansard* (the official record of parliamentary proceedings) contains many pages of ministerial answers to parliamentary questions. While Britain has only recently adopted freedom of information legislation (the Freedom of Information Act 2000 came fully into force only in 2005), written answers to parliamentary questions have long been a highly important means of eliciting information from ministers.

The committee work of the House of Commons has become much more important in the past thirty years. Since the 1979 reorganization of committees of the House of Commons, a departmental select committee for each government department has been charged with examining in detail the expenditure, administration, and policy of the department in question. Since 1979, the committees have been enormously successful. They are the unique preserve of the backbenches (no ministers may serve on them) and allow cross-party groups of MPs to develop specialist knowledge; no parliamentary mechanism achieves more detailed, expert, and rigorous scrutiny of government departments than the committees. The committees have full control over their own agendas and decide subjects of and methods for investigation. They employ a small staff and take written and oral evidence from a wide range of sources. A good select committee with an active chair can undertake four or five major inquiries each year. Such inquiries produce reports, which may be debated in Parliament and which may attract substantial media attention. Significantly, almost all select committee reports are unanimous. Recently, a number of select committees have scored important hits, leading to changes in government policy in areas as diverse as export control, child welfare, public transport, and reform of the public services. Where necessary, select committees can follow up their recommendations, keeping political pressure on the government to make concessions. In recent years they have started to work together, reinforcing each other's insistence that the government change track or make improvements.[14]

The importance of these practices is reflected in the *Ministerial Code*, a rule book of ministerial behavior given to all government ministers by the prime minister.[15] Paragraph 1 of the *Ministerial Code* provides *inter alia* that "Ministers have a duty to Parliament to account, and be held to account, for the policies, decisions and actions of their departments and agencies." Ministers are both accountable and responsible to Parliament for their own policies, decisions, and actions and for the policies, decisions, and actions of their departments. The duty of accountability is a duty to give an account of what has happened or of what is proposed to happen; it is a duty to provide information. The liability to be held to account is an obligation to take responsibility when things go wrong. Sanctions are imposed to enforce these rules, the ultimate sanction being a minister's resignation from office. Ministers who contravene the duties laid down in paragraph 1 of the *Ministerial Code* are expected to resign.[16]

Parliamentary Citizenship

What is the origin of, or explanation for, Britain's constitutional preoccupation with distinctively political or parliamentary means of governmental accountability? Why does Britain have this historical preference for parliamentary over (say) legal or judicial means of doing constitutional business? What has this to do with citizenship, and what does it suggest about practices and values of citizenship in Britain?

This last question is not difficult to answer. In Britain, citizenship has traditionally been seen mainly in *parliamentary* rather than in directly *popular* or *legal* terms. Citizenship has been neither about electing a government nor about having the power to expel the government. To repeat, the government is not directly elected. The House of Commons, not the people directly, decides when to withdraw confidence from the government. Neither has citizenship been conceived primarily in terms of conferring rights to sue or to seek judicial review in the courts of law. Citizenship in Britain has not principally involved the enjoyment of constitutional, fundamental, or human rights; it has not been guaranteed by ensuring that citizens can go to court to have such rights protected or enforced. Citizenship has been about having a representative—a Parliament—principally tasked with keeping the government under constant review. Parliament exists not only to legislate (although that is an important aspect of its work) but also to provide an essential, daily link between governed and government. In this sense, Parliament has been the institutional embodiment of citizenship in Britain. This sense of parliamentary citizenship, however, has recently come under challenge as the more "juristocratic" model of citizen-as-litigant has emerged. I return to this point below.

The origins of and explanations for parliamentary citizenship constitute difficult and contested territory. One matter must be cleared up straightaway. Whatever its motivations, British parliamentary citizenship is not, or at least was not conceived as, an expression of mass democracy. Its beginnings and development predate the emergence of democracy in Britain by at least two centuries. If it may now be regarded as an expression of mass democracy, this is by accident rather than by design.

Parliament and, in particular, the House of Commons emerged as the principal locus in the attempt to hold the Crown to some form of constitutional accountability in the seventeenth century.[17] It was not always thus. But Parliament felt compelled to adopt this role upon the demonstrable failure of the common-law courts to perform the task satisfactorily over the course of the first four decades of the seventeenth century, the rhetoric and efforts of Sir Edward Coke notwithstanding.[18] Somebody had to stop the abuses that occurred over the eleven-year period (1629–40) during which Charles I governed without calling Parliament. This was the period that saw, for example, the notorious ship-money, a form of extraparliamentary taxation whose legality the common-law judges upheld in the much-derided *Case of Ship-money*.[19]

If the courts would not or could not stop such abuses, the House of Commons would have to. When the House was finally recalled in 1640, political conflict between the Commons and the Crown was inevitable. What was *not* inevitable in 1640 was the conflict's escalation into the full-blown Civil War that consumed not only England but also Scotland and Ireland from 1642 to 1648, and that led to the trial and execution of the king in 1648–49.

Amid the chaos and violence of this period of English history, what we now recognize as the doctrines of ministerial accountability and responsible government emerged. As far as I have been able to discover, the first demand for these doctrines was expressed by Parliament in June 1642, in a document called the *Nineteen Propositions*.[20] The *Nineteen Propositions* included the following demands: that no one should serve in the Privy Council without express parliamentary approval; that the "great affairs of the kingdom . . . may be debated, resolved and transacted only in Parliament, and not elsewhere," ruling out any return to the nonparliamentary government of the 1630s; and that ministers and senior judges should be appointed only after having received parliamentary approval. To these claims should be added Parliament's insistence, in its Militia Ordinance of March 1642, that control of the militia should be vested exclusively in persons approved by the two houses. This was as direct an attack on the royal prerogative as Parliament had ever dared to mount. It was a bold and unambiguous declaration of intent that the king's government should rule exclusively *through* Parliament, thereby making it subject to—accountable to—Parliament's views.

Nearly half a century later, after a period of significant political turmoil, many of these claims found their way into legislation, albeit only after the Stuarts were finally expelled from the throne in the Glorious Revolution of 1688–89. Under the Bill of Rights of 1689, "levying money for or to the use of the Crown by pretence of prerogative, without grant of Parliament . . . is illegal,"[21] "raising or keeping a standing army within the kingdom in time of peace . . . is against law,"[22] and "the freedom of speech and debates or proceedings in Parliament ought not to be impeached or questioned in any court or place out of Parliament."[23] These provisions, which remain law to this day, outlaw any repetition of the policies of Charles I. It should be noted, however, that Parliament in 1689 did not win everything that it had claimed in 1642. Neither government ministers nor judges are required (as the *Nineteen Propositions* had posited) to have their nominations to office ratified before assuming their duties. In Britain ministers, if not judges, are required to account to Parliament *during* their period in office, but no formal procedure of prior parliamentary ratification exists.

Parliament's bold claims of 1642 and its equally bold legislation of 1689 did not sprout from a theoretical vacuum. Seventeenth-century England was a hotbed of radical political theory. This was the era, after all, of such luminaries as Thomas Hobbes (1588–1679) and John Locke (1632–1704), among others. One of the era's most significant currents of political thought was a particular variant of republicanism, whose understanding of the relationship between the Crown and Parliament both informed and was in turn informed by Parliament's claims and actions. And as it happens, seventeenth-century republican constitutionalism had something significant to say about citizenship.[24]

The central preoccupations of English seventeenth-century republican writers were political liberty, civic virtue, constitutional form, and the political theory of rebellion.[25] A desire to construct a constitutional means whereby the forces of monarchism could be substantively limited and subjected to parliamentary account was a constant and central theme. Thus, for John Milton, writing on the eve of the trial and execution of King Charles I,

> since the king or magistrate holds his authority of the people, both originally and naturally for their good in the first place, and not his own, then may the people, as oft as they shall judge it for the best, either choose him or reject him, retain him or depose him, *though no tyrant*, merely by the liberty and right of free-born men to be governed as seems to them best.[26]

Here Milton weaves together three of the core themes of republican constitutionalism: that the king or magistrate is the delegate of the people and should rule only in their interests rather than his own;[27] that the people may rebel against the king or magistrate—may reject, retain, or depose him—at any time, even if he is not acting tyrannically; and that this right is a natural manifestation of the essence of political liberty, namely, being governed as the people (or, at least, as the free-born people) consider best.

Eleven years later, on the eve of the restoration of the monarchy,[28] Milton advocated "the excellence" of a free commonwealth "compared with the inconveniences and dangers of readmitting kingship in this nation." He argued that

> it is well and happy for the people if their king be but a cipher, being ofttimes a mischief, a pest, a scourge of the nation and, *which is worse, not to be removed, not to be controlled,* much less accused or brought to punishment, without the shaking and almost subversion of the whole land; whereas in a free common-wealth, any governor or chief councillor offending may be removed and punished without the least commotion.[29]

The cardinal importance to republican constitutionalism of the practice of political accountability and the notion of responsible government is clear: those in office hold power in trust, and their exercise of it should, *as a matter of wholly unexceptional routine,* be regularly subjected to forms of account.

Milton's argument about the incompatibility of freedom with hereditary monarchy was further developed by Algernon Sidney in his *Discourses Concerning Government,* composed in 1681–83:

> Liberty consists only in being subject to no man's will, and noth-ing denotes a slave but a dependence upon the will of another; if there be no other law in a kingdom than the will of a prince, there is no such thing as liberty. . . . If the safety of the people be the supreme law, and this safety extend to, and consist in the preser-vation of their liberties, goods, lands and lives, that law must nec-essarily be the root and beginning, as well as the end and limit of all magistratical power, and all laws must be subservient and sub-ordinate to it. The question will not then be what pleases the king, but what is good for the people; not what conduces to his profit or glory, but what best secures the liberties he is bound to pre-serve: he does not therefore reign for himself, but for the people; he is not the master, but the servant of the commonwealth.[30]

Here again we find the republican themes that the king is subject to the law (and not the other way around) and that government should be for the good of the people, not the private gain of the ruler. Sidney was refreshingly (or perhaps alarmingly) clear about the consequences should it be otherwise. In another passage he stressed that

> when nations fall under such princes as are either utterly unca-
> pable of making a right use of their power, or do maliciously
> abuse that authority with which they are entrusted, those nations
> stand obliged, by the duty they owe to themselves and their pos-
> terity, to use the best of their endeavours to remove the evil.[31]

That "this may sometimes cause disorders," he acknowledged: "but . . . it [is] much better that the irregularities and excesses of a prince should be restrained or suppressed, than that whole nations should perish by them."[32]

Like Milton, Sidney saw the king as a delegate and, as such, accountable to the source from which he derived his power: "The king can have no . . . power, unless it be given to him. . . . 'Tis not therefore an inherent, but a del-egated power; and whoever receives it, is accountable to those who gave it."[33] The law which Sidney saw as being the "root and beginning, as well as the end and limit" of "all magistratical power" was the law as set down by Parliament. Likewise, the institution that gave power to the king, and to which the king was accordingly accountable, was Parliament.[34] Sidney wrote that "'there must . . . be a judge of such disputes as may . . . arise in every kingdom: and tho 'tis not my business to determine who is that judge in all places, yet I may justly say, that in England it is the Parliament."[35] He maintained that "the power of altering, mitigating, explaining or correcting the laws of England, is only in the Parliament, because none but the Parliament can make them."[36] For Sidney, this was good: "Parliament, . . . being the representative body of the people, and the collected wisdom of the nation, is least subject to error, most exempted from passion, and most free from corruption."[37]

In Milton and Sidney, we see the emergence of and the justification for Britain's practices of "parliamentary citizenship." The citizenship of a free-born people is freedom from the domination of a ruler you cannot choose, reject, retain, or depose.[38] Such a right to rebellion may on occasion have bloody consequences (as in the 1640s) but—and this is the crucial point—the constitution should be designed such that violence does not necessarily ensue. Hence the conversion of Machiavellian force into parliamentary power. Through Parliament, the free-born people choose and subsequently decide whether to reject, retain, or depose the government of the day. Through Parliament, citizenship is realized.

Rights

When Gordon Brown became prime minister in June 2007, he immediately initiated a review of British citizenship. Brown appointed former attorney general Lord Goldsmith QC to undertake a review of citizenship, and the ensuing report was published in March 2008.[39] It categorized the rights of citizenship into four broad classes: the right of abode and free movement; the right of protection (and the concomitant duty of allegiance); civic rights; and (most problematically, we shall see) social and economic rights.

Several issues prompted this initiative. First, a concern had developed that British multiculturalism as practiced since the 1960s had diluted notions of "Britishness" to such an extent that Britain hosts thousands and perhaps hundreds of thousands of British citizens who do not feel British and, in some instances, display outright hostility to Britain. (The 7/7 bombers on the London Underground were British nationals.) This concern was compounded by long-standing popular discontent with immigration and asylum policy as well as with the effects on Britain of the 2004 enlargement of the EU, which had resulted in significant numbers of Eastern Europeans coming freely to Britain seeking work and an improved standard of living. Additionally, there was a concern that measures such as the Human Rights Act 1998 had inappropriately skewed notions of citizenship in the political imagination, emphasizing rights and entitlements and underplaying civic duties, responsibilities, and obligations. Low-level social disorder, antisocial behavior, and late-night town- and city-center drunkenness are problems with high political salience at the moment in Britain (at least, if the newspapers are to be believed). Many felt that a heightened sense of belonging and a deepening of civic pride could attenuate these problems. Finally, a number of commentators seemed to think that Gordon Brown's identity as a *Scottish* prime minister was potentially problematic among English voters, as Scotland has since 1999 enjoyed considerable devolution of legislative and executive power; some wondered whether there was a "legitimacy deficit" in a Scottish MP being prime minister of the entire United Kingdom. Allied to this concern was that the fact that, despite the new devolutionary scheme for Scotland, calls for Scottish independence were once more on the rise, and unionist parties were struggling to defend the Union and to explain what Britain (as opposed to England or Scotland) stood for.

From a point of view sensitive to British constitutional history, one is tempted to introduce the *Goldsmith Review* with Monty Python's tagline: "And now for something completely different." The review says little about the development and importance of what I have dubbed "parliamentary citizenship," and very little of its substance links contemporary British citizenship to the history and development of Britain's parliamentary constitution. It is all rights talk; it focuses on the rights and liabilities of citizenship as if citizenship in Britain were little different from citizenship in any other member state of the European Union—though perhaps Britain's imperial heritage has bequeathed a legacy of legal peculiarities pertaining to the immigration status (and related matters) of certain classes of Commonwealth citizens.

Lord Goldsmith identified the right of abode as "the most central and important right of citizenship."[40] While citizenship is not required for an individual to live in Britain, only citizens have the fullest right of abode. Citizens' right of abode includes the rights to move freely around the United Kingdom, to leave the United Kingdom, and to reenter it at any time, for any length of time.[41] Citizens do not lose the right of abode even if they leave the country for years.[42] Connecting the full right of abode to nationality, Lord Goldsmith stated, "It is not possible to deprive a British citizen of his right to abode without first depriving him of his citizenship status."[43] Nationals cannot be deported. No British citizen may be deprived of his citizenship if that step would render him stateless.[44] EU citizens and aliens granted "indefinite leave to enter" or "indefinite leave to remain" in the UK also enjoy extensive rights of abode in Britain.[45] Such individuals are regarded as being "settled" in the UK—that is, "ordinarily resident in the UK without restriction under immigration laws as to the length of that stay."[46] However, a settled person, unlike a citizen, will likely lose his right of abode if he leaves Britain for more than two years without returning.

The second category, rights of protection, includes the right to diplomatic protection and other forms of consular assistance. As with the right of abode, citizenship is not a prerequisite for all forms of consular assistance. Citizens enjoy Britain's fullest diplomatic protection, but other British residents may also benefit from British consular assistance. A recent example is Britain's pressure on U.S. authorities to release from Guantanamo Bay not only British citizens but also noncitizens formerly resident in the UK.[47]

The third category, civic rights, includes the rights to vote and stand as a candidate in elections, to donate to a political party, to hold public office (as in the civil service), and to undertake jury service. While all of these rights are connected to citizenship, they may also be enjoyed by certain other classes of persons. British citizens and Commonwealth and Irish citizens resident in the United Kingdom may vote in parliamentary elections.[48] A person may vote in British elections while also subject to immigration control.[49] Donating to political parties is treated similarly. Citizenship is not a requirement for the franchise but, generally, membership in the franchise is a prerequisite for an individual's donation to a British political party.[50]

The final category of rights is welfare rights. Britain, like its nearest neighbors and like all of its closest allies except for the United States, is a welfare state. Herein lies the greatest challenge for citizenship. If citizenship is, in Lord Goldsmith's words, a "common bond," who is bound? How far does such "commonality" extend? To whom are citizens of a welfare state obligated, such that they should pay taxes to fund public services which may be freely accessed by . . . well, by whom? Should the welfare state's manifold benefits be available only to citizens? Only to citizens and tax-paying residents? Should its services be available (free of charge?) to "settled" aliens, irrespective of whether they are taxpayers? Or to all residents? Including very short-term visitors? These are the questions posed by what might be termed "welfare citizenship."

In Britain the legal answer to the questions posed here is complex. Much depends on the sort of public service at issue. A state education (a free place in a state primary or secondary school) is much more widely available to noncitizens, whether "settled" or not, than are most forms of social security. Why this should be the case is not immediately obvious.[51]

Social security provision is perhaps the most inaccessible aspect of the welfare state for those who are neither citizens nor settled. Residents who are not settled in the UK generally cannot obtain "public funds,"[52] including child benefit, council tax benefit, disability living allowance, housing benefit, income-based job-seeker's allowance, and income support. Exceptions exist for certain asylum seekers who would otherwise be destitute, among others.

Noncitizens may have more access to certain forms of community care services, although access is liable to be limited. For example, access to residential accommodation, to welfare arrangements for disabled persons, and to services promoting the welfare of the elderly may be available. In these areas much depends on the discretion of the local authority (the city or county council).[53] Access to public housing is likewise restricted (but not wholly unavailable) in the cases of persons who are neither citizens nor settled.[54]

Access to health care is different. Goldsmith writes:

> The general principle is that all those who are ordinarily resident in the UK enjoy full entitlement to health care [under the National Health Service]. The test of "ordinary residence" covers all those who are lawfully present and settled in the UK, and is not dependent on nationality. . . . In relation to primary health care treatment, GPs [general practitioners] have a discretion to register any new patient, regardless of immigration status or nationality and may provide free treatment to any person where it is necessary, even where the person is not registered. As such, this basic health care provision is available to all. The provision of hospital treatment is governed by the NHS (Charges to Overseas Visitors) Regulations 1989, which provide that charges will be levied in relation to health care provided to overseas visitors, defined as those who are not ordinarily resident. Certain types of treatment are exempted and are thus free to all.[55]

Finally, education is different: education for children between the ages of five and sixteen is compulsory and not restricted by the immigration status of either parent or child.[56] Further education, including university education, is no longer free in England and Wales (in Scotland the state pays for much of such education), but "home" and "overseas" students pay different rates. For this purpose, "home" includes EU students.

A complex web of legal rights associated with citizenship exists. Even within the category of welfare rights, citizenship is not an absolute prerequisite. Noncitizens settled in the UK may have access to most welfare rights in Britain, including those implicating "public funds," and health care and free schooling are much more widely available. Perhaps this is what it means to be a citizen of a welfare state: to contribute to a civilized polity that extends assistance to all those who need it, irrespective of nationality, while they are the guests of the host nation.

Conclusions

In its abstraction from British constitutional traditions, the *Goldsmith Review* exemplifies recent trends in the constitutional debate. Since the mid-1990s there has been a monumental and perhaps decisive shift away from Britain's traditions of parliamentary and political constitutionalism to a more legal or rights-based constitutionalism—a constitutionalism which is less distinctive and which has more in common with the constitutional orders found in the United States, in the Commonwealth, and elsewhere in the EU.

There are probably four main reasons why a more legal constitutionalism (or "juristocracy") has come in the view of most contemporary British commentators to be preferred to Britain's traditions of political or parliamentary constitutionalism.[57] First, there is a sense, not altogether supported by the data but nonetheless often genuinely felt, that the political constitution has failed—in that Parliament cannot effectively hold the government to account—and, accordingly, that courts should step in to take a greater role in this regard. Second, the influence of the great nineteenth-century constitutional lawyer A. V. Dicey began to wane in the last quarter of the twentieth century. Although he was a great enthusiast of the power and authority of the common law, Dicey advocated a doubly limited role for the courts in constitutional terms in that he propounded a very strong notion of the sovereignty of Parliament (meaning, for example, that no court could overturn or set aside a provision of an act of Parliament) while at the same time giving only a rather weak definition of the rule of law.[58] As many have observed, Dicey's work effectively stymied the development of a strong public law in the United Kingdom for much of the twentieth century; his hold on the senior judiciary began to loosen only in the 1980s and 1990s. Third, the recent experience of certain leading Commonwealth jurisdictions has had a spillover effect. Canada adopted its Charter of Rights and Freedoms in 1982. New Zealand passed its Bill of Rights Act in 1990, and South Africa adopted a new constitution and bill of rights in 1994. The influence of these countries' courts on the British courts has been significant. Finally, and perhaps most important, is the influence of Europe, specifically that exerted by the European Convention on Human Rights and what is now the EU, to which Britain has belonged since 1972. All of these influences have pushed in much the same direction—to encourage a greater role for the judiciary in constitutional affairs generally and in the enforcement of fundamental rights in particular, such that the focus of constitutional attention has moved from Parliament to courts of law.

Admittedly, this account is quite broad. It is not the case that the courts played no role in the constitution before 1990, or that Parliament now plays no role. Still, the relative weight of their respective roles has changed since the early 1990s. The courts' constitutional role has increased significantly, in some respects at the expense of Parliament. This is the combined effect on the British constitution of both European law and the unprecedented constitutional reform within Britain since the mid-1990s (in particular since the Labor government led by former prime minister Tony Blair came to power in 1997). Ground-breaking legislation, including the Human Rights Act 1998, the Scotland Act 1998, and the Constitutional Reform Act 2005, has conferred a range of new powers and duties on the courts. Examples include a judicial duty to read, interpret, and apply legislation subject to fundamental rights, wherever possible; a power to declare legislation to be incompatible with fundamental rights where no such interpretation is possible; a power to quash any action or decision of a public authority (including government ministers) where the action or decision is incompatible with fundamental rights; a power to police the legislation of the Scottish Parliament to ensure that it does not trespass onto territory reserved to the United Kingdom Parliament in Westminster (the beginnings of a new jurisprudence of federalism, perhaps); and a formal strengthening of the rule of law and the judicial separation from the institutions of parliamentary government. The courts have also continued to develop the common law so as to subject both government and Parliament to closer judicial supervision and scrutiny than ever before.[59]

What does this mean for citizenship? Among other things, it means that litigation is beginning to replace political participation as the mechanism of choice in seeking to challenge government actions and decisions: "parliamentary citizenship" is beginning to give way to the citizen-as-litigant. The recent *Shayler* case offers a telling example of both the prevalence and the (to my mind) significant drawbacks of this shift in emphasis.[60] *Shayler* concerned a legal challenge to Britain's notorious official secrets legislation, in which it was argued that parts of the Official Secrets Act 1989 are so broadly defined as to be incompatible with the fundamental right to freedom of expression as enshrined in Article 10 of the European Convention on Human Rights. (Article 10 of the ECHR was incorporated into domestic UK law under the Human Rights Act 1998.) The right to freedom of expression is not an absolute right under Article 10, but is rather a qualified right; the state may lawfully interfere with its exercise if certain conditions apply: (a) the interference must be "prescribed by law"; (b) the interference must be for the sake of a certain (listed) public good, such as safeguarding national security; and (c) the interference must be "necessary in a democratic society."[61] The last condition has been interpreted by the European Court of Human Rights (and, by extension since the Human Rights Act 1998, by the UK courts) as a condition of proportionality. Disproportionate interferences with a right such as freedom of expression will not be lawful even if conditions (a) and (b) are satisfied.

Shayler concerned Section 1 of the Official Secrets Act 1989, which makes it a crime for a member or former member of Britain's security and secret intelligence services to disclose any information relating to security or intelligence if it came into his possession by virtue of employment in the service. No damage to the UK's national security need actually or even potentially be caused by the disclosure, and the "public interest" provides no defense to a charge under Section 1. The House of Lords unanimously ruled that, notwithstanding the breathtaking scope of this section, it was not a disproportionate interference with freedom of expression.

When the Thatcher government introduced the bill that became the Official Secrets Act 1989, it was condemned by civil liberties lawyers and human rights activists throughout the United Kingdom. Coming on the back of that government's ludicrous chase of former MI5 officer Peter Wright through the British, Australian, and American courts for publishing his memoirs, the legislation hardly portrays Britain's commitment to liberty in a positive light.[62] Civil liberties lawyers immediately began a campaign to have the legislation amended or repealed, to be replaced with a statute that achieves a more mature and balanced relationship between safeguarding national security and protecting freedom of expression.[63] Such a campaign was always likely to be difficult. Few votes are gained in liberalizing such laws, and it is in the government's own interest to maintain tough laws in this area. But at least, under the political constitution, the argument for liberalization could have been made. The judgment of the House of Lords in *R v. Shayler* makes such an argument more or less impossible. The House of Lords ruled that the interference with free speech was not disproportionate and in so doing gave the government a trump card which, it seems, can defeat any argument by civil liberties lawyers. How could Parliament be persuaded, no doubt against the wishes of the government of the day, that the law needs to be amended or repealed in order to achieve a better balance between security and free speech? Citizens aggrieved at the illiberal nature of this law now have no recourse. This is a critical difference between politics and law. Politics is the world of debate; the law, of judgment and precedent. Debate can always be revisited. Judgment offers finality and closure—which few can challenge or reopen. Debate includes citizens; judgment tends to exclude them.

Shayler is alarming to those who fear that something precious has been lost in the rush to move away from Britain's traditions of political constitutionalism and its attendant "parliamentary citizenship" to embrace the new juristocracy of legalism and judicial review. Moreover, it should not be thought that *Shayler* is a one-off. In numerous recent instances, remarkably illiberal judicial decisions have effectively cut off political and parliamentary debate about reforming the law to offer greater protection to civil liberties. *Gillan*, concerning rights to peaceful protest,[64] and *JJ*, concerning the government's scheme of "control orders" (which subjects a number of suspected international terrorists to various forms of house arrest),[65] are instances of judicial decision making that render the parliamentary argument for reform of the law significantly harder to make and less likely to succeed. Both decisions raise grave concerns about the state of liberty in the UK; yet, like *Shayler*, they are decisions the judges could make only because of the powers conferred on them by the Human Rights Act. It is a horrible irony that twenty-first century human rights law, ostensibly enacted in order to *enhance* the protection of the rights of citizens (and others), seems to have the reverse effect, thus undermining a core achievement of Britain's historic, political constitution.

Notes

1. John A. G. Griffith, *The Political Constitution* 42 Mod. L. Rev.1 (1979); Adam Tomkins, Our Republican Constitution ch. 1 (2005).

2. Only the constitution of New Zealand comes close to resembling it, and even here, there are important differences.

3. Bruce Ackerman, *The Rise of World Constitutionalism*, 83 Va. L. Rev. 771 (1997).

4. For an overview, *see* Colin Turpin and Adam Tomkins, British Government and the Constitution ch. 5 (6th ed. 2007).

5. Ran Hirschl, Towards Juristocracy: The Origins and Consequences of the New Constitutionalism (2004).

6. On the ways in which this is changing, *see* Adam Tomkins, *The Rule of Law in Blair's Britain* 26 U. Queensland L. Rev. 255 (2007) and *see* further below.

7. Entick v. Carrington 19 Howell's St. Tr. 1029 (1765).

8. An excellent recent example is *R (Corner House Research) v. Director of the Serious Fraud Office* [2008] UKHL 60 (U.K).

9. The name derives from the case *Associated Provincial Picture Houses Ltd v. Wednesbury Corporation* [1948] 1 K.B. 223 (U.K.), in which the test was laid down.

10. *See, e.g.,* Council of Civil Service Unions v. Minister for the Civil Service [1985] A.C. 374 (U.K.). Additional grounds of review exist where a claimant wishes to argue that government decisions have been taken in a manner that is procedurally unfair.

11. The advent of the Human Rights Act 1998 has led to an expansion of the grounds of judicial review, at least in cases which are claimed to touch on rights under the European Convention on Human Rights. In such cases the UK courts now use "proportionality" rather than "*Wednesbury* unreasonableness" as the main standard of review: *see* R (Daly) v. Secretary of State for the Home Department [2001] 2 A.C. 532 (U.K.). This change has made some difference, but whether the difference is more than marginal is open to debate.

12. Walter Bagehot, The English Constitution (1867).

13. The government comprises about 110–120 ministers, of whom about 90–95 are MPs in the House of Commons; the remainder are peers in the House of Lords. The House of Lords remains wholly unelected. Membership of the House of Lords is by appointment of the Crown.

14. At the beginning of the decade this happened with great effect over export controls. In 2006–8 it happened with regard to the constitutional governance of the prime minister's power to wage war and to send the armed forces into combat overseas.

15. Until 1997 this document was known as *Questions of Procedure for Ministers*. The current version of the *Ministerial Code* is available from the Web site of the Cabinet Office, a department of the UK government: *see* www.cabinetoffice.gov.uk/propriety_and_ethics/ministers/ministerial_code.aspx.

16. For fuller discussion of the operation of these rules, *see* Adam Tomkins, Public Law ch. 5 (2003).

17. This is the argument of Tomkins, *supra* note 1, at ch. 3.

18. *Id., esp.* 69–87.

19. R v. Hampden 3 Howell's St. Tr. 825 (1637) (U.K.).

20. For the text, *see* John Phillips Kenyon, The Stuart Constitution: Documents and Commentary 222–26 (2d ed. 1985).

21. Bill of Rights 1689, art. IV (U.K.).

22. *Id.*, art. VI.

23. *Id.*, art. IX.

24. The following paragraphs draw on Adam Tomkins, *On Republican Constitutionalism in the Age of Commerce*, in Legal Republicanism: National and International Perspectives ch. 14 (Samantha Besson and José Luis Marti eds., 2009).

25. Jonathan Scott, Commonwealth Principles: Republican Writing of the English Revolution chs. 5–8 (2004).

26. John Milton, *The Tenure of Kings and Magistrates* (1648), in Milton: The Major Works 281 (Stephen Orgel and Jonathan Goldberg eds., 1991) (emphasis added).

27. Earlier in the tract, Milton wrote that "the power of kings and magistrates is nothing else but what is only derivative, transferred, and committed to them in trust from the people to the common good of them all." *Id.*, 279.

28. Charles II, elder son of Charles I, was restored to the throne in 1660.

29. John Milton, *The Ready and Easy Way to Establish a Free Commonwealth* (1659) in Milton: The Major Works, *supra* note 26, at 337 (emphasis added).

30. Algernon Sidney, Discourses Concerning Government (1683) 402–3 (T. West ed., 1996).

31. *Id.* at 546–47.

32. *Id.* at 523.

33. *Id.* at 529.

34. Sidney attached considerable importance to the fact that it was Parliament that *invited* Charles II to return to the throne in 1660.

35. Sidney, *supra* note 30, at 430.

36. *Id.* at 451.

37. *Id.* at 557.

38. On the claim that freedom as nondomination is the central leitmotif of republican political thought, *see* Philip Pettit, Republicanism: A Theory of Freedom and Government (1997); *see also* Quentin Skinner, Liberty before Liberalism (1998).

39. Entitled *Citizenship: Our Common Bond* (hereafter referred to as *Goldsmith Review*), the review is available at the Web site of the Ministry of Justice of the UK government, www.justice.gov.uk..

40. *Id.* at 20.

41. This is not an unqualified right. Statutory provisions allow for the right to be overridden in certain, specific circumstances in the interests of preventing public disorder: for example, known football hooligans may be temporarily prevented from traveling abroad to attend certain football matches.

42. Immigration Act 1971, ch. 77, § 1.

43. *Goldsmith Review*, at 23.

44. British Nationality Act 1981, ch. 61, § 40, as amended; *see Goldsmith Review*, at 23.

45. On EU citizenship, see the chapter by Markus Kotzur in this volume.

46. *Goldsmith Review*, at 30.

47. *Id.* at 12.

48. Representation of the People Act, 1983, ch. 2, § 1.

49. *Goldsmith Review*, 45–46.

50. *See* the Political Parties, Elections and Referendums Act, 2000, ch. 41; for commentary, *see* Keith D. Ewing, *Transparency, Accountability and Equality: The Political Parties, Elections and Referendums Act 2000*, 2001 Pub. L. 542 (2001).

51. On similar perplexities in the U.S. context, *see* Diane Wood's contribution to this volume.

52. Asylum and Immigration Act, 1999, ch. 33, § 115, as amended; *see Goldsmith Review*, at 57.

53. *See* National Assistance Act, 1948, ch. 29, and National Health Service and Community Care Act, 1990, ch. 19, as well as other measures; *see Goldsmith Review*, 62.

54. Housing Act 1996, ch. 52; *see Goldsmith Review*, at 64–65.

55. *Goldsmith Review*, at 66.

56. Education Act, 1996, ch. 56.

57. I have explored these issues at length in a series of previous publications and no attempt will be made here to reproduce the argument in full. *See, e.g.*, Tomkins, *supra* note 1, at ch. 1; Tomkins, *supra* note 6; Adam Tomkins, *British Constitutionalism*, in Oxford Handbook of British Politics (Matthew Flinders, Colin Hay, Andrew Gamble, and Michael Kenny eds., forthcoming 2009); and Adam Tomkins, Public Law (2003), esp. chs. 1, 5, and 6.

58. *See* Entick v. Carrington, supra note 7 and associated text.

59. A leading example is *Jackson v. Attorney General* [2006] 1 A.C. 262 (U.K.). For discussion, *see* Turpin and Tomkins, *supra* note 4, at 66–74.

60. R v. Shayler [2003] 1 A.C. 247 (U.K.).

61. Art. 10(2) Eur. Ct. H.R. Many other convention rights are structured (i.e., qualified) in the same way: *see, e.g.*, Article 8 (privacy), Article 9 (freedom of thought, conscience, and religion), and Article 11 (freedom of assembly and association). Only a minority of convention rights are absolute: the right to freedom from torture (art. 3 Eur. Ct. H.R.) is an example.

62. For the full, dismal story, *see* Keith D. Ewing and Conor A. Gearty, Freedom under Thatcher: Civil Liberties in Modern Britain chs. 5–6 (1990).

63. *See, e.g.*, John A. G. Griffith, *The Official Secrets Act 1989*, 16 J. L. Soc'y 273 (1989).

64. R (Gillan) v. Metropolitan Police Commissioner [2006] 2 A.C. 307 (U.K.); *see* Turpin and Tomkins, *supra* note 4, at 277.

65. Secretary of State for the Home Department v. JJ [2007] UKHL 45 (U.K.); *see* Keith D. Ewing & Joo-Cheong Tham, *The Continuing Futility of the Human Rights Act*, Pub. L. 668 (2008).

10

Structural Constitutional Principles and Rights Reconciliation

Robert R. Gasaway and Ashley C. Parrish

This paper is about contrasting approaches to constitutional rights. We contend that the American Constitution achieves an often underappreciated reconciliation both among individual rights and between individual rights and representative democracy—a reconciliation rooted in structural principles that emerge, on one hand, from the Constitution's pattern of rights inclusion and omission, and, on the other, from canonical statements of the Constitution's larger purposes. Our sense is that modern Europeans have largely embraced an alternative, rights-proliferating approach to individual rights—more rights are better. That approach inevitably triggers the sort of conflict among rights, and between rights and democracy, that the American Constitution properly seeks to avoid.

We hope to make two contributions to the transatlantic discussion. First, we hope to dispel a possible misconception among Europeans. Europeans appreciate that our Constitution declines to recognize many rights proposed for inclusion in the ultimate arrangements for future Europe. They appreciate that rights can conflict and that more rights can lead to more conflict. Their possible misconception, we believe, is a too-ready assumption that conflicts between democratic rights and other rights are inevitable and that differences between rights-scarce and rights-laden constitutions reduce to matters of degree. We argue, in contrast, that the structural principles of the American Constitution help to avoid such conflicts altogether by recognizing only those rights that can achieve a large degree of peaceful coexistence.

Second, we cast onto the American side a good share of blame for what we perceive as European misconceptions. "Originalism," the dominant

American school of constitutional interpretation, threatens to shortchange the Constitution's structural principles—principles that are essential for explaining to non-Americans and non-specialists the Constitution's reconciliation of rights. We therefore aim to go beyond the received practices of academic originalism, elevate the interpretive stature of structural principles, and show how structural principles are rooted in the four corners of the Constitution and other legitimate, objective sources of constitutional meaning.

We conclude with a soft (but important) suggestion that the American Constitution has endured precisely because it avoids specifying a long, conflicting roster of individual rights and, instead, safeguards each generation's ability to debate and decide the pressing issues of the day. The structural principles we identify confine our Constitution to a less comprehensive role than that filled by constitutions in other nations. But they ensure that constitutional rights are for the most part reconciled; that democratic outcomes are perceived as fair and reasonable; and that citizens enjoy the right *not* to have substantive constitutional law, etched in stone, governing their everyday lives.

We begin with a brief description of the current constitutional landscape in Europe and America. Europe's tendency is to insulate citizens from vagaries of democracy by cataloguing a vast array of individual rights. This approach, we contend, threatens to compromise democratic self-government by empowering legal elites to determine how myriad rights are reconciled, prioritized, and enforced. In contrast, the most prominent approach to interpreting the American Constitution—originalism—is a useful balm for rights-proliferation syndrome. In its purest, most "academic" form, however, originalism threatens to truncate the quest for objective constitutional meaning and to obscure America's most profound constitutional achievements.

European Constitutionalism: A Focus on Rights

The 2004 Treaty establishing a Constitution for Europe, endorsed by member states in Rome and rejected by voters in France and the Netherlands, merits continued attention. Undaunted by the fact that their constitutional moment is becoming a drawn-out movement, Europeans appear determined to achieve an avowedly political unification, however long that might take. We do not claim to be scholars of European law in its constitutional or other dimensions. But we do claim to be interested students and sometime practitioners of a constitutionalism that should be and is, however awkwardly, the principal supplier of signposts on the road ahead for unified Europe—American constitutionalism.[1]

Those who have confronted constitutional questions only in academic or judicial settings may not appreciate how effectively constitutional rights can bind the feelings and prejudices of a community to its foundational laws, or how they can link a nation's highest ideals to its citizens' most concrete concerns. The American Founders understood that even "the most rational government will not find it a superfluous advantage to have the prejudices of the community on its side" in a manner that induces a civic "reverence for the laws."[2] Rights creation can indeed build nations precisely because rights sweep broadly and touch deeply.

But if Europe's constitutional architects are on the right track in looking to constitutional rights as political adhesives, surely they should consider with care America's centuries-old experience with such rights. Although the definition and enforcement of rights can effectively build nations, constitutional rights can also threaten to impinge democracy by assigning legal elites the most important tasks of governance. Certain rights—such as rights to vote, worship, speak freely, and enjoy the full measure of citizenship—are essential prerequisites for a free society. But apart from this finite list of essential prerequisites, the definition of rights should be left to the push and pull of democratic processes, allowing for governmental accountability, citizen participation, improvements in civic understanding and virtue, and change over time. Every credit to the ledger of constitutionally protected freedoms is, by definition, a debit on the ledger of issues subject to democratic decision making. By cutting off democratic debate over the most important economic, social, cultural, and political issues of the day, prodigality in bestowing enforceable rights can restrict "opportunities for the sort of ongoing dialogue upon which a regime of ordered liberty ultimately depends."[3] It risks giving rise to a government, not for the people, but for the governing elites.

The 2004 constitutional treaty, which incorporates the Charter of Fundamental Rights of the Union, includes a lengthy catalogue of constitutional rights. From an American perspective, many of these rights—for example, a right to protection of personal data, a right to join trade unions, a right to access vocational and continuing training, a right for children to express their views freely and to have those views taken into consideration, and a right to paid maternity leave and to parental leave[4]—should be left for democratic decision making, not surrendered to judicial definition. The slogan most heard on this side of the Atlantic during the debates over Europe's draft constitution was that a proper constitution was needed to narrow the "democratic deficit" in Europe's existing institutions. From this side of the Atlantic, it appeared that the rights-laden document ultimately proposed threatened to widen the very deficit it was intended to narrow.

American Constitutionalism

Properly interpreted, the American Constitution enshrines its citizens' rights to a *decision-making* ballot, not merely a *consultative* one. In America, many of those who worry about an erosion of this bedrock principle, and the opening of an American "democratic deficit" brought about by constitutional rights proliferation, have rallied under the jurisprudential banner of "originalism." Originalism's impact is readily seen in the Supreme Court's increasingly frequent citations to originalist sources and reliance on originalist methods of interpretation.[5] Commentators and jurists alike have noted that "originalism has become authoritative, both inside and outside of courts,"[6] and that it can be viewed as "the prevailing approach to constitutional interpretation."[7] In the broadest, most inclusive sense of the term, "we are all originalists now."[8]

It is important to distinguish two subtly but fundamentally different species of originalist interpretation. One might be referred to as judicial, or nonexclusive, originalism. This version insists that, although original understandings of texts are essential and central to constitutional interpretation, the real or attributed contemporaneous understandings of those who were the political handmaidens of individual constitutional provisions (like framers, ratifiers, or voters) cannot serve as the exclusive source of constitutional meaning. Although they are self-described originalists, both Justice Scalia and Justice Thomas subscribe in one degree or another to this avowedly "faint-hearted" mode of originalism.[9] Faint-hearted originalism's competitor might be termed academic or pure originalism. This version holds that the Constitution's text, along with contemporary understandings of its "public meaning" at the time of ratification, constitutes the sole legitimate grounds for constitutional interpretation.[10]

The difference between these competing modes of interpretation implicate important disagreements over the extent to which neutral principles of law can effectively and legitimately be derived from the Constitution's structure. Terms such as "structural principles" and "structuralism," as used in this paper, encompass a pair of related meanings. Structural constitutional principles include those foundational presuppositions that lie beyond or behind the Constitution but properly inform its interpretation. Lincoln's insistence that the Declaration of Independence and Constitution were related, like the biblical "apple of gold" in a "picture of silver," exemplifies this type of interpretive structuralism.[11] Structuralism, in a related but narrower sense, signifies the interpreter's reliance on patterns of neighboring or related textual provisions including, importantly, what is omitted as well as what is included.

We contend that structural principles are important because they can provide a foundation for the basic units of constitutional analysis (constitutional "doctrines") that is at once rooted, objective, and enduring while at the same time flexible in application to ever-changing circumstances. The Framers themselves and, as described below, our most authoritative constitutional interpreters, would have expected constitutional interpretation to identify structural principles and draw corresponding doctrinal implications. The Framers of the United States Constitution could have, but chose not to, follow the example of John Adams in the Massachusetts constitution by including an express, textual affirmation of the structural principle of separation of powers.[12] They chose instead to leave the principle implicit, but hardly less apparent, in the Constitution's structure. They did so by beginning its three first articles with parallel linguistic constructions referring sententiously to "all legislative powers herein granted," "the executive Power," and "the judicial Power of the United States." This conscious decision to convey meaning through structural parallelism, as opposed to express text, must be read as an invitation to discover a separation-of-governmental-powers principle and to find that principle's doctrinal scope and meaning by exploring the *relationship* between the concept of legislative power, the concept of executive power, and the concept of judicial power as the three are delineated in the Constitution.

But if the Framers have directed us to seek constitutional meaning in a *relationship*, it follows that we might possibly understand that relationship better than did the Framers themselves. Unlike the Framers, we have had the benefit of post-ratification separation-of-powers experiences. We, unlike the Framers, have profited from observing the results of divergent separation of powers innovations, such as the enactment and implementation of a law providing for prosecutions of high government officials by "independent" counsels operating outside the Department of Justice. And we, unlike the Framers, have benefited from eloquent criticisms of such innovations.[13] In some respects, then, we are better positioned to understand the enduring meaning (and perhaps enduring wisdom) of the Framers' original choices. Accordingly, while we must regard ourselves as confined by the Framers' understandings, we should not feel confined to those understandings.

Originalism in its judicial form accords not only with the choices of the Philadelphia Framers, but also, we contend, with the interpretive practices of our foremost constitutional interpreters, President Lincoln and Chief Justice Marshall. But we are not blind to the legitimate fears that impel the purer, more academic version of originalism. On the academic view, originalism unmodified is the only reliable bulwark against raw judicial lawmaking. Legal radicalism in the American academy marched not so long ago under the banner of the Critical Legal Studies movement. That movement was useful precisely because in fact, if not in the minds of adherents, it was exclusively critical as opposed to constructive. It was appreciated even by nonadherents for its combination of thought-provoking intellectual critiques and often (humorously) ridiculous reform proposals. Legal radicalism today, at least in the law schools, is not so much a movement but an increasingly pervasive mindset. It is the specter of legal radicalism, loosed from its ivory cage to hound the bar and bench, that academic originalists rightly fear. On this view, to fail to embrace pure originalism is to open the door to the menace of a twenty-first century "Marxist-Brennanism"—that pulsating, action-inspiring, elitist dream of socialist utopia brought about not by the blood and rubble of proletarian revolt but by the sophistry and assurances of a bloodless, velvet, judicial usurpation.

The stakes in the debate we have joined are large. Given all the efforts invested, all the notoriety gained, and all the multidimensional doctrinal progress achieved under the banner of originalism, the term has become almost sacrosanct. But the fact remains that clause-by-clause inquiry into contemporaneous public meanings can never be a complete answer to every problem of constitutional construction. Unless another, expanded originalism is brought to bear—call it structural originalism, if you like—originalism will remain inscrutable to non-Americans, unreconciled with our centuries-wide corpus of Supreme Court precedent, and inadequate to the full dimensions of constitutional interpretation.

Our side will prevail in this debate, as against the clause-by-clause purists, only if we can convince our friends that the structural conclusions we draw are not airy, rootless bromides, but concrete, well-grounded, higher-level principles—principles concrete enough to beget doctrines that constrain judicial discretion and well grounded enough to inspire confidence in their legitimacy. One measuring stick of success will be whether our principles can be defended with a persuasiveness remotely approaching that with which Lincoln defended the far more paradoxical proposition that slavery, while constitutionally protected, nonetheless remained an "unqualified evil" contrary to the Constitution's fundamental presuppositions. Ideally, we should be able to defend our structural principles the same way Lincoln criticized the Court's *Dred Scott* decision—both as a matter of simple, commonsense appreciation of American democracy and as a matter of rigorous interpretation rooted in the most authoritative sources of constitutional understanding.

Individual Rights Anomalies in the American Constitution

A serious criticism of using structural principles in constitutional construction is the fear that, in comparison to inquiries into text and historical meaning, the derivation of structural principles is too malleable to be reliable. We respond to this challenge by looking for structure in places where structural principles are *not* under direct examination. By relying on patterns of text and judicial decision that take no direct cognizance of the principles we elicit, we hope to inspire confidence that our principles, and the judicial doctrines to which they give rise, are legitimate components of our constitutional architecture—doctrines arising not from someone's philosophy or a phantom in the eye of an interpreter but from objective sources of constitutional understanding.

Our search for structural principles focuses on what we regard as the five most instructively anomalous aspects of America's experience with individual rights. We contend these anomalies illuminate two of our Constitution's most

well-grounded, readily applied, and frequently overlooked structural princi-
pals: *first*, that decisions as to whether to proscribe or permit almost any type
of future, private action should be left for democratic determination; *second*,
that decisions as to what economic, social, or cultural goals should be accomplished by private action, as opposed to state action, also should be left for
democratic determination.

The first three anomalies we discuss appear on the face of amendments
to our original Constitution: (i) the Eighteenth Amendment's singular effort to
regulate private conduct (the manufacture, sale, and transportation of
liquors); (ii) the Second Amendment's singular inclusion of a preamble introducing the substantive right to keep and bear arms; and (iii) the Bill of Rights'
inclusion of two singularly underutilized rights, the Second Amendment's
right to bear arms and the Third Amendment's right to be free from the billeting of troops in private homes.

The final two anomalies appear not in the Constitution's text but in the
Supreme Court's decisions: (i) a notable exception (the right to travel) to the
general rule that individual rights to engage in private conduct are controversial; and (ii) a recurring pattern in which the Court has held that textual rights
are *not* violated in circumstances involving bona fide governmental efforts to
regulate future, private conduct.

An Anomalous Amendment and Its Singular "Repeal." The Constitution's
Eighteenth Amendment formerly "prohibited," by its terms, not some over-
reaching or abusive governmental practice, but the private "manufacture,
sale, or transportation of intoxicating liquors." The Eighteenth Amendment
was on the books a mere fourteen years before its "repeal" by the Twenty-First
Amendment, which expressly states, in language that knows no parallel elsewhere in the Constitution, "the eighteenth article of amendment to the
Constitution of the United States is hereby repealed."

Since 1791, when the first ten amendments were added in the Bill of
Rights, the United States has approved only seventeen further amendments
to its Constitution. The first of these seventeen corrected not the the constitutional text itself but rather an early Supreme Court interpretation of
federal courts' jurisdiction.[14] The two most important amendments corrected
the original Constitution's defects in affording protections for slavery and failing to prohibit racial and other invidious discrimination (Amendments XIII,

XIV). Five other amendments have expanded the franchise (Amendments XV, XIX, XXIII, XXIV, XXVI); four have modified, modernized, elaborated, or made more workable the machinery for selecting a president and ensuring continuity in the executive branch (Amendments XII, XX, XXII, XXV). One amendment provided for the direct election of senators to the upper house of Congress (Amendment XVII); another expanded Congress's power to levy direct taxes (Amendment XVI); and the most recent amendment provides that congressional pay increases cannot take effect before an intervening election occurs (Amendment XXVII). Taken collectively and from a two-century vantage, these fifteen amendments carry an air of Whiggish historical inevitability. They all address issues recognized since the founding as being of constitutional moment, arriving at different and hopefully better answers to what have been enduring constitutional concerns.

The exception to this evolution is the odd couple of the Eighteenth and Twenty-First Amendments. The Eighteenth Amendment's direct and unabashed prohibition on private conduct—the manufacture, sale, and transportation of intoxicating liquors—knows no analogue in our tradition. Had James Madison prevailed in the First Congress, our Constitution's amendments might have been interwoven into the original text, like amendments to a statutory code, instead of being appended at the end as sequentially numbered "articles of amendment."[15] Under that approach, natural constitutional homes might readily have been found for all fifteen "ordinary" constitutional amendments. But there is no easy answer for where to put the Eighteenth Amendment, for there is no ready precedent for constitutionalizing an express, nationwide prohibition on private conduct. Viewed from the vantage of two centuries of constitutional history, the Twenty-First Amendment, the only amendment to use the word "repeal," can be seen as an admission that the Eighteenth Amendment did not merely arrive at a wrong constitutional answer; it asked a constitutional question that should have never been posed.

An Anomalous Preamble. Our Constitution is notable both for the brevity of its initial preamble and for the absence throughout the document of other prefatory statements of purpose. The Second Amendment's preamble, the only other preamble found in the document, has thus confounded scholars and divided the judiciary.[16] Because introductory preambles have long been viewed as interpretive or explanatory guides,[17] one might have predicted the appearance of a strong prefatory statement introducing, say, the Thirteenth Amendment's abolition of slavery or the Nineteenth Amendment's grant of suffrage to women. But no similar clause appears in those or any other amendment. The Second Amendment's preamble is truly and literally extraordinary.[18]

Absent its preamble, the Second Amendment would do nothing more than grant an individual the right to keep and bear private arms principally as a matter of self-defense. That would accord with Blackstone's fundamental understanding of a "right of having and using arms for self-preservation and defence."[19] Viewed from this perspective and in point of form, the Eighteenth and Second Amendments are mirror images: the Eighteenth uniquely *prohibits* purely private conduct (involving "intoxicating liquors") and the Second uniquely *protects* purely private conduct (involving privately keeping and bearing arms).

When viewed in light of its preamble, however, the Second Amendment is seen to serve a second purpose—one tied to the Constitution's broader structural design. As the 1788 ratification debates highlighted, the Anti-Federalists were concerned that the government could disarm the people in order to impose rule through a standing army or select militia.[20] Because it protects the right of citizens to participate in the creation of a well-regulated militia under local control,[21] the Second Amendment is consistent with the general rule that the rights granted under the Constitution are held first and foremost as rights against the state. Against this backdrop, the Second Amendment's preamble can be seen as an essential *apologia* for what might otherwise appear as an improper constitutional entrenchment of a decision that ought to be left to ordinary legislative processes—whether citizens should be permitted to engage in private self-protective conduct using firearms.

Two Rights Rarely Invoked. A closely related, but distinct, anomaly involves the rarity of litigation under the Second and Third Amendments, two of the eight rights-granting amendments added in the Bill of Rights. The other Bill of Rights amendments establishing individual rights—the First, Fourth, Fifth, Sixth, Seventh, and Eighth—have all been dissected and closely interpreted in thousands of judicial decisions. In contrast, the meaning and effect of the Second and Third Amendments have been left comparatively unexplored.[22]

Scholars have suggested various reasons for the Second and Third Amendments' relative desuetude, including that plaintiffs often lack standing to assert rights under the Second Amendment,[23] and that the Third Amendment is "in fact of no current importance whatsoever (although it did, for obvious reasons, have importance at the time of the founding)."[24] Those explanations, while correct to some degree, underemphasize the more fundamental reasons for these amendments' anomalous status.

The Second and Third Amendments parallel the other Bill of Rights amendments in that they safeguard individual rights; namely, the right to keep and bear arms, and the right to be free from forced billeting. In another respect, however, both amendments serve what is essentially a regulatory purpose involving military forces—to ensure the possibility of forming a well-regulated militia, and permit billeting only in "times of war" in a "manner . . . prescribed by law."[25] The signal contrast between these two rights and other rights enshrined in our Constitution is that these rights uniquely address situations where the distinction between civilian and military, public and private, government and governed, has become blurred. The First, Fourth, Fifth, Sixth, Seventh, and Eighth Amendments all leave little doubt about the difference between the government and the governed: the government is that group which might someday use or try to use the force of law to (for example) prohibit your religion; abridge your speech; search your house; seize your person; deprive you of life, liberty, or property; take your property without compensation; improperly force you to stand as the accused in a criminal prosecution; improperly adjudicate your suit at common law; or inflict on you a cruel or unusual punishment. The governed are citizens like you and me, persons who might someday have to fend off such tyrannical government behaviors.

The Second and Third Amendments contemplate, by contrast, situations where the distinction between the people making up the government and those making up the citizenry, or the property belonging to the government and that belonging to the citizenry, gives way to the demands of military necessity. The Second Amendment recognizes that these demands can take the form of personnel needs for a ready "militia" composed of persons who keep and bear arms in time of peace. The Third Amendment recognizes that these demands can take the form of needs for property interests in buildings to be used both as an owner's "house" and a soldier's quarters in time of war.

But both amendments narrowly target situations where the distinction between government and governed, between public and private—a distinction implicit but fundamental to the enforcement of any individual right *against the government*—has become blurred by military exigencies. Precisely because their function is to prevent governmental abuses in these gray areas, these rights should be viewed as different from, but structurally consistent with, the other rights included in our Constitution.

An Anomalously Uncontroversial Implied Right. Constitutional rights permitting or prohibiting private action—like anomalous rights to live in a society free of intoxicating liquors or to keep and bear private arms—have been the subject of intense discussion, scrutiny, and controversy. But so have parallel rights rooted in more ambiguous texts or in multiple texts.

For example, Judge Michael McConnell has contended on originalist grounds that the Supreme Court has too grudgingly interpreted the free exercise clause by excluding from constitutional protection private conduct undertaken for religious reasons. Judge McConnell urges that the free exercise clause be interpreted to require the government to grant exceptions from generally applicable laws for the exercise of private, religiously inspired practices.[26] After the Supreme Court rejected this view, Congress responded by passing legislation seeking to "restore" free exercise rights of the type that the Court has been unwilling to recognize.[27]

In another controversial line of authority tracing its origins to the 1920s, the Supreme Court has defined constitutionally protected "liberty" to include, among other things, a person's right "to acquire useful knowledge, to marry, establish a home and bring up children, to worship God according to the dictates of his own conscience, and generally to enjoy those privileges long recognized at common law as essential to the orderly pursuit of happiness by free men."[28] Since its early decisions in this line, the Supreme Court has struggled to define the contours of an individual right to "privacy," especially as regards private, consensual sexual activity.[29] These implied rights have been a focus of intense controversy on grounds they short-circuit democratic decision-making without clear textual warrant in the Constitution.

By contrast, the Supreme Court has also recognized what it calls an implied "right to travel," but in so doing it has engendered little criticism. Although not grounded in any single constitutional provision, the "right to travel" has drawn remarkably few accusations of improper judicial legislating.[30] As with the right of privacy, the Supreme Court has sought to ground the right to travel in multiple textual provisions, including privileges and immunities, the Article I commerce clause, and the citizenship clause of the Fourteenth Amendment.[31] But confusion over the textual parentage of the right to travel has prompted few accusations of bastardy. As Justice Stewart explained in an oft-quoted passage, "the constitutional right to travel from one State to another . . . occupies a position fundamental to the concept of our Federal Union" that is "elementary."[32] The Supreme Court has thus explained, "We are all citizens of the United States, and as members of the same community must have the right to pass and repass through every part of it without interruption."[33] Although the "sources and dimensions of right to travel as a constitutional entitlement" have been described as "mysterious and indeterminate,"[34] as a general matter, the existence of the right in some form is widely accepted.[35]

There undoubtedly are multiple reasons for the comparatively uncontroversial status of this particular implied constitutional right. But any explanation must include the critical fact that this right cannot be seen merely as a matter of personal freedom, like the free exercise of religion or an implied right to privacy. It must also and primarily be seen as a fundamental *political* right. Viewed as a political right, the right to travel aims essentially to protect the affirmative right of citizens to choose the body of state law that might or actually does govern them by, for instance, engaging in out-of-state advocacy or undertaking a temporary or permanent relocation. Viewed from the other side, the right prohibits state governments from infringing on the freedom of United States citizens to make these fundamental political choices.[36] But however it is viewed, the right can best be analogized, not to personal freedoms, but to political rights such as rights to vote and hold office.[37] These fundamental political rights are nowhere stated in affirmative terms by our Constitution.[38] They instead "must be inferred from the structures of self-government that underlie our Constitution's architecture and its animating premises."[39] Nonetheless, because they are self-evidently central to a democratic constitution, the Supreme Court has encountered little criticism in elaborately enforcing implied political rights with an expansive jurisprudence.[40] Something akin to the same dynamic, we believe, is at work in the widespread acceptance of the Court's recognition of an implied right to travel.

Future "Action" as a Recurring Counterpart in Constitutional Rights Decisions. Our final anomaly, at once more elusive and potentially more telling than the others, is the Supreme Court's tendency in a variety of doctrinal contexts to assume the presumptive legitimacy of governmental attempts to regulate future, private conduct. Remarkably, but with little notice, constitutional doctrines in entirely unrelated contexts define an array of rights in contradistinction to the same adjudicatory counterpart—the permissible state regulation of the future activities of private citizens. By contrast, state regulation that targets things deemed different from private action (such as speech, opinion, religious practice and belief, disfavored groups, disfavored persons, and so forth) is almost always held constitutionally infirm. Although we are not aware of any Supreme Court decision recognizing this recurring pattern, the bona fide, nondiscriminatory regulation of future private action is undeniably an important adjudicatory counterpart in a wide variety of constitutional contexts.

To be clear about what we mean by an adjudicatory counterpart, recall that constitutional adjudication is essentially common-law adjudication. An initial presumption that state action is constitutional may be rebutted by showing that one or more constitutional "doctrines" apply to invalidate the state action. Significantly, the application of these (potentially) invalidating doctrines is binary in form—either the doctrine applies and the state action is struck down or it does not apply and the state action is upheld.

This analytical procedure parallels the application of common-law doctrines. In a stylized common-law suit, a plaintiff must prove the elements of (i) the existence of a duty; (ii) breach of that duty; (iii) causation of damages; and (iv) amount of damages. The common-law court must therefore determine, in binary fashion, the presence or absence of each of these elements. Precisely because all relevant determinations are binary, the doctrines as to what constitutes the presence of a given element are equally defined by the cases finding the element absent. Many memorable holdings and statements defining common-law rules and doctrines are thus drawn from definitions of the *absence* of some essential element of liability.[41] Because constitutional adjudication occurs in this same mode as common-law adjudication— background presumption, doctrinal delineation, binary doctrinal application— our constitutional cases define "adjudicatory counterparts" for each constitutional right. Constitutional doctrine is thus defined by decisions holding what is *not* an establishment of religion, *not* a prohibition on the free exercise of religion, *not* an invasion of the freedom of speech, and so forth.

The anomaly here is that an important adjudicatory counterpart is consistently, albeit unconsciously, recognized by Supreme Court decisions spanning a wide variety of constitutional rights doctrines—namely, a finding that the law under scrutiny constitutes a bona fide effort to regulate future, private activity. One may defeat an equal protection challenge by arguing that the law at issue targets not the race of the persons affected, but only the activities in which those persons will engage.[42] One may defend against a free speech challenge on grounds that the challenged law targets not speech, but action;[43] against a free exercise challenge on grounds that the challenged law targets not religious belief or practice, but the secular aspects of the regulated action;[44] a regulatory takings challenge on grounds that the challenged law does not seek to confiscate a property's value but to regulate activities occurring on it;[45] and against a bill of attainder challenge on grounds that the law targets not disfavored persons, but those persons' activities.[46]

The Significance of Persisting Anomalies

The anomalies just sketched suggest that a powerful underlying logic may account for what appear at first to be constitutional oddities, mistakes, and happenstance. They suggest in particular that the Constitution exerts a powerful gravitational field centered on two structural principles: (i) decisions to permit or proscribe future, private action should be left for democratic determination, and (ii) decisions as to what economic, social, or cultural goals should be accomplished by private action also should be left for democratic determination. These principles appear nowhere in the Constitution's text. But the anomalies suggest they are part of a foundational constitutional architecture that can and must inform constitutional adjudication.

Democratic Control of Future, Private Action. Commentators have remarked that, with a few notable exceptions, specifically the now-repealed Eighteenth Amendment, the United States Constitution is "concerned only with the exercise of public authority."[47] Although constitutional rules may influence the panoply of private actions affected by lawmaking processes, our

Constitution, quite unlike constitutions in Europe, "has no formal, juridical *Drittwirkung*, imposing its values on the interpretation of private law rules."[48] The anomalies discussed above not only reinforce this received wisdom, they qualify it, color it, and help refute the contention that written constitutions are necessarily chains on the living forged by the dead.

Four of the five anomalies traced above suggest a significantly sacrosanct constitutional status for private activities. The anomalous repeal of the Eighteenth Amendment, the anomalous preamble that introduces and colors the Second Amendment, and the anomalously uncontroversial acceptance of an implied right to travel (in contrast with raging controversies over the right to bear arms, free exercise exceptionalism, and implied "privacy" rights) all suggest that the Constitution's structure disfavors, not implied rights as such, but implied rights to engage in private activities. The recognition and enforcement, without controversy, of implied rights to vote and hold office confirm this conclusion. And the conclusion is further reinforced by every constitutional lawyer's unthinking response to a wide and varied set of constitutional challenges—that the law under scrutiny is *not* unconstitutional because it *is* a bona fide regulation of future, private activity. The Court's repeated willingness to accept the validity of that answer, if justifiable, can only be rooted in a structural principle that transcends particular clauses.

The upshot is what might be termed one of the foundational principles of American, as opposed to European, democracy: a citizen's right to vote means a citizen's right to choose representatives for properly constituted democratic bodies that, taken collectively, enjoy the authority to determine (with a few possible exceptions) whether *any* and *every* future, private action will be lawful or unlawful, so long as the determinations are made according to laws that are properly compensatory, tailored, prospective, and applied to the specific facts of the case.

This structural principle recognizes the role and importance of *political rights*, the citizen's right to influence and control the bodies making governmental decisions. It recognizes the role and importance of *civil rights*, the rights that channel the mode, as opposed to controlling the outcome, of governmental decision making. And it recognizes most critically an individual's *personal freedoms,* rights for blocking as opposed to channeling democratic outcomes. As seen in the anomalies, the essential prerequisite for successfully enforcing a personal freedom is often establishing that the asserted freedom protects something *other than* private action, such as private belief, opinion, worship, speech, and the like. If our structural principle is valid, the haunting specter of "rights in conflict" gives way to a more cheery prospect of rights in remarkably harmonious alignment, at least insofar as the American Constitution is concerned.

The Public-Private Dividing Line. Our emphasis on the distinction between action and nonaction is complemented by emphasis on the location of the public-private dividing line. Civil rights channel *governmental* action by requiring that it be properly compensatory, well tailored, prospective, and applied to the facts of a specific person's case. Civil rights thus constrain governmental actions, but not private actions.[49] The practical scope of application of a person's civil rights therefore depends, in part, on the scope of governmental activities undertaken in the public sector.

The remaining anomaly traced above, that of the Second and Third Amendments, serves to underscore another foundational principle of our Constitution—the proposition that practically *every* decision as to what economic, social, or cultural goals should be accomplished by private action, as opposed to state action, should be left for democratic determination. Viewed in this light, the Second and Third Amendments, unlike the Eighteenth Amendment, are appropriate candidates for inclusion in a constitution because they answer a significant, recurring constitutional question: where does the public sphere end and the private sphere begin? As seen above, the Second and Third Amendments clarify the constitutional rules as to both persons and property in situations where the usual distinctions between public and private, military and civilian, government and governed, have become blurred by military necessity. The amendments underscore the critical constitutional importance of the public–private boundary.

A related structural proposition is that democratic processes should determine where to draw this boundary. This principle must be elicited not from an individual-rights anomaly but from features of our Constitution that appear anomalous only when viewed in comparison to the constitutions of other nations.

The American Constitution is unusual in that it provides only for a government in embryo, not for a government at maturity. Our Constitution establishes only one legislative body (the Congress); only one recipient of executive authority (the president); only one federal court (the United States Supreme Court). If regulations are to be enacted, if the vice president is to do anything other than break voting deadlocks in the Senate, if subordinate executive officers are to be appointed, if an executive officer other than the president is to be given authority, if inferior federal courts are to be constituted—all these embodiments of an ordinary, functioning government must be supplied, not by constitutional recipe, but by the workings of democracy. In a related vein, the Constitution establishes no mandated taxes and provides for no mandated spending; if taxes are to be collected and revenues are to be spent, they must *all* be approved in democratic deliberations.[50] Legislative, executive, and judicial powers are granted, to be sure, but these constitutional grants encompass only the irreducible institutional minimum necessary for the government to constitute itself and begin to deliberate. The institutions established by the Constitution must be democratically elaborated if a meaningful federal public sector is to come into existence at all.

In short, the American Constitution assigns to democratic processes almost the entirety of the decision as to where to draw the public-private dividing line. Admittedly, this aspect of constitutional design provides especially expansive scope for the play of democracy, confining our Constitution to less comprehensive political, economic, social, and cultural roles than those filled by more rights-laden instruments. But this very confinement, in conjunction with the other structural principle discussed above, enhances the Constitution's ability to avoid direct collisions among individual rights.

Lincoln's Originalism and Structuralism

Our contention that America's constitutional rights coexist in harmony and our appeal to structural principles in explaining that harmony is grounded first and foremost in the four corners of the Constitution and patterns in the decisions of our Supreme Court. But it is also sanctioned by President Lincoln. It is sanctioned especially by Lincoln's instructive, often poetic, appeals to higher-level constitutional principles, notwithstanding his remarkably firm command of and adherence to constitutional text and historical understandings. Lincoln read the Constitution very carefully, by the light of its historical meaning, and as a whole. This multidimensional approach is most evident in his reconciliation of an unqualified denunciation of slavery as inconsistent with the "first principles of free government," on the one hand, and his equally unqualified concession of slavery's constitutionally protected status on the other.

An important influence on Lincoln's constitutional understandings was Chief Justice Marshall's earlier willingness to look behind the Constitution's text to structure, function, and presuppositions in the course of constitutional decision making. Although Marshall's jurisprudence is too voluminous to encapsulate, his approach clearly influenced Lincoln, including his heavy reliance on what we call structural reasoning.[51] Marshall's critical presupposition that (in one scholar's words) "the Framers were too wise and too patriotic to have created an imperfect Constitution"[52] introduced into Marshall's constitutional decisions a strand of logic running from structural understandings of what *ought* to be found in democratic constitutions to what in fact *is* found in ours.

One of Lincoln's most important debts to Chief Justice Marshall arises from Lincoln's canonical description of our Constitution as establishing government "of the people, by the people, and for the people." This characterization of our democracy is a reworking of a famous passage from Marshall referring to the Constitution's preamble, which in turn recalls the Declaration of Independence's own preamble, affirming "the right of the people to alter or abolish" existing forms of government and "institute" new ones.[53] The characterization is thus in an important sense *the* canonical encapsulation of American democracy: there could hardly be a more authoritative interpretive statement than Lincoln quoting Marshall quoting the Constitution quoting the Declaration. It is therefore significant that Lincoln's epigrammatic characterization is a subtle but ringing endorsement of the right of each generation to make its own world for itself—presumably by invoking the aid and not surmounting the hindrance of their Constitution. Critically, "People" in this canonical description cannot refer to an eternal *Volk*, or an intergenerational amalgam of the living, dead, and yet to be born. It can refer only to living persons acting in their political capacities, as is clear from the preamble to the Constitution's unambiguous distinction between "We the People" and "our Posterity." Lincoln's speech at Gettysburg is an important rejoinder to those who contend that constitutional rights necessarily impose the specific political priorities of the dead upon the living.

Lincoln's more targeted and legalistic constitutional pronouncements—a model for our own—were rooted not only in structural understandings of republican government, but also in the Constitution's text and history. Despite decrying slavery as an "unqualified evil" fundamentally antithetical to the Constitution, Lincoln nonetheless recognized slavery as protected by both explicit and implicit constitutional guarantees. He stated in a pivotal 1860 speech that "all" the constitutional "guarantees" the "fathers gave" slavery should be "not grudgingly, but fully and fairly maintained."[54] Lincoln's view thus differs starkly from those of present-day academics who permit perceived structural principles to trump constitutional text, by identifying more or less favored constitutional provisions and advocating correspondingly more or less robust constitutional constructions.[55]

Lincoln's willingness to abide by text and history, even in the face of a countervailing structural principle, is particularly remarkable in light of Lincoln's unrelenting denunciations of slavery—an institution he described as "an unqualified evil" tending "to subvert *the first principle of free government.*" In an 1858 Senate campaign speech, Lincoln declared:

> The Republican party . . . hold that this government was instituted to secure the blessings of freedom and that slavery is *an unqualified evil* to the negro, to the white man, to the soil, and to the State. Regarding it an evil, they will not molest it in the States where it exists; they will not overlook the constitutional guards which our forefathers have placed around it; they will do nothing that can give proper offence to those who hold slaves by legal sanction; but they will use every constitutional method to prevent the evil from becoming larger and involving more negroes, more white men, more soil, and more States in its deplorable consequences.[56]

Lincoln closed the campaign with a summary of his position:

> The legal right of the Southern people to reclaim their fugitives I have constantly admitted. The legal right of Congress to interfere with their institution in the states, I have constantly denied. In resisting the spread of slavery to new territory, and with that what

appears to me to be a tendency to subvert *the first principle of free government itself* my whole effort has consisted.[57]

Lincoln's invocation of his power as commander-in-chief to suspend the writ of habeas corpus and emancipate slaves has sometimes provoked charges of interpretive libertinism. In fact, Lincoln flatly denied that in times of peace, including very turbulent times of peace, even the strongest structural considerations could water down express or clearly implied constitutional protections. Despite his moral and political rejection of slavery, Lincoln pledged to use only "every *constitutional* method" to arrest its enlargement.

Lincoln's insistence on adhering to constitutional means, combined with his concessions of the express and implied constitutional protections afforded slavery, left him in something of an exposed position in the wake of the Supreme Court's *Dred Scott* decision. *Dred Scott* forced Lincoln to explain precisely why the Constitution permits the federal government to outlaw slavery in federal territories but forbids it from outlawing slavery in states, even though the document addresses neither question in express terms. Lincoln rose to the challenge by marshaling perhaps the first extended "originalist" argument to deploy a person-by-person analysis exploring the Framers' individual historical understandings. Within a mere four months of the decision, Lincoln declared that the "*Dred Scott* decision was, in part, based on assumed historical facts which were not really true."[58] His assault culminated three years later in a renowned speech at New York's Cooper Institute in which he painstakingly argued from the historical understandings of Congress's power to outlaw slavery in federal territories. Lincoln combed congressional voting records and similar sources to support his declaration that "a clear majority" of our "fathers who framed the original Constitution" certainly understood that no "part of the Constitution, forbade the Federal Government to control slavery in the federal territories."[59] Lincoln's reliance on careful historical inquiry into contemporaneous understandings of constitutional texts mark him an early practitioner of "originalist" interpretation.

But while Lincoln respected the Constitution's text and plumbed its historical understandings, he did not hesitate to look beyond the Constitution's operative clauses for foundational presuppositions that support and inform its meaning. We have seen that Lincoln coupled his denunciation of slavery as "unqualified evil" with a paraphrase, not of an operative constitutional clause, but of the Constitution's preamble: "The Republican party . . . hold that this government was instituted to secure the blessings of freedom." Forced by *Dred Scott* to rebut charges that he was obstinately refusing to accept the Constitution's authoritatively declared meaning, Lincoln turned not to constitutional text and history alone, but also to the higher principles of liberty enshrined in the Constitution's preamble and the Declaration of Independence.

Lincoln's most evocative description of the relationship between the written Constitution and its higher, unwritten principles was referred to briefly above. It is his characteristically biblical image of an "apple of gold" in a "picture of silver."[60] The apple of gold in the image is the Declaration of Independence and its "most happy and fortunate" expression of the principle of "Liberty to all." The picture of silver is the Union and Constitution, which were made "not to conceal, or destroy the apple but to adorn and preserve it." "The picture was made for the apple—not the apple for the picture." The salient point of the image is that the Constitution reflects and embodies principles that are not spelled out by their terms in its text. Although the Constitution might entrench the "unqualified evil" of slavery, and although that entrenchment must be respected, the entrenchment need *not* be accepted, much less perpetuated, much less revered.

Lincoln's most important, and narrow, dispute with Chief Justice Taney's logic in *Dred Scott* was his complete rejection of Taney's assertion that "the right of property in a slave is distinctly and expressly affirmed in the Constitution."[61] Conceding that the South's position might be "fully justified" if its citizens stood to be deprived of "some right, plainly written down in the Constitution," Lincoln countered that "no such right is specifically written into the Constitution."[62] In fact, the "instrument is literally silent about any such right" and, according to Lincoln, the historical record showed that no such right has any existence "in the Constitution, even by implication."[63] It was based on his belief that the express constitutional text *was* silent, and even abashed, regarding "the right of property in a slave," and that the historical understandings of the Framers were in his favor, that Lincoln felt free to invoke higher constitutional principles in his nuanced but unrelenting denunciation.[64]

Stated in its most famous and expansive terms, Lincoln's constitutional conception was of a government of (living) people by (living) people for (living) people. This conception, far from being divorced from the raging controversies of his era, was instead an essential jumping-off point for Lincoln's understanding of the Constitution. The central paradox of Lincoln's constitutional thinking—his simultaneous complete acceptance and utter rejection of slavery's constitutional status—cannot be understood except through his belief that higher structural principles lay beneath and behind the express and implied constitutional protections that slavery enjoyed in its day. Unless rights-granting constitutions carefully select and circumscribe the rights they entrench, and abide by the structural principles Lincoln championed, they unavoidably will depart from Lincoln's democratic constitutionalism. In so doing, they will produce some incalculable combination of government by the dead on the living or else government by legal elites on everybody else.

Conclusion

The Charter of Fundamental Rights of the European Union, as noted above, confers protective rights regarding personal data. It states that "everyone has the right of access to data which has been collected concerning him or her, and the right to have it rectified," and "the right to the protection of personal data concerning him or her."[65] Not surprisingly, the U.S. Congress has enacted legislation along similar lines in the Buckley Amendment, which establishes rights of parents and students as regards schools' practices in compiling and sharing educational records.[66] The Buckley Amendment creates mechanisms both for forcing educational records disclosures (to the relevant students and their parents) and for limiting such disclosures (to everyone else). At one level, then, it can be said that both Europe and America, as advanced Western democracies in an information age, have adopted rights granting laws concerning the accuracy, confidentiality, and disclosure of personal data.

A critical difference, however, is that Europeans have mounted efforts to *constitutionalize* privacy protections and disclosure interests of the sort the Buckley Amendment addresses in statutory law. To a European eye, these rights may be both uncontroversial and easily reconciled with each other; hence, there should be little problem with their constitutional entrenchment. But the result of such entrenchment is an encroachment on a more fundamental right—citizens' right to a decision-making vote. Ordinary American citizens may, in the future, mobilize their democratic representatives to alter America's rules regarding confidentiality and disclosure of educational records—just as ordinary New Yorkers once mobilized the attention of Senator Buckley and his colleagues. But ordinary Europeans, stripped of this political right, or of the full entirety of this right, might well be consigned to the tender mercies of less democratic, less accountable, and less transparent governance.

Who believes this is a good idea? Why is it that ordinary Europeans cannot be trusted to make sensible policy decisions about educational records confidentiality and disclosure? And who has mounted a persuasive case for constitutions with opposing democratic and antidemocratic elements, with educational records confidentiality and disclosure policy landing on the undemocratic side of the line? What astounds many Americans about Europe's current round of constitution making is its apparent departure from the European ideals of democracy they admire—ideals that inspired America's own founding and that continue to inspire an appreciation for "active liberty" and cognate ideas in our contemporary judiciary and academy.[67]

The fact that European democracy is departing almost off-handedly from the European-inspired American model brings us full circle to a final thought regarding the academic approach to originalist interpretation. We worry that academic originalism's tendency to undervalue the salience of structural principles may obscure the unity and harmony of our Constitution, rendering its profoundest meanings opaque even to, or perhaps especially to, academic specialists. All of Lincoln's intelligence, and all of his eloquence, wisdom, patience, and compassion, might well have come down to a historical footnote had he simply offered an effective, lawyerly, originalist critique of *Dred Scott*, while omitting also to explain why slavery violates the first principle of free government. Originalism can be, should be, and is being brought to bear to determine outcomes in specific cases. But unless something else is also brought to bear on the public mind, we do not see how either Europeans or future Americans will come to share Americans' traditional readiness to debate ferociously every proposed exception—from booze, to guns, to God, to sex—to the rule that the lawfulness of private activities should be determined democratically, by the lights of each succeeding generation.

Notes

1. Europeans have an ambivalent attitude toward the American legal system. *See, e.g.*, Fernanda G. Nicola, *Transatlanticisms: Constitutional Asymmetry and Selective Reception of U.S. Law And Economics in the Formation of European Private Law*, 16 Cardozo J. Int'l & Comp. L. 87, 139-153 (2008) (discussing the extent to which Europeans have both relied on and resisted mainstream American legal insights).

2. The Federalist No. 49 (James Madison).

3. Mary Ann Glendon, Rights Talk: The Impoverishment of Political Discourse (1991).

4. *See* Elizabeth F. Defeis, *A Constitution for the European Union? A Transatlantic Perspective*, 19 Temp. Int'l & Comp. L.J. 351, 378 (2005).

5. Lawrence Rosenthal, *Does Due Process Have An Original Meaning? On Originalism, Due Process, Procedural Innovation . . . And Parking Tickets*, 60 Okla. L. Rev. 1, 3–4 (2007) (discussing the rise of public-meaning originalism).

6. Robert Post and Reva Siegel, *Originalism as a Political Practice: The Right's Living Constitution*, 75 Fordham L. Rev. 545, 550 (2006).

7. Troy L. Booher, *Putting Meaning in Its Place: Originalism and Philosophy of Language*, 25 L. & Phil. 387, 387 (2006); *see also* Steven G. Calabresi, *A Critical Introduction to the Originalism Debate*, 31 Harv. J. L. & Pub. Pol'y 875 (2008).

. 8. Laurence H. Tribe, *Comment to Antonin Scalia*, in A Matter of Interpretation 65, 67 (Amy Gutmann ed., 1997).

9. David B. Rivkin and Lee A. Casey, *Mr. Constitution*, Wall. St. J., Mar. 22, 2008 (The Weekend Interview: Clarence Thomas); *see also* Bradley P. Jacob, *Will the Real Constitutional Originalist Please Stand Up?* 40 Creighton L. Rev. 595 (2007); Antonin Scalia, *Originalism: The Lesser Evil*, 57 U. Cin. L. Rev. 849 (1989); Clarence Thomas, *Judging*, 45 U. Kan. L. Rev. 1 (1996).

10. Our sense is that pure originalists tend to see the faint-hearted originalism of its judicial adherents as a bow to the expediency required of those who have ascended the bench. *See* Gary Lawson, *Mostly Unconstitutional: The Case Against Precedent Revisited*, 5 Ave Maria L. Rev. 1, 17 (2007) (rejecting the pragmatic concerns of "faint-hearted" originalists as "the province of moral and political theorist[s]"); Randy E. Barnett, *Scalia's Infidelity: A Critique of "Faint-Hearted" Originalism*, 75 U. Cin. L. Rev. 7, 23 (2006) (criticizing judicial approaches that depart from the original meaning of the "entire Constitution"); Gary Lawson and Guy Seidman, *Originalism as a Legal Enterprise*, 23 Const. Comment. 47 (2006) (arguing that the "reasonable American person of 1788 determines, for 1788 and today, the meaning of the federal Constitution"); Vasan Kesavan and Michael Stokes Paulsen, *The Interpretive Force of the Constitution's Secret Drafting History*, 91 Georgetown L.J., 1113 (2003) ("to avoid creeping or lurching anachronism infecting the interpretation of an authoritative legal text, the proper approach must be one of 'originalist' textualism—faithful application of the words and phrases of the text in accordance with the meaning they would have had at the time they were adopted as law"); Vasan Kesavan and Michael Stokes Paulsen, *Is West Virgina*

Unconstitutional? 90 Cal. L. Rev. 291, 398 (2002) ("If the object is to ascertain the meaning of the Constitution as a written document . . . the appropriate search is for the original public meaning . . . [of what the Constitution's] language would have had (both its words and its grammar) to an average, informed speaker and reader of that language at the time of its enactment into law.").

11. Roy P. Basler, ed., The Collected Works of Abraham Lincoln vol. iv, 513.

12. *See* Constitution of the Commonwealth of Massachusetts, art. XXX ("In the government of this commonwealth, the legislative department shall never exercise the executive and judicial powers, or either of them: the executive shall never exercise the legislative and judicial powers, or either of them: the judicial shall never exercise the legislative and executive powers, or either of them: to the end it may be a government of laws and not of men.").

13. *See Morrison v. Olson*, 487 U.S. 654, 697 (1988) (Scalia, J., dissenting).

14. U.S. Const. amend. XI; *see Chisolm v. Georgia*, 2 U.S. (2 Dall.) 419 (1793).

15. Akhil R. Amar, The Bill of Rights: Creation and Reconstruction 27, 37 (1998).

16. Compare *District of Columbia v. Heller*, 128 S. Ct. 2783, 2801–2802 (2008), with *id.* at 2824–2826 (Stevens, J., dissenting); *see also* Andrea Moates, *Second Amendment Jurisprudence: The Possible Destruction of the Rights of "The People,"* 30 Okla. City U. L. Rev. 363 (2005) (summarizing cases and scholarship concerning the Second Amendment).

17. David Thomas Konig, *The Second Amendment: A Missing Transatlantic Context for the Historical Meaning of "The Right of the People To Keep And Bear Arms,"* 22 Law & Hist. Rev. 119, 155–56 (2004) (arguing that Thomas Jefferson, like Blackstone before him, regarded preambles as reliable and necessary indications of lawmakers' intent).

18. Michael C. Dorf, *What Does the Second Amendment Mean Today?* 76 Chi.-Kent L. Rev. 291, 302 (2000) ("In the case of the Second Amendment as it appears in the federal Constitution, the text is striking for containing its own preamble.").

19. William Blackstone, Commentaries on the Laws of England 136, 140 (1765).

20. Heller, 128 S. Ct. at 2801 (citing Letters from the Federal Farmer III (Oct. 10, 1879, in 2 The Complete Anti-Federalist 234, 242 [H. Storing ed., 1981]).

21. *See* Konig, *supra* note 17, at 143–53 (arguing that American colonists looked to the Scottish experience of resisting British authority and viewed local militias as a natural bulwark against federal authority).

22. *See* Tom W. Bell, *The Third Amendment: Forgotten But Not Gone*, 2 Wm. & Mary Bill Rts. J. 117 (1993) (explaining that while the "other amendments of the United States Constitution's Bill of Rights inspire public adoration and volumes of legal research," the "Third Amendment languishes in comparative oblivion"); Kenneth A. Klukowski, *Armed by Right: The Emerging Jurisprudence of the Second Amendment*, 18 Geo. Mason U. Civ. Rts. L.J. 167 (2008) (noting that with the Supreme Court's *Heller* decision, the "nation may be in the early stages of a new legal regime: the emergence of a coherent and meaningful jurisprudence concerning the Second Amendment").

23. Klukowski, *supra* note 22, at 172–73.

24. Sanford Levinson, *The Embarrassing Second Amendment*, 99 Yale L.J. 637, 640 (1989).

25. Amar, *supra* note 15, at 62.

26. Michael W. McConnell, *The Origins and Historical Understanding of Free Exercise of Religion*, 103 Harv. L. Rev. 1409 (1990); Michael W. McConnell, *Free Exercise Revisionism and the* Smith *Decision*, 57 U. Chi. L. Rev. 1109 (1990).

27. *See* Religious Freedom Restoration Act of 1993, 42 U.S.C.A. §§ 2000bb, *et. seq.*; Religious Land Use and Institutionalized Persons Act of 2000, 42 U.S.C.A. § 2000cc.

28. *Meyer v. Nebraska*, 262 U.S. 390, 399 (1923); *see also Pierce v. Society of Sisters*, 268 U.S. 510 (1925).

29. *Griswold v. Connecticut*, 381 U.S. 479 (1965); *Lawrence v. Texas*, 539 U.S. 558 (2003).

30. *Edwards v. California*, 314 U.S. 160 (1941); *see also id.* at 169 (Douglas, J., concurring) ("The right to move freely from State to State is an incident of national citizenship protected by the privileges and immunities clause of the Fourteenth Amendment against state interference."). The implied right to travel stands at an intersection of the Supreme Court's individual rights jurisprudence and its dormant commerce clause jurisprudence, but has generated less noticeable controversy than either of these other doctrines.

31. *Senz v. Roe*, 526 U.S. 489 (1999) (describing different aspects of, and constitutional bases for, the right to travel).

32. *United States v. Guest*, 383 U.S. 745, 757–68 (1966).

33. *Crandall v. State of Nevada*, 73 U.S. 35, 49 (1867).

34. Bryan H. Wildenthal, *State Parochialism, The Right to Travel, and the Privileges and Immunities Clause of Article IV*, 41 Stan. L. Rev. 1557, 1575 (1989).

35. Francesca Strumia, *Citizenship and Free Movement: European and American Features of a Judicial Formula for Increased Comity*, 12 Colum. J. Eur. L. 713, 728 (2006) (describing the history of the right of travel as understood in Europe and in the United States).

36. Laurence H. Tribe, *Saenz Sans Prophecy: Does the Privileges or Immunities Revival Portend the Future—Or Reveal the Structure of the Present?* 113 Harv. L. Rev. 110, 154 (1999) (the "component of the right to travel . . . involved the elaboration of a structural principle of equal citizenship more than the protection of an individual right").

37. *See Dunn v. Blumstein*, 405 U.S. 330, 360 (1972) (striking down state durational residency requirements as violating citizens' rights to vote and travel).

38. *See Harper v. Va. State Bd. of Elections*, 383 U.S. 663, 665 (1966) (the right to vote in state and local elections "is nowhere expressly mentioned" in the Constitution); *Saenz*, 526 U.S. at 498 (the "word 'travel' is not found in the text of the Constitution).

39. Tribe, *supra* note 36, at 154.

40. John Hart Ely, Democracy and Distrust 177–79 (1980); *see also Crandall v. Nevada*, 73 U.S. (6 Wall.) 35, 43–44 (1868) (describing right to travel as guarantee for citizens to exercise their political rights at the seat of government).

41. For example, the doctrines holding that a duty of care is not owed to Mrs. Palsgraf (*Palsgraf v. Long Island R. Co.*, 248 N.Y. 339, 162 N.E. 99 (1928)); that negligence does not occur when one takes care to "stop, look, and listen" before crossing train tracks (*Baltimore & Ohio R. R. Co. v. Goodman*, 275 U.S. 66 (1927) (Holmes, J.)); and that recoverable damages are not caused when one's business suffers because of consequential damages arising from a late delivery (*Hadley v. Baxendale*, 156 Eng. Rep. 145 (1854)).

42. *Washington v. Davis*, 426 U.S. 229 (1976).

43. *United States v. O'Brien*, 391 U.S. 367 (1968).

44. *Church of Lukumi Babalu Aye, Inc. v. City of Hialeah*, 508 U.S. 520 (1993); *Employment Div., Dep't. of Human Res. v. Smith*, 494 U.S. 872 (1990).

45. *Lucas v. S.C. Coastal Council*, 505 U.S. 103 (1992).

46. *United States v. Brown*, 381 U.S. 437, 442 (1965).

47. William B. Fisch & Richard S. Kay, *The Constitutionalization of the Law in the United States*, 46 Am. J. Comp. L. 437, 452 (1998). The German concept of *Drittwirkung* (third-party effect) is a legal theory that, in simple terms, eliminates the requirement of state action and presumes a private party's human rights are protected against violations by other private parties.

48. *Id.*

49. The Civil Rights Cases, 109 U.S. 3, 13 (1883).

50. *See* U.S. Const. art. I, § 8, cl. 1 (the "spending clause"); *see also* U.S. Const. art. I, § 8, cl. 12 (the "military appropriations clause").

51. Structuralist reasoning is preeminent in Marshall's most important judicial decisions: *Marbury v. Madison* and *McCulloch v. Maryland. See Marbury v. Madison*, 5 U.S. (1 Cranch) 137, 2 L. Ed. 60 (1803); *McCulloch v. Maryland*, 17 U.S. 316 (1819).

52. David P. Currie, *The Constitution in the Supreme Court: The Powers of the Federal Courts*, 1801–1835, 49 U. Chi. L. Rev. 646, 694 (1982) (*discussing Cohens v. Virginia*, 19 U.S. (6 Wheat.) 264 (1821), and *Marbury v. Madison*, 5 U.S. (1 Cranch) 137 [1803]).

53. *See McCulloch v. Maryland*, 17 U.S. 316, 403–4 (1819) ("The government of the Union . . . is emphatically, and truly, a government of the people. In form and in substance it emanates from them. Its powers are granted by them, and are to be exercised directly on them, and for their benefit."). This passage's repeated references to "the people" recall the opening words of the Constitution's Preamble ("We the People of the United States"). The connection to the Preamble is made even stronger by the immediately preceding passage in Marshall's opinion, which paraphrases the Preamble by remarking that the Constitution derives its whole authority "directly from the people; is 'ordained and established' in the name of the people; and is declared to be ordained, 'in order to . . . secure the blessings of liberty to themselves and to their posterity.'" *Id.* at 403. Similarly, the reference to "ordain and establish," which appears in both the Preamble and *McCulloch*, recalls the "right of the people to alter or to abolish" old forms of government and "institute" new ones as declared by the Preamble to the Declaration of Independence.

54. Abraham Lincoln, *Address at Cooper Institute* (New York, Feb. 27, 1860), reprinted in Abraham Lincoln: His Speeches and Writings 526 (Roy P. Basler ed., 1969).

55. *See* Ronald Dworkin, Freedom's Law: The Moral Reading of the American Constitution (1996); *see also* Alexander Meiklejohn, *The First Amendment Is an Absolute*, 1961 Sup. Ct. Rev. 245, 255.

56. Abraham Lincoln, *Fragment: Speech at Edwardsville, Illinois* (Sept. 11, 1858), reprinted in Abraham Lincoln: His Speeches and Writings, *supra* note 54, at 470 (emphasis added).

57. Abraham Lincoln, *Last Speech in Springfield, Illinois, in the Campaign of 1858* (Oct. 30, 1858), reprinted in Abraham Lincoln: His Speeches and Writings *supra* note 54, at 480–81 (emphasis added).

58. Abraham Lincoln, *The* Dred Scott *Decision: Speech at Springfield, Illinois* (June 26, 1857), reprinted in Abraham Lincoln: His Speeches and Writings, *supra* note 54, at 352–66; *see also Dred Scott v. Sandford*, 60 U.S. (19 How.) 393 (1857) (decided March 6, 1857).

59. Lincoln, *supra* note 54, at 523. By contrast, an effective originalist defense of *Brown v. Board of Education*, based on a similar person-by-person analysis of congressional voting records, first arrived more than four decades after *Brown* was decided. *See* Michael W. McConnell, *Originalism and the Desegregation Decisions*, 81 Va. L. Rev. 947 (1995).

60. Abraham Lincoln, *Fragment on the Constitution and the Union*, in The Collected Works of Abraham Lincoln 169 (Roy P. Basler ed., 1953).

61. *Dred Scott*, 60 U.S. (19 How.) at 451.

62. Lincoln, *supra* note 54, at 532–33.

63. *Id.*

64. *Id.*

65. Charter of Fundamental Rights of the European Union, Dec. 7, 2000, 2000 O.J. (C 364) 2, 8(2).

66. Family Educational Rights and Privacy Act, 20 U.S.C. § 1232(g) (2000).

67. Stephen Breyer, Active Liberty: Interpreting Our Democratic Constitution 3–4 (2005); *see also* Michael W. McConnell, *Active Liberty: A Progressive Alternative to Textualism and Originalism*, 199 Harv. L. Rev. 2387 (2006) (book review).

11

Concluding Remarks

Kenneth W. Starr

My theme will be the perhaps startling proposition that true Americans can be and indeed must be true cosmopolitans, owing ultimately to the fact that the American creed is itself cosmopolitan—rooted in neither blood nor soil, but providing instead a universal statement of self-evident truths applicable at all times, in all places, to all human beings. I begin with one of my favorite Public Broadcasting System television shows, *Think Tank with Ben Wattenberg*. A few years ago, Ben Wattenberg had a gathering of authors discussing one of my favorite personages from the American founding, the estimable Dr. Benjamin Franklin.[1] He asked the renowned historian H. W. Brands, now at the University of Texas Law School, why he referred to Franklin as "the first American" in the title of his book about Franklin.

Professor Brands explained that he did so for three reasons: First, "he was the most illustrious [and] best-known American of his day." Second, he established "a model for the American character": practical, self-reliant, self-educated, unimpressed with wealth and title, optimistic, endowed with a great sense of humor and great enthusiasm for civic virtue. Third, he was the first person "to have a real sense of American identity separate from that of Englishmen." According to another guest, Claude-Anne Lopez, an author and editor of the Franklin Papers at Yale, Franklin "was also the first American to become cosmopolitan. [He was] the first one to go to Europe, live there as minister to Paris, to be admired immensely, to this day, by the Europeans and to bring back this larger vision when he came back to Philadelphia."

This then is the paradox: the first American, the first person to be endowed with American character and identity, was also America's first cosmopolitan—a transnational figure recognized abroad for his uniquely American identity.

The *Oxford English Dictionary* defines "citizen" first as "an inhabitant of a city or (often) of a town," and second as "a member of a state, an enfranchised inhabitant of a country, as opposed to an alien." The first, etymologically derived definition seems fairly loose, referring as it does to a mere "inhabitant" rather than to someone who genuinely belongs to a place. (I will briefly return to this point at the end of my remarks.) For me, the best and highest definition of citizenship involves community—moral connectedness as well as legal connectedness. It may suggest a national character or identity, but at a minimum, it suggests moral and/or legal attachment to a community, and thus necessarily implies boundaries that define and separate those inside the community from those outside the community.

The modern citizenship narrative, of course, is one of extending citizenship's boundaries and expanding outer perimeters. But, as the comments about Dr. Franklin suggest, this urge to extend the boundaries of citizenship—and to overcome the difference between those inside and outside the communal perimeter—has been underway for centuries, indeed, for millennia. Consider the observation a few millennia ago of a certain person who met his demise in his beloved Athens. Socrates was put to death for (among other reasons) the radicalism of his statement, "I am neither Athenian nor a Greek. I am a citizen of the world."[2] Or to choose a more modern example, consider those who seek to transcend national boundaries and write a meta-narrative for the entire human race, whether for environmental reasons or, as in the case of Albert Schweitzer, a personal favorite of mine, for compelling reasons of faith. Shortly before his death in Gabon, Africa, Schweitzer wrote, "As long ago as my student days, it struck me as incomprehensible that I should be allowed to live in one country such a happy life while I saw people around the world suffering. And there grew up within me an understanding that we must not treat our lives as being for ourselves alone."[3]

A few years ago, these larger questions of identity and citizenship were examined at a conference sponsored by, of all institutions, the United Nations. A Nobel laureate in economics, Amartya Sen, described the many "spaces" through which a single human being living in our time "travels" or even "wanders" over the course of his or her lifetime. A person can be at the same moment a person of Asian background, a Christian, a liberal, a woman, a vegetarian, and so on, with endless links to other individuals all over the globe.[4] And we must acknowledge that those global links may in some instances be more morally significant to that individual than the fact that he or she happens to be a "citizen" of a particular country. Another participant at that same conference, Princeton philosophy professor Kwame Anthony Appiah, suggested that a strong tendency exists to overstate the importance of national allegiance in identifying and describing the identities of individuals. He spoke of the enduring significance of cosmopolitan loyalties. Raw demographic data can be marshaled to reinforce this conception of a multiplicity of "citizenships" or identities. A recent survey found that "among young Americans ages 15 to 19, . . . barely half expected to live in the country of their birth."[5] Sociologists tell us that all across the United States, there are now metropolitan melting pots assimilating immigrants from various backgrounds.

But we know as well that the nation-state remains a powerful force in the world; hence the continuing paradox with which I opened my remarks. What does it really mean to be, for example, a British citizen? A minister in the Labor government recently said that Britain must "clarify the contract between our country and newcomers. . . . We need to do more to help newcomers understand *our values and our British way of life*."[6] What about a French citizen? While the *Economist* reports that the French president "has made immigration a centerpiece" of his presidency,"[7] other news stories report on Faiza Silmi, an applicant for French citizenship who was turned down for wearing an Islamic veil: "When Faiza Silmi applied for French citizenship, she worried that her French was not quite good enough or that her Moroccan upbringing would pose a problem. 'I would never have imagined that they would turn me down because of what I chose to wear.'"[8] And German citizenship, it seems, is now being put to the test with a new multiple-choice examination. Among the questions: "Why did former Chancellor Willy Brandt kneel down at the former Warsaw Ghetto in 1970?" Another: "What does Stasi stand for?"

There is, in short, a recurring and seemingly irreducible assertion of national identity in various countries, notwithstanding the increasingly flat world with its global economic arrangements. I want to suggest that, contrary to what some might suppose, such assertions have quite venerable, respectable, nonnativist roots here in the United States.

Interestingly enough, the Constitution of the United States does not speak about citizenship. We get around to it only in the Fourteenth Amendment. And now citizenship is governed by statute, meaning that it can be changed at any time. There has undoubtedly been a historical march constitutionally toward greater inclusiveness within the American polity. We see that inclusiveness in the post–Civil War constitutional amendments. We see it as well in the expansion of the franchise, the fundamental right to vote. But there remains in the Constitution a provision that excludes foreign-born individuals from the office of president.[9]

Professor Akhil Amar of Yale Law School has written very thoughtfully about this anomaly. "The Constitution," he reminds us, "was, by the standards of the time, hugely pro-immigrant. Under the English Act of Settlement . . . no naturalized subject in England could ever serve in the House of Commons, the Lords, the Privy Council, or a wide range of other offices. The Constitution repudiated this tradition across the board, opening the House, the Senate, the Cabinet. and the federal judiciary to naturalized and native alike."[10] As Amar further notes, "Seven of the 39 signers of the Constitution in Philadelphia were foreign-born, as were countless thousands of voters who helped ratify the Constitution. Immigrant Americans accounted for 8 of America's first 81 members of Congress, 3 of our first 10 Supreme Court justices, [and] 4 of our first 6 secretaries of the treasury"[11]— including of course, famously, Mr. Hamilton.

In the second *Federalist* paper, John Jay, who became our first chief justice, described Americans as a providentially guided "band of brethren"— "descended from the same ancestors, speaking the same language, professing the same religion, attached to the same principles of government, very similar in their manners and customs."[12] Likewise, Jay's contemporary, the enlightened Mr. Thomas Jefferson, feared America becoming "a heterogeneous, incoherent, distracted mass."[13] This emphasis on national unity was later transformed—during times of heavy immigration—into an emphasis on assimilation of the new arrivals to our shores. "Americanization" became Theodore Roosevelt's rallying cry in the latter years of his presidency. He railed repeatedly against what he termed "hyphenated" Americans. Faintly echoing President Jefferson, President Roosevelt warned of the nation being "brought to ruins by a tangle of squabbling nationalities."[14] As a cure, he advocated the compulsory learning of English: "Every immigrant who comes here should be required within five years to learn English or to leave the country."[15]

The upshot of this centuries-old discussion is a very widely held view, perhaps even approaching a consensus, favoring immigration and allowing new Americans to become full Americans comparatively quickly—provided that they undertake an ill-defined but vitally important set of steps called "Americanization." This certainly suggests that Americanism is a creed that can be believed in, and to a certain extent practiced, from afar, setting the stage offshore for the later onshore "Americanization" of new arrivals.

The idea of an American creed being in some sense universal brings to mind, in this its sixtieth anniversary year, the United Nations' *Universal Declaration of Human Rights*. The Universal Declaration's language will be familiar to our friends from France and, more importantly for present purposes, to students of our own Declaration of Independence.

"Article 1. All human beings are born free and equal in dignity and rights." One striking feature of the Universal Declaration is the textually parallel expressions of universalism at the beginning of so many of its thirty articles: "No one should be denied"; "Everyone"; "all"; "everyone"; "no one"; and so on and so forth. Judging just from the repeated textual framing of its pronouncements, the declarations set forth in the Universal Declaration aim to be just that—universal. The idea of universal rights suggests to many people a cognate idea of universal citizenship. I recognize that "world citizenship" can strike some as pure fantasy floating on thinnest air. But I find it inspiring to think and voice thoughts of shared humanity and human dignity. Indeed, I find myself inspired by the Universal Declaration, even as I recognize the grave dangers it poses to democracy whenever its aspirations are interpreted as the terms of a directly judicially enforceable roster of worldwide citizenship rights.

Which brings us back to communities and perimeters, to the idea that the very notion of citizenship carries and sometimes conceals a notion of limits. I will close with words from a beautiful address that captures for me the distinctive American spirit that Dr. Franklin is said to have inaugurated. In his farewell address to the nation on January 11, 1989, President Ronald Reagan remarked, "People ask how I feel about leaving and the fact is parting is sweet sorrow. The sweet is California and the ranch and freedom. The sorrow: the goodbyes, of course, and [the] notion of leaving this beautiful place because down this hall and up the stairs is the part of the White House where the president and the family live. There are a few favorite windows I have up there that I like to stand at and look out of early in the morning. The view is over the grounds here to the Washington Monument, and then the Mall, and then the Jefferson Memorial. But on mornings when the humidity is low, you can see past Jefferson to the river, to the Potomac, and the Virginia shore. . . . And I have been thinking a bit at that window. I have been thinking on the past eight years and what they have meant. . . . The past few days when I have been at that window upstairs, I have thought a bit about the 'shining city upon a hill.' The phrase comes from John Winthrop, who wrote it to describe the America he imagined. What he imagined was important because he was an early Pilgrim, an early friend of freedom. He journeyed here on what today we would call a little wooden boat, and like the other Pilgrims, he was looking for a home that would be free."[16]

The word "city" is derived, of course, from the Latin *civitas*, closely akin to *civis*, citizen. A citizen by etymological definition is thus a city dweller. And just as the idea of a city means city *limits*, beyond which lie distinct noncity spaces, so the idea of citizenship means legal and moral *boundaries*, beyond which lie persons called noncitizens. I remain unabashedly taken with John Winthrop's imagery, because the metaphor conveys with subtlety and poetry both the bonds and boundaries of cities and citizenship. The sightlines—back and forth—from an upraised city are clean and clear. The denizens of the surrounding countryside can look into and up to their shining-city neighbors for inspiration. But just as important, the city's citizens may and must look out in the other direction. To remain the type of moral exemplars Winthrop had in mind, they are obliged (especially in times of trouble, famine, or despair) to emerge and come to the mutual aid and support of their neighbors. This mutual aid and support are *not* legal obligations. They do *not* arise from a legal relationship. They do *not* constitute a kind of shared citizenship. But they remain nonetheless a vital necessity for any city that expects to shine forth as a beacon. This relationship can perhaps be best described, not as one of some higher, more encompassing citizenship, but by the term our French friends call *fraternité*. By whatever name, the relationship truly and surely inspires, and it is at the foundation of Dr. Franklin's cosmopolitan world.

Notes

1. PBS, Think Tank: Transcript for "Think Tank with Ben Wattenberg" (May 29, 2003), http://www.pbs.org/thinktank/transcript956.html. *See id.* for quotations that follow.

2. Plutarch, Morals 19 (William Goodwin ed., 2007).

3. Albert Schweitzer, Memoirs of Childhood and Youth 61 (2007).

4. Melissa Gorelick, *The Idea of Global Citizenship: Scholars Debate Notions of Identity and Tolerance at Secretary-General's Lecture*, U.N. Chronicle, June 2, 2006, at 51.

5. *Movement at Warp Speed: Young Americans Move Frequently*, American Demographics, Aug. 2000, at 1.

6. Liam Byrne, Minister of State for Immigration, Citizenship & Nationality, remarks to KPMG London, June 4, 2007.

7. *Letting some of them in*, The Economist, Oct. 2, 2008, *available at* http://www.economist.com/world/europe/displaystory.cfm?story_id=12342253.

8. Katrin Bennhold, *A Veil Closes France's Door to Citizenship*, N.Y. Times, Jul. 19, 2008.

9. U.S. Const. art II, § 1, cl. 5. The provision is especially controversial today because of a certain European-born governor of California.

10. Akhil Reed Amar, *Natural Born Killjoy*, Legal Affairs, March 2008, at http://www.legalaffairs.org/issues/March-April-2004/argument_amar_marpar04.msp.

11. *Id.*

12. The Federalist No. 2 (John Jay).

13. Thomas Jefferson, Notes on the State of Virginia, 84–85 (William Peden ed., 1954) (1782).

14. Theodore D. Roosevelt, Speech before the Knights of Columbus, Carnegie Hall, New York (Oct. 12, 1915).

15. Theodore D. Roosevelt, A Square Deal for All Americans (Apr. 27, 1918) in Roosevelt in the Kansas City Star 142 (1921).

16. Ronald Reagan, Farewell Address to the Nation (Jan. 11, 1989), *at* http://www.reaganlibrary.com/reagan/speeches/farewell.asp.

Index

About the Authors

Jean-Claude Bonichot is a judge at the European Court of Justice. Before his appointment in October 2006, he was president of the Sixth Subdivision of the Judicial Division at the Council of State. He has authored numerous publications on administrative law, community law, and European human rights law. He is the founder and chairman of the editorial committee of the *Bulletin de jurisprudence de droit de l'urbanisme*. From 1998 through 2000, Judge Bonichot was a lecturer at the University of Metz.

François-Henri Briard is an attorney before the Supreme Courts of France with the law firm Briard, Delaporte et Trichet, chairman of the Paris chapter of the Federalist Society, and president of the Vergennes Society, which he cofounded with U.S. Supreme Court Justice Antonin Scalia. Mr. Briard is an auditor at the French National Institute for Defense High Studies. He has written many lectures and contributions dealing with the friendship between the United States and France. Mr. Briard is a knight of the Legion of Honor and knight of the French National Merit. He is also a member of honor of the Sons of the American Revolution.

William Galston is the Ezra K. Zilkha chair in governance studies and senior fellow at the Brookings Institution, and also College Park Professor at the University of Maryland. Prior to joining Brookings in 2006, he was the Saul Stern Professor and dean at the University of Maryland's School of Public Policy. He is the author of eight books, of which the most recent is Public Matters (Rowman & Littlefield, 2005), a coauthor of *Democracy at Risk: How Political Choices Undermine Citizen Participation and What We Can Do About It* (Brookings, 2005), and has published more than one hundred articles on questions of moral and political philosophy, American politics, and public policy.

Robert R. Gasaway is a partner at Kirkland & Ellis LLP. He has represented and advised corporate clients on a wide variety of matters before federal courts, state courts, federal administrative agencies, and federal and state legislative bodies. Mr. Gasaway focuses his practice on appellate litigation, representing clients in the preparation of integrated, multiforum trial, and appellate strategies in high-risk sets of related cases.

Michael S. Greve is the John G. Searle Scholar at AEI. His research and writing cover constitutional law, federalism, and business regulation. Mr. Greve cofounded and, from 1989 to 2000, directed the Center for Individual Rights, a public interest law firm that served as counsel in many precedent-setting constitutional cases, including *United States v. Morrison* and *Rosenberger v. University of Virginia*. He also serves on the board of directors of the Competitive Enterprise Institute. His publications include numerous law review articles and books, including *The Demise of Environmentalism in American Law* (AEI Press, 1996) and *Real Federalism: Why It Matters, How It Could Happen* (AEI Press, 1999.) Mr. Greve is the coeditor, with Fred L. Smith, of *Environmental Politics: Public Costs, Private Rewards* (Praeger, 1992) and, with Richard A. Epstein, of *Competition Laws in Conflict: Antitrust Jurisdiction in the Global Economy* (AEI Press, 2004) and *Federal Preemption: States' Powers, National Interests* (AEI Press, 2007).

Ayaan Hirsi Ali is a resident fellow at AEI. At AEI, Ms. Hirsi Ali researches the relationship between the West and Islam; women's rights in Islam; violence against women propagated by religious and cultural arguments; and Islam in Europe. An outspoken defender of women's rights in Islamic societies, Ms. Hirsi Ali was born in Mogadishu, Somalia, where she escaped an arranged marriage by immigrating to the Netherlands in 1992, and served as a member of the Dutch parliament from 2003 to 2006. In parliament, she worked on furthering the integration of non-Western immigrants into Dutch society, and on defending the rights of women in Dutch-Muslim society. In 2004, together with director Theo van Gogh, she made *Submission*, a film about the oppression of women in conservative Islamic cultures. The airing of the film on Dutch television resulted in the assassination of van Gogh by an Islamic extremist.

Josef Joffe is publisher-editor of the German weekly newspaper *Die Zeit*, an adjunct professor of political science at Stanford University, a senior fellow of the Freeman Spogli Institute for International Studies, and Abramowitz Fellow of the Hoover Institution, Stanford. He is also co-founder and executive board member of the *American Interest* and serves on the board of *International Security*. Previously, he was a columnist and editorial page editor of *Süddeutsche Zeitung*. His essays and reviews have appeared in a wide number of publications including the *New York Review of Books*, *Times Literary Supplement*, *Commentary*, *New York Times Magazine*, *The New Republic*, *The Weekly Standard*, and the *Prospect* (London). His scholarly work has appeared in many books and journals, such as the *American Interest*, *Foreign Affairs*, the *National Interest*, *International Security*, and *Foreign Policy*, as well as in professional journals in Germany, Britain, and France. He is the author of *The Limited Partnership: Europe, the United States and the Burdens of Alliance* (Ballinger, 1987). His most recent book is *Überpower: The Imperial Temptation in American Foreign Policy* (W.W. Norton, 2007).

Jürgen Kaube has been an editor at the *Frankfurter Allgemeine Zeitung* newspaper since 1998. Mr. Kaube is also a professor of sociology at the University of Lucerne in Switzerland. He is responsible for higher education, sciences, and the humanities. Previously, Mr. Kaube studied economics, philosophy, German literature, and art history at the Free University of Berlin. He has also served as an assistant professor for sociology at the University of Bielefeld.

Martin Klingst the Washington bureau chief for the German weekly newspaper *Die Zeit*. Previously, he worked for the North German Television and Broadcasting Corporation and taught German law at the University of Hamburg. He has covered many constitutional and supreme courts and the Balkan Wars for *Die Zeit*. Mr.Klingst was a Bucerius Fellow at the Minda de Gunzburg Center for European Studies at Harvard University in 2006.

Markus Kotzur is a professor of law at the University of Leipzig, where he serves as chair of public international law, European law, and foreign public law. Mr. Kotzur is the author of numerous articles, including "Decisive for the World—On Rationality and Legitimacy Regarding the Resolutions of the UN Security Council" in the 2007 edition of the *Annual Book of Current Public Law*.

Ashley C. Parrish is a partner in the Washington, D.C. office of King & Spalding, LLP, and a member of the firm's national appellate practice. His practice focuses on general appellate and administrative litigation; on the preparation of high-risk cases for eventual appeal; and on strategic, complex commercial litigation. Before joining King & Spalding, Mr. Parrish was a partner at Kirkland & Ellis LLP and, earlier in his career, clerked for the Honorable Emilio M. Garza on the U.S. Court of Appeals for the Fifth Circuit.

Robert von Rimscha is national spokesperson and communications director for the Freie Demokratische Partei (FDP), Germany's centrist liberal party. He is also editor-in-chief of *Liberale Depesche*, a monthly German political magazine. Before joining politics in August 2004, he was Berlin bureau chief for the daily *Der Tagesspiegel*. Mr. von Rimscha served as its U.S. correspondent from 1996 to 2000. Mr. von Rimscha is the author of eight books on current international politics, most recently family biographies of the Kennedys and the Bushes, which have been translated into several languages. He regularly appears on German and American media outlets and has contributed editorial writing to, among other publications, the *Los Angeles Times* and the *International Herald Tribune*. He was awarded the Arthur F. Burns Prize for distinguished commentary on transatlantic issues in 2003.

Peter H. Schuck is the Simeon E. Baldwin Professor of Law at Yale Law School, where he has served as deputy dean and has held the chair since 1984. His major fields of teaching and research are tort law; immigration, citizenship, and refugee law; groups, diversity, and law; and administrative law. He has written and edited numerous books, including *Agent Orange on Trial: Mass Toxic Disasters in the Courts* (Belknap, 1985); *The Limits of Law: Essays on Democratic Governance* (Westview, 2000); *Foundations of Administrative Law* (Foundation Press, 2004); *Diversity in America: Keeping Government at a Safe Distance* (Belknap Press, 2006); and *Meditations of a Militant Moderate: Cool Views on Hot Topics* (Rowman & Littlefield, 2006). His most recent book, co-edited with James Q. Wilson, is *Understanding America: The Anatomy of an Exceptional Nation* (PublicAffairs, 2008). He is a contributing editor to *The American Lawyer*. Before teaching at Yale, he was principal deputy assistant secretary for planning and evaluation in the U.S. Department of Health, Education, and Welfare, and practiced public interest law in Washington, D.C.

Peter Skerry is a professor of political science at Boston College and a non-resident senior fellow at the Brookings Institution and at the Kenan Institute for Ethics at Duke University. He previously taught at Claremont McKenna College and the University of California at Los Angeles. He was formerly a research fellow at AEI and legislative director for Senator Daniel Patrick Moynihan (D-N.Y.) His book *Mexican Americans: The Ambivalent Minority* (Harvard University Press, 1995) was awarded the *Los Angeles Times* Book Prize. He has written about race, religion, ethnicity and immigration for a variety of publications, including the *New York Times*, the *New Republic*, the *Public Interest*, *National Review*, *Foreign Policy*, the *Washington Post*, and *Time*. Mr. Skerry serves on the editorial advisory boards of *Society*, *American Politics Research*, the *Forum*, and the *Wilson Quarterly*, to which he is also a frequent contributor. He has also served on the Advisory Council on European/Transatlantic Issues of the Heinrich Böll Foundation, an affiliate of the German Green Party. He is currently a member of the board of the United Neighborhood Organization, a Chicago-based Latino community organization and charter school operator. His most recent book on the politics of the U.S. census, *Counting on the Census? Race, Group Identity, and the Evasion of Politics*, was published by Brookings. He is currently completing a book about the social and political integration of Muslims in the United States, entitled *Will Allah Bless America?* During the 2006–7 academic year, he was a visiting scholar at the Russell Sage Foundation in New York. He is currently co-director of the Brookings-Duke Immigration Policy Roundtable.

Kenneth W. Starr is dean of the Pepperdine University School of Law, where he teaches current constitutional issues and civil procedure. Mr. Starr's areas of expertise are constitutional law, federal courts, federal jurisdiction, and antitrust. While in private practice, he was a partner at Kirkland & Ellis LLP and Gibson, Dunn & Crutcher. In addition to working in the private sector, he has served as counselor to Attorney General William French Smith; judge for the U.S. Court of Appeals, D.C. Circuit; solicitor general of the United States; and independent counsel on the Whitewater matter. As solicitor general, he argued twenty-five cases before the U.S. Supreme Court. Mr. Starr is a member of numerous professional organizations and boards, including the American Law Institute, the Supreme Court Historical Society, and the

American Inns of Court. He has authored many law review articles, and his best-selling book is *First Among Equals: The Supreme Court in American Life* (Grand Central Publishing, 2003).

Francesca Strumia is a post-graduate research fellow at Harvard Law School, where she obtained her S.J.D. in June 2009. She writes on issues relating to free movement, citizenship and immigration in the European Union. She taught a course of European Union Law at New England School of Law as an adjunct professor and was President of the Harvard European Law Association from 2007 to 2008. Her article "Citizenship and Free Movement: European and American Features of a Judicial Formula for Increased Comity" was published in 2006 in the *Columbia Journal of European Law.*

Adam Tomkins has been the John Millar Professor of Public Law at the University of Glasgow since 2003. He previously taught at King's College London (1991–2000) and at the University of Oxford, where he was a fellow and tutor in law at St. Catherine's College (2000–2003). He is a specialist in constitutional law, especially British constitutional law, but he has also published on EU law, comparative constitutional law, and administrative law. His books include *Public Law* (Oxford University Press, 2003), *Our Republican Constitution* (Hart Publishing, 2005), and *British Government and the Constitution* (Cambridge University Press, 2007). He is currently working on projects concerning constitutional law and national security, republican constitutionalism in theory and practice, and the idea of the mixed constitution.

Diane P. Wood is a circuit judge on the U.S. Court of Appeals for the Seventh Circuit and a senior lecturer in law at the University of Chicago Law School. Previously, she clerked for Judge Irving L. Goldberg on the U.S. Court of Appeals for the Fifth Circuit (1975–76), and for Justice Harry A. Blackmun of the U.S. Supreme Court (1976–77). Judge Wood spent a brief period at the Office of the Legal Adviser in the U.S. Department of State. In 1980, she began her career as a legal academic at Georgetown University Law Center. She moved to the University of Chicago Law School in 1981, serving as a full-time professor until 1995 and as associate dean from 1989 through 1992. In 1990, she was named to the Harold J. and Marion F. Green Professorship in International Legal Studies, becoming the first woman to hold a named chair at the school. From 1993 until her appointment to the Seventh Circuit in 1995, she served as deputy assistant attorney general in the antitrust division of the U.S. Department of Justice. Judge Wood is a fellow of the American Academy of Arts & Sciences and is on the council of the American Law Institute.

Michael Zöller is a professor of political sociology at Bayreuth University, president of the American-European Council on Public Policy, and an adjunct professor of government at the Catholic University of America. Previously, he was a junior editor with *Bayerischer Rundfunk* and then with *Frankfurter Allgemeine Zeitung*. He serves on the board of the Mont Pelerin Society and received fellowships from Notre Dame University, the University of Chicago, Stanford University's Hoover Institution, the International Center of Economic Research, the Woodrow Wilson International Center, and the University of Erfurt. He has published mainly on social thought, including political economy, comparative public policy, sociology of religion, and the American polity.